DEEP DESCENT

Adventure and Death Diving the Andrea Doria

KEVIN F. McMURRAY

A TOUCHSTONE BOOK
Published by Simon & Schuster
New York London Toronto Sydney

Touchstone
Rockefeller Center
1230 Avenue of the Americas
New York, NY 10020

First Touchstone Edition 2002

TOUCHSTONE and colophon are registered trademarks
of Simon & Schuster, Inc.

For information regarding special discounts for bulk purchases,
please contact Simon & Schuster Special Sales at 1-800-456-6798
or business@simonandschuster.com

Designed by Jaime Putorti
Map by Paul J. Pugliese

Manufactured in the United States of America

10   9   8   7

The Library of Congress has cataloged the Pocket Books
edition as follows:

Deep descent : adventure and death diving the Andrea Doria/
Kevin F. McMurray.
p.   cm.
Includes bibliographical references.
1. Scuba diving—Accidents—Atlantic Coast (U.S.) 2. Andrea Doria
(Steamship) 3. Shipwrecks—Atlantic Coast (U.S.) I. Title.
GV838.673.A75 M36   2001
363.14—dc21   2001021621
ISBN-13: 978-0-7434-0062-6
ISBN-10:   0-7434-0062-3
ISBN-13: 978-0-7434-0063-3 (Pbk)
ISBN-10:   0-7434-0063-1 (Pbk)

*With heartfelt thanks to my father, Joseph,
and my wife, Victoria*

A venturesome minority will always be eager to get off on their own. . . let them take risks, for godsake, let them get sunburnt, stranded, eaten by bears, buried alive under avalanches – that is the right and privilege of any free American."

—16 IDAHO LAW REVIEW 407, 420-1980

CONTENTS

CONTENTS

FOREWORD

ON WRECK DIVING

Over five-hundred years of man's ceaseless strivings to better himself can be found on the desolate sandy bottoms off the coast of the northeastern United States. Only an intrepid few dare risk this watery corner of our planet's last frontier. I count myself among those lucky, reckless few.

There are many examples of wealth resting at the depths of the Atlantic. The *Titanic* and the *Lusitania* and the circumstances surrounding their untimely demises are known to millions. Yet thousands of other shipwrecks have broken the hearts of those who knew their passengers and crews. Those wrecks have also captured the imagination of those of us who refuse to let their memories die.

We divers who explore these wrecks consider ourselves the lucky ones. We plumb the depths in search of history and adventure. The dark, gloomy abyss, the threatening elements, and the dangerous sea creatures that lord over this realm have become our friends, for they have kept away the hordes and the weaker of heart and left us the spoils. These wrecks have become glorious testaments to human ingenuity, moments in time snatched from their rightful place, and underwater monuments to human striving, lost but not forgotten.

I, for one, have endured more than one query on why I partake in such a seemingly dangerous activity as wreck diving. As a husband and father of two I find it difficult to answer. To the uninitiated, the allure of the deep that protects these former vessels of humanity is minimal compared to the risk.

Most people understand the spell of the depths as long as it has to do with the warm, gin-clear waters of places such as the Caribbean that come complete with colorful reefs and exotic fish. But compared to wreck diving in the North Atlantic, warm-water reef exploration is like snowplowing down the bunny slope.

George Mallory, the mountain climber who mounted the first serious attempt to summit Everest and died as a result, was once quoted as saying that he climbed "because it's there," to which the first ascendant of the fabled El Capitan in Yosemite, Grover Cleveland (not the president), added his two cents' worth: "Because it's nowhere." The same applies to wreck diving, surely the most obscure and dangerous of amateur activities: it's there and it's nowhere.

But the pithy replies are easy evasions for a true explanation of the attraction of wreck diving. Too many have died exploring the ocean's deep secrets to write it off as a frivolous activity of the idle and foolhardy.

The *Andrea Doria* sank under tragic circumstances over four decades ago. As someone who remembers her dramatic sinking and yearns to keep a piece of that precious time close to heart, I can think of no more fitting tribute than beholding the magnificent lady up close and touching her now silent remains, and maybe if lucky and bold enough even bringing back some artifact from her to preserve and display.

The *Andrea Doria* is often called the "Mount Everest of wreck diving," although there are deeper and more challenging wrecks for divers to explore. Yet the *Andrea Doria* has a mystique about her: her untimely demise, the tragic loss of life, the rescue of her survivors by her heroic brethren, and of course the whims of the open oceans that brought about her destruction.

The risks are many. Are they worth it? Perhaps not. As one diver related to me after attending one too many funerals of fellow deep-wreck divers, "If I buy the farm diving, I told my wife, if someone in their eulogy says I died the way I would have wanted, she should stand up and yell, 'Bullshit!' "

No deep-wreck diver wants to die diving. Drowning while lost inside a wreck, being convulsed by oxygen toxicity, or falling victim to decompression sickness is no way to pass into the hereafter. Then why do we risk it?

I can speak only for myself. I trust my training, my skills, my equipment, my judgment, my ability to react, my luck, and possibly the kind hand of God to interfere when respectfully implored. I like going where few dare to tread. It makes my life unique and vibrant in this world of sameness where most people think that adventure is just getting to work on time. I like to think Sir Edmund Hillary and Warren Harding (again not the president) had the same feelings.

This book is about those who blazed new paths, challenged the odds, explored new frontiers, and pushed the envelope of deep-sea exploration. Unfortunately, many of them have died as a result of their quest. I write this book so that they will not be forgotten.

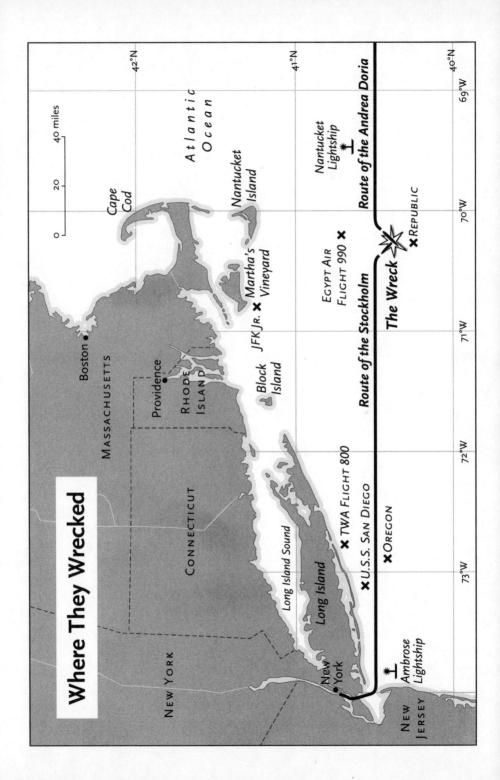

Where They Wrecked

40 miles

42°N

41°N

40°N

69°W

70°W

71°W

72°W

73°W

Atlantic Ocean

Cape Cod

Nantucket Island

Nantucket Lightship

Route of the Andrea Doria

X REPUBLIC

Martha's Vineyard **X**

JFK JR. **X**

EGYPT AIR FLIGHT 990 **X**

Route of the Stockholm

The Wreck

MASSACHUSETTS

Boston •

Providence •

RHODE ISLAND

Block Island

CONNECTICUT

Long Island Sound

TWA FLIGHT 800 **X**

X U.S. SAN DIEGO

X OREGON

Long Island

NEW YORK

New York •

Ambrose Lightship

NEW JERSEY

ONE

DEATH ON THE *DORIA*

It is not death, but dying, which is terrible.
—Henry Fielding

Wearing close to two-hundred pounds of scuba gear, Gary Gilligan was anxious to make his ungainly entry into the rolling seas of the Atlantic. The neoprene dry suit and his heavy undergarments had him sweating bullets under the hot July-afternoon sun. Prior to his giant step outward and down from the deck of the dive boat *RV Wahoo,* Gary glanced around and surveyed his surroundings with only the narrow range of vision that his dive mask afforded him.

Land had long since disappeared over the horizon, and no other vessel was in sight. The glare of the sun reflecting off the glassy seas made him wince behind his faceplate. He of course was aware of the activity around him. Getting into the water is always a major hassle for deep divers, and attendance by crew members and fellow divers prior to entry is a necessity, not a luxury. Still, it was tough for Gary Gilligan to be patient, overburdened as he was with gear, not to mention with anxiety. Gary had to remind himself to be cool: getting all bent out of shape before entering the water was a bad idea, he knew. It had a way of biting you back in the ass.

1

Gary Gilligan aboard
the *Wahoo.*
*(Photo © Kevin
McMurray)*

Gary tried to maintain his balance, but he felt encumbered
with all the hardware, encased from head to toe in the suffocating
dry suit. It was not easy what with the three-foot swells gently lifting up the fifty-five-foot fiberglass boat, only to drop it back down
into the following trough, making the deck of the vessel an unstable platform. The cerulean skies high overhead, Gary noticed, still
had contrails vectoring eastward to Europe, left behind by the
streaking Concorde whose sonic booms had rocked the boat just
minutes earlier.

Then the dorsal and caudal fins of the circling blue sharks and
their ominous forms beneath suddenly disappeared. They had

descended into the depths, Gary thought, knowing full well that he would catch glimpses of their skittish shadows on his long swim to the bottom. Steadying himself on the gunwale, he was relishing the thought of immersion in the cold, blue-green waters of the Atlantic. Finally he would be on his way down the distance of a seventeen-floor skyscraper to the wreck of the *Andrea Doria*.

Gary checked to see if his buddy Sally Wahrmann was ready. They gave each other the thumb-to-forefinger salute indicating that everything was okay. Gary pressed his mask tight to his face, snugged his double tanks to his back, and entered the ocean.

With only twenty-five minutes allotted for bottom time, Gary and Sally quickly emptied their bloated dry suits of air and kicked hard for the bow anchor line that led down to the sunken luxury liner. Gary was surprised to see three divers lingering on a line running from the anchor line aft at the fifty-foot mark.

Kicking down past them, Gary gave a quick glance back up. He could see the three men were having difficulties. Just a mere hour ago the three had rigged the two long sets of hoses and breathing regulators that were hooked to a tank of pure oxygen aboard the *Wahoo* and had secured them to a weighted line amidships at the desired depth of twenty feet. Gary could now see that one of those divers, twenty-seven-year-old John Ormsby, one of the charterers of the trip, had gotten hung up in the traverse line. Another diver, Billy Deans, had come to his aid to untangle him. Gary could see they were handling the situation and continued his descent.

In deep diving it was a radically new practice to use supplemental oxygen in water. Breathing pure oxygen after a dive was always known to be beneficial, but using it underwater had only recently been advocated, by Billy Deans of Key West, Florida. Deans knew it was a quick way to expunge the nitrogen gas that had been absorbed by the blood and soft tissues under the crushing load of the ocean. The tiny nitrogen bubbles released by the rapid reduction of pressure, if not compensated for by a slow ascent and a supply of oxygen, could spread through the body, crippling or even killing the diver. Divers called it getting "bent," but the medical community referred to it as decompression sickness.

Sally Wahrmann never saw the unfolding drama above her. She was focused on the dark abyss beneath her. Only later would she hear the story and think about how it was a tragic foreshadowing of what was to happen just minutes later, more than two-hundred feet beneath the surface deep within the holds of the sunken steel sarcophagus of the *Andrea Doria*.

No one would ever guess that Sally Wahrmann was a pioneer in the world of deep diving. At thirty-nine, Sally looked more like the accounting professor she actually was in the professional world. Only five foot five and edging precipitously toward two hundred pounds, Sally was one of the most accomplished scuba divers—male or female—in the rarefied world of deep-wreck diving. She had logged over sixty dives alone on the Doria.

On July 31, 1985, Sally was again on the *Wahoo*. She was more excited than usual as several Florida diving luminaries were also aboard.

Spencer Slate from Key Largo had chartered the *Wahoo*. Slate owned the Atlantis Diver Center in Key Largo, which was a popular tourist destination for divers in the Florida Keys. It had always been a dream of Slate's to dive the *Andrea Doria*, so he had put the group together to charter the *Wahoo*. Billy Deans owned Key West Diver, a dive shop and training business. Deans was a trailblazer in deep diving, and his exploits in Florida-water shipwrecks were the stuff of legend. Neal Watson, the owner of Undersea Adventures, which consisted of diving resorts in Florida and the Caribbean, also had the record at the time for the deepest dive on scuba at 437 feet. John Ormsby, Deans's best friend, dive buddy, and instructor at his shop, had the record for free diving, or skin diving, down to 170 feet on just one breath. Rick Frehsee was an internationally acclaimed underwater

Left to right: Sally Wahrmann, Steve Bielenda, and Billy Deans.
(Photo courtesy Billy Deans)

photographer, whose work had appeared in *National Geographic* among others. Also in the charter were Dick Masten, a police officer, and Lou Delotto, an airline pilot, both well-known in the Florida dive community. It was a first trip for all of them to the *Andrea Doria*. For all his deep-water experience, Billy Deans had never dove outside the state of Florida.

The group made the trek up to Montauk at the tip of New York's Long Island, where the *Wahoo* was to pick them up.

Spencer Slate, who had chartered the boat, wasn't with them. On one of his training dives for the *Doria*, Slate had taken a minor hit of decompression sickness in 250 feet of water off Key West, and his doctor thought for safety's sake Slate should back out of the deep *Andrea Doria* dive.

The Florida group was there for one reason: china. Pieces of china, crystal, and silverware with the mark of the Italia steamship company

First-class demitasse and spoon.
(Courtesy of Joel Silverstein Photography)

are more precious than Spanish doubloons to wreck divers. The
Floridians had discussed the china the day before departure with veteran *Doria* diver Gary Gentile, who was crewing on the *Wahoo*.
Gentile had already made a trip out to the wreck the week before, and
he had his recovered artifacts from the first-class gift shop. Deans
remembered the trinkets had stirred up "a fever, a frenzy, a rabidity,"
among the Florida group. On the way out to the wreck site the only
topic of conversation was the *Andrea Doria* ship plans and how to get
some artifacts off her.

Rick Jaszyn, another deep diver with *Doria* experience, was also
crewing aboard the *Wahoo*. A New Jersey resident, Jaszyn was only
twenty-seven years old, but he had logged hundreds of dives on the
deep wrecks found in the waters of the North Atlantic. He was the
only diver, besides Gary Gentile and Steve Bielenda, who knew the
Florida contingent personally. He had made a pilgrimage to Deans's

Key West Diver and dove the USS *Wilkes-Barre* with Deans and Ormsby. He had the highest regard for their diving skills. Jaszyn was amazed when Ormsby made a free dive to the top of the *Wilkes-Barre,* a depth of 150 feet. But on this *Doria* trip Jaszyn was alarmed by Ormsby's "gung ho" determination to collect some artifacts on his first visit to the wreck. It was not Ormsby's diving talents he doubted. Jaszyn knew that Ormsby's experience came from the totally different Florida environment. Up north, diving in higher latitudes was an "equipment-intensive" experience, plus visibility and cold water factored in as well. Rick Jaszyn tried to cool Ormsby's jets, but knew he had the "fever."

Having *Andrea Doria* china in one's collection of wreck artifacts is a testament to one's diving prowess, as close to an Olympic gold medal as a diver can get. However, diving the recumbent luxury liner is outside the realm of recreational diving. Unlike on a recreational

Doria china (left to right: tourist, cabin, first class).
(Courtesy of Joel Silverstein Photography)

dive, on a *Doria* dive you have to contemplate the very real possibility that you may not get out alive.

The *Doria*, as veteran wreck divers simply refer to her, lies in 235 feet of frequently storm-tossed waters. From the *Wahoo*'s home port in Captree Boat Basin on New York's Long Island, it was a torturous eighteen-hour trip out to the wreck site. Even from Montauk it was still a ten-hour trip.

"Getting beat up" on the trip out is a rite of passage for *Doria* divers. It isn't just the mercurial Atlantic that conspires against you. The sleeping quarters aboard the speedy fiberglass *Wahoo* are laughingly referred to as "spice racks." The *Wahoo*'s bunks are stacked like trays below the decks, and diesel fumes mingle with the odor of dozens of sweating bodies in the claustrophobic space. The smell of fear pervades belowdecks preceding any *Doria* dive. The common belief is that if you are not scared about doing the dive, you are either lying or stupid. Few get much sleep before the dive, and the fatigue adds to the likelihood of a mishap.

Aft deck of the *Wahoo* strewn with diving gear.
(Photo courtesy Billy Deans)

• • •

The *Andrea Doria* is one shipwreck the mainstream diving community prefers to ignore—and for good reason. Travel magazines and publications like *Skin Diver Magazine* promote scuba diving as a nice, safe recreational sport. Scuba advertisers—the equipment manufacturers and Caribbean resorts in particular—tend to illustrate their ads with curvy, bikini-clad models and smiling families suited up in color-coordinated dive gear. *Doria* divers in bulky, ugly dry suits, shouldering backbreaking double tanks, bedecked with crowbars, hammers, chisels, goodie bags, and big, powerful underwater lights look like intimidating creatures from another planet. These explorers of the deep also violate the widely accepted maximum depth of diving of 130 feet. Going beyond that limit is a dangerous heresy to the diving industry.

Below 130 feet, the risks to divers with a limited air supply are substantial. Nitrogen narcosis, the "rapture of the deep" as scuba inventor and underwater cinematic chronicler Jacques Cousteau called it, intoxicates divers to varying degrees at those depths, often impairing judgment with fatal results.

Nitrogen routinely makes up almost 80 percent of the air we breathe in, with obviously no ill effects. But when nitrogen is compressed into a steel cylinder and transported down to that depth, it becomes a gaseous anesthetic. In the infancy of scuba, divers used to refer to it as Martini's Law: every fifty feet down was equal to drinking one dry martini on an empty stomach. A diver on the *Doria* would suffer the effects of four to five martinis.

But narcosis is sneaky for most people because it induces a pleasant euphoric feeling, inability to concentrate, and a short attention span. Being easily distracted can mean big trouble to someone who is down deep under the surface of the ocean. Like people with their liquor, some divers hold their nitrogen better than others. Most *Doria* divers manage getting "narced" by systematic thinking, taking everything slowly and step by step. A deep diver's ability to operate while narced is his or her badge of courage.

Nitrogen has another insidious effect on the diver; under pressure, nitrogen is dissolved from the lungs into the blood and soft tissues. On a diver's return to the surface he must allow for the nitrogen to slowly migrate back to the lungs, revert to its gaseous state, and then be exhaled. This is why divers make decompression stops. Failing to decompress and returning to the surface too quickly is analogous to opening a well-shaken bottle of soda. Millions of tiny bubbles escape into the blood system and can cause blockages in the heart, brain, and central nervous system, preventing the flow of life-giving oxygen. Getting bent is, in effect, a stroke of cataclysmic proportions.

Decompression illness can also have chemical side effects, which could include blood clotting, formation of fat emboli, activation of platelets and leukocytes, and lactic accumulation. The circulatory system can be impaired, and when blood flow is hampered, cells die and irreversible damage can occur.

According to U.S. navy diving tables, a twenty-minute dive down to 220 feet requires a one-minute stop at forty feet, a three-minute stop at thirty feet, an eleven-minute stop at twenty feet, and a twenty-four minute stop at ten feet—or almost double the time spent on the bottom. This is all done on a limited air supply carried on the diver's back. Running out of air before you can surface is always the foremost worry to a deep diver. Getting bent or drowning when diving the *Doria* are real possibilities, and precautions must be taken and followed to the letter.

Getting narced and bent are not the only problems that breathing compressed air present. Life-giving oxygen can also be treacherous at extreme depths. Down at two atmospheres (thirty-three feet below the surface), 100 percent oxygen is toxic. In compressed air the oxygen is diluted to about 21 percent. Still, according to Dalton's law of physics, in a mixture of gases, each gas exerts a pressure proportional to the percentage of the total gas that it represents. So at two hundred feet, or seven atmospheres absolute, oxygen approaches the same dangerous toxicity it has at two atmospheres. Simply put, oxygen is needed to support life and cells, but too much of it initiates cell destruction. Oxygen toxicity can convulse a diver, and drownings at deep depths on compressed air are often blamed on oxygen toxicity. Portraying scuba as a potentially dangerous activity is not the face the travel industry wants to put on the sport. Therefore diving the *Doria* is bad for the lucrative business of scuba diving. Unable to stop it, the industry simply pretends it does not exist. To people like Sally Wahrmann, the appeal of that outlaw tag made diving the *Doria* all the more exciting.

Sally was crewing on the *Wahoo* for the fourth year in a row. In exchange for her time in the galley as cook, getting the boat ready for the charter, helping in the tedious job of hooking the grapple to the hull of the wreck, and getting client divers in the water, Sally got a free bunk aboard the boat and all the diving she could squeeze in. The paying clients shelled out $700 for the four-day charter. One of Sally's other jobs was signing in divers, collecting the waivers of risk, and checking certification cards and logbooks—the onerous task of making sure the divers had documentation.

Sally remembers that everyone from the Florida group on the trip was gracious about the indignity of having their credentials checked except one—John Ormsby. The tall, tan, and muscled Ormsby waved her off the first time she asked him for his certification cards and log, saying they were down below with his gear and he would get them later, a scenario that would be repeated several times over the next few hours. "It was like he couldn't be bothered," Wahrmann remembered. "Here he is this big-shot diver from Florida being asked for his c-cards [scuba certification cards] by this little nobody from New York. It really bothered me."

Sally made a visit to the bridge, where the master of the *Wahoo*, Captain Steve Bielenda, and regular pilot Captain Janet Bieser were busy negotiating the seas on the trek eastward. The ocean east of Montauk Point and south of Block Island and Martha's Vineyard is a mariner's nightmare: unpredictable seas, frequent fog banks, and a heavily trafficked shipping lane meant that one's captain's skills and focus have to be sharp. Problems below with clients on the trip out are the crew's problem, and Sally was hesitant to bother Captains Bielenda and Bieser with the seemingly trivial problem she was having with Ormsby.

Gary Gentile was also in the wheelhouse. Of all aboard the *Wahoo*, Gentile was by far and away the most experienced deep-wreck diver in the group, if not in the world. Gentile had been diving the *Doria* since 1974 and had more dives logged on the ocean liner than anyone else. Gentile had enough artifacts from the *Doria* to fill a small museum.

Captain Steve Bielenda was a legend. Dubbed "the king of the deep" by local newspapers in New York, Bielenda was well-known for his diving history in the wreck-strewn bottom of the New York Bight, the city's underwater environs. True to his reputation, he had the first charter dive boat to run regular trips out to the *Doria* in 1981, no small task since locating the bottom-dwelling ship was difficult. Other boats ran *Doria* trips, but Steve Bielenda's *RV Wahoo* was considered the best.

Janet Bieser, Bielenda's usual pilot out to the *Doria*, was the second woman ever to dive the *Andrea Doria*. Bieser was a stereotypical sea captain. Huge by any standards and as strong as an ox, Bieser also captained the *Wahoo* in the bitterly cold winters to fish for cod. Captain Janet tolerated no bullshit aboard the *Wahoo*. If you crossed her, you were told to stay the "fuck" off her boat. Bielenda always supported her.

When Bielenda asked Sally how everything was below, she reported that she had checked out all the divers but one, John Ormsby, and related her problems in getting him to cooperate. Gary Gentile remarked that of all the divers aboard, Ormsby was the last one that Sally had to worry about, but Bielenda was not so accommodating. He told Sally to demand his credentials and stop the bullshit or Ormsby wouldn't dive.

Ormsby finally produced his c-cards and log just a few hours

Billy Deans (left) and John Ormsby in Key West.
(Photo courtesy Billy Deans)

before arriving at the destination. Sally took the time to sit down and read it, as Sally said, "just to break his balls." It was the only log of the entire charter group she actually read.

The *Wahoo* arrived at the wreck site at around 1 P.M., in time for one dive after lunch. Deans, Ormsby, and Lou Delotto quickly suited up and looked as if they would be the first to enter the water.

After cleaning up from lunch, Sally got permission from Bielenda to get a dive in before she had to prepare the evening meal. She buddied up with fellow crew member Gary Gilligan, and they planned to follow the Florida trio into the water but go to a different location in the wreck.

Unlike Sally, thirty-three-year-old Gary Gilligan fit the image of a death-defying deep diver. A lean, muscular six-footer, suntanned to the texture of leather, with blond hair and blue eyes, he looked every bit the part. When not crewing on the *Wahoo,* Gary "banged nails" as an independent carpenter at construction sites. He made his home on a boat, christened none too surprisingly the SS *Minnow*, in a marina in Bridgeport, Connecticut. This was his third year diving the *Doria*. He also had many artifacts liberated from the hold of the sunken vessel.

Sally and Gilligan were getting antsy after waiting almost forty-five minutes for the Florida contingent to get into the water. All dives on the *Doria* were carefully planned with the idea not to have different teams of divers in the same place on the same dive. Getting into each other's way and stirring up the muck inside the ship obscures visibility for the next team and is to be avoided at all costs. So Gary and Sally waited.

Gilligan remembered that the Florida group were "fucking around with their gear." John Ormsby, in particular, fussed with his weight belt. Gary Gentile remembers that Ormsby's belt looked like a carpenter's tool belt. A hammer, an adjustable wrench, a crowbar, and pliers were slung from the spring-gated snap hooks that hung from his belt. This kind of gear configuration was popular with Florida cave divers, who were responsible for most technical diving innovations in the Sunshine State. But it was not the same in the cold depths of the Northeast. Wreck divers who frequent the *Doria* call the snaps "suicide clips."

In Florida there was little chance of "danglies," such as Ormsby's snap hooks or tools, snagging the smooth limestone walls of an underwater cave, but in the dark, confining passages of a wreck, all the twisted and collapsed steel seems to almost reach out and grab you. Streamlining your gear and minimizing the chance of snagging yourself with danglies is foremost in a *Doria* diver's mind.

Mounted between John Ormsby's tanks was an emergency ascent line, called "Jersey upline" in the Northeast. The ascent line was to be deployed if the diver could not locate the anchor line or he was too far from it and low on air. To the right of his ascent line, Ormsby secured a power source for his underwater light. The configuration gave him a

Left: John Ormsby suiting up for the fatal dive with Gary Gentile assisting.
Right: Ormsby's gear belt—notice the "suicide clips."
(Photos © Steve Bielenda)

wide profile, making him extremely susceptible to snagging himself in tight quarters. But none of the locals ventured his opinion, not even Gary Gentile, who had assisted Ormsby in donning his gear. Other divers must have noticed the "suicide clips" but said nothing. Ormsby's ballyhooed reputation had preceded him. His comportment aboard the *Wahoo* on the trip out had put an exclamation point on it.

Under the hot sun, cooking in their stifling dry suits and thermal underwear, Sally appealed to Bielenda for a go-ahead with their dive since dinner-preparation time was nearing. The master of the *Wahoo* gave the okay. Sally and Gilligan needed another fifteen minutes to ready their gear, and in the meantime, and much to their relief, Deans, Ormsby, and Delotto finally entered the water.

The Florida trio's entry was made from the starboard side of the

Wahoo, not the usual port side where there was a cutout on the gunwale. Deans had made the special request so they could inspect their oxygen rigging, which was on a weighted line on that side of the boat. The oxygen regulators were cinched to the line at twenty feet, the ideal depth for the purging of nitrogen using oxygen. According to their dive plan, once the oxygen lines were inspected, they would deploy a traverse line from the decompression line to the anchor line and then make their descent to the wreck.

The *Wahoo* crewmates gave the Floridians another ten minutes so they would not be crowding the anchor line during decompression, so Gary was surprised to see them struggling with the traverse line at fifty feet.

Ormsby and Delotto had dropped down the anchor line with one end of the traverse line that was to be deployed and secured it at fifty feet. Billy Deans, at the other end of the line, was to tie it off to the decompression line at the same depth, then swim over to join them for their descent.

When Deans arrived at the anchor line, he saw that Ormsby was fouled in the transverse line. Somehow it had gotten snagged on his tank manifolds. Deans says that Ormsby was annoyed since the fouling was delaying his timetable on the wreck.

"You can read a guy's eyes and hand signals in the water," Deans said, "and I could see that he was obviously agitated because he was fouled up. Lou couldn't really unfoul him. So I held up my hands, like saying 'Hey, relax!' and then untangled him, and he started down the anchor line hand over hand real fast. I looked at Lou and signaled with exasperation to just let him go."

Sally Wahrmann remembered that Ormsby kicked past her and Gilligan "like a bat out of hell." Ormsby's reputation as a strong swimmer was realized firsthand. Once he disappeared below her into the watery abyss, Sally focused on her own efforts.

Dropping down to the *Doria* was always an emotional experience for the fun-loving and gregarious accountant. Keeping a firm grip on the anchor line, equalizing the pressure in her mask and her inner ears, and blasting air into her dry suit to offset the squeeze from the weight of the ocean never prevented Sally from enjoying the rapid drop down to the wreck.

The light streaming down from the surface in refracted broad beams made her feel as if she were in a vast cathedral. The ethereal light humbled her, making her feel so small and the ocean so big. During the long four minutes before she set finned foot on the black hull of the *Doria*, she watched the passing parade of jellyfish, plankton, and sharks with a wondrous gaze.

The remains of the *Andrea Doria* were always a spellbinding sight to Sally. Seven hundred feet in length—longer than two football fields—lying on her starboard side, the carcass of the old ship stretched into the blue-green void farther than underwater visibility would permit Sally to see. Schools of bergalls, blackfish, cod, pollock, and ling hovered over the Doria like bees on a hive harvesting her bounty of algae and bait fish. Sally and Gary caught a glimpse of a swift-swimming dusky shark who had been patrolling its domain. It darted off at the sight of the interlopers. The wreck was pocked with thousands of portholes that sprouted countless sea anemones, and portions of her amidships were shrouded in tattered fishing nets. The ghostly appearance of the once grande dame of the transatlantic fleet brought a lump to Sally Wahrmann's throat.

She could not help but wonder what it must have been like to be aboard her on that panic-stricken night of July 25, 1956, when the Swedish liner *Stockholm* suddenly appeared out of the heavy fog and stabbed her reinforced bow deep into the *Doria*'s starboard flank. It was a lingering death. Fifty-one people died, but more than eleven hundred escaped from the sinking ship. It took eleven hours for the *Andrea Doria* to reluctantly succumb to her fate. The plucking of survivors from the stricken ship that night is still considered the greatest sea rescue of the twentieth century. Sally surveyed the scene as she hovered over the recumbent, silent lady and felt as if she were walking on hallowed grounds. Sally was one of the few who dared the danger-ous elements and the laws of physics to visit the *Doria*, and each time she felt honored.

Gary Gentile had first discovered the cache of gold, silver, and pre-cious stones in the first-class gift shop on a previous dive. Gentile was intimate with the ship's layout, having studied its plans and made dozens of forays down its darkened passages. He was generous with his expertise of the ship with those he thought worthy, and he thought Gary Gilligan was worthy. This was to be his second excursion into the gift shop. Sally also begged him to take her there. Gilligan had confi-dence in Sally's ability and agreed to buddy up with her.

Sally and Gary Gilligan knew the Florida contingent was supposed to be making only an exploratory dive, so they would not run into them inside the ship. After all, Bielenda had given his customary talk to beginners before hooking into the wreck: visit the shallow end of the wreck—the Promenade Deck. Since the wreck lay on its starboard side, all the corridors were vertical shafts, and the staircases were all muck-filled labyrinths, too much of a challenge to first-time explorers of the wreck.

Bielenda was also a proponent of "progressive penetration," a hotly debated subject in the wreck-diving community. In progressive penetration, divers make successively deeper forays inside the ship, familiarizing themselves with its layout. In theory, several dives were necessary on a wreck before deep penetration could be made. Progressive-penetration divers also eschewed employing dive reels, handheld spools of line. Cave divers had pioneered the dive-reel prac-tice, and most wreck divers religiously used the reels: the end of the line was secured outside the wreck, and line was spent upon entering the ship, laying out an escape route.

Bielenda believed, and expounded upon with little prompting, that dive reels were an unreliable crutch for divers. They were great for cave divers because they could run out several hundred feet of line over limestone and not worry about them being cut, but it was different inside a wreck. Lines could easily be snagged and cut on the sharp edges found inside sunken ships. Because of oxidation, steel corroded away to razor-sharp edges, which meant that a wreck diver would have to spend an inordinate amount of time tying off every several feet so that one cut in the line would not mean disaster.

Reel lines were also aesthetically unsightly. Most popular wrecks had become "spaghetti cities" with all the abandoned penetration lines laid out and left behind. There was also a hefty bit of machismo among progressive-penetration adherents, not unlike among mountain climbers who forgo the use of fixed ropes on ascents.

At the Promenade Deck, Bielenda would lecture, first-time *Doria* divers could get a feel for the wreck and get accustomed to the low visibility and the swift currents that buffet her. Bielenda made a point to the assembled listeners: this was not Florida.

"I gave them my pat speech," he said, "that their first dive on her should be just a touch dive to dispel the myths of diving the *Doria*, reducing it to just another dive."

Bielenda used to reason back then, "You think you know, but you don't know what a diver will do once they are on the wreck. Of course I know now that a wreck diver is gonna do whatever they want to. I could only hope that maybe some of them will go down with some of my words of warning, but most of them won't. And in Ormsby's case, he definitely paid me no heed."

Gimbel's Hole was a wide opening cut out by underwater adventurer, cinematographer, and department-store heir Peter Gimbel. The hole had been the double doors of the first-class gangway, where the passengers entered the vessel. Gimbel and his crew had broken the portholes out, burned off the hinges, secured a chain through the portholes, and pulled out the doors for a 1981 documentary, an effort that had almost killed Gimbel. During one of the dives Gimbel took an oxygen toxicity hit and had to be pulled from within the wreck and up to the surface by a fellow diver. Gimbel would later say that the ship-wreck had a "malevolent spirit."

Sally and Gary dropped down the corridor shaft through a jungle of hanging cables and wires. At one point, fifty feet in, the corridor branches off aft to the first-class dining room and forward to the chapel. The first-class dining room, located near the center of the ship to provide the most stability for the wealthy diners, was the mother lode for divers seeking china. Hence, the corridor just inside Gimbel's Hole was the most logical entry point for divers seeking artifacts.

Below the branch-off point, Sally and Gary had to duck under some collapsed beams dropping into an area that fell off to a watery blackness. From there they had to rely on their depth gauges to bring them to a spot on the wall at 223 feet. The room was once glass-enclosed. Shelves from the gift shop had slid down, dumping their contents onto the walls. That was where Gary and Sally began to dig.

Sally was shoulder to shoulder with Gary when they started dig-ging through the muck for the precious artifacts. While she was con-centrating on digging through the now billowing silt, something big suddenly slammed into Sally Wahrmann.

"At the time I didn't know what it was," she said. "Whatever it was, it really whacked me hard, it was all over me. It was almost like I got socked in the jaw. My regulator got knocked out of my mouth, my mask flooded, I lost my buoyancy, and I went barreling down to the bottom of the corridor coming to rest in a pile of rotting wood and debris."

Stunned, Sally was still able to get her regulator back in her mouth, then she cleared her mask of the invading seawater. It was no small task, but Sally had presciently secured her mask to her face by pulling her neoprene hood over the mask strap, a practice Bielenda ardently endorsed. Had she not had the mask under her hood, she would probably have lost her mask, her underwater vision—and any hope of escaping death from deep inside the ship.

Sally frantically tried to orient herself to where she was. Telling herself to calm down, she located the telltale stream of air bubbles spent from her regulator in the silt-blackened waters, which told her which way was up. Following the bubbles and making a slow, cautious ascent, she was finally able to make out the faint green glow of light from the surface. The glow of light was no bigger than the circumference of a tablespoon but its welcome sight added to the flood of adrenaline that was furiously pumping through her system. Sally was sucking down air at an alarming rate. She knew she had to get out of there—and fast.

Sally swam up and out of the hole, "faster than I should have," and thought about heading right for the anchor upline and to the surface. She hesitated and thought that whatever had slammed into her might have got her buddy. Without giving it another thought, Sally reentered Gimbel's Hole. Almost immediately she saw a bright beam from a diving light coming up at her. Sally held her breath, and Gary Gilligan emerged from the darkness.

Gilligan could see that Sally was excited, her eyes still wide with fear. "She kept waving her arms and pointing to her depth gauge. The needle was nailed at two hundred fifty-three-feet, way deeper than I had been. All I could think was 'Fuck! What happened to her?' "

Weighed down with a bag full of artifacts, Gilligan followed Sally to the anchor line, just twenty to thirty feet away, and up one hundred thirty feet to their first decompression stop at the forty-foot depth.

Upon alighting on the wreck, Deans and Delotto, not finding Ormsby at the tie-in point, shrugged to each other their ignorance of his whereabouts and proceeded with their dive plan. They dropped into the wide-open Promenade Deck and followed the vertical teak decks aft. Deans noticed that no stirred-up silt billowed in the darkened passage, a sure indication that no one had been there before them. Deans, at that moment, knew that Ormsby was not following their dive plan.

Reaching the one-third limit of their air supply, they retraced their way back to the anchor line, where Deans indicated to his buddy that he was going over to the hole to take a peek in. Delotto gave him the okay signal, then started his ascent. Delotto was a good ten years older than Deans and Ormsby, and he had made it quite clear before the expedition set sail that he would be diving conservatively. Deans kicked over to the hole and dropped in eighteen minutes into his dive. He immediately saw a light. Dropping down deeper into the hole, he then saw Ormsby, and that he was in trouble.

Ormsby, floating faceup, was tangled in cables. His regulator gave off intermittent trails of bubbles, and his eyes were shut. Deans cautiously came down behind him and shook him. The response he got was, in his words, "not from a highly cognitive individual but from a person that was unconscious."

Deans told himself to stay calm, stopped, looked, and tried to assess the situation. Seeing the amount of cable wrapped around Ormsby's body reminded Deans of a fork that had been stuck in a plate of spaghetti and twisted. Deans tried to release his friend's weight belt, but because the two quick-release buckles were cinched too tight, Deans could not get the belt off. Every pull just torqued John's body. Deans pulled frantically on the cables and cut at them with his knife—all to no avail. He remembers saying to himself, "There's no fucking way, he's dead, and there's no fucking way I'm getting him out." With tears welling in his eyes he reluctantly swam out of the hole and made his ascent.

Deans, pulling himself hand over hand up the anchor line, ran into divers Gary Gilligan and Sally Wahrmann. Deans pulled out his writing slate and quickly scrawled, "HELP BUDDY STUCK IN HOLE." Gilligan nodded his understanding, then Deans swam to the traverse line at fifty feet and followed it under the boat. He made it to the weighted end and swam up the line, reaching the surface amidships.

It was an extremely dangerous chance to take, making that ascent without decompressing. But Deans knew if he did not spend much time on the surface and quickly returned to the depths to decompress, he might be spared from getting bent.

At the starboard side of the *Wahoo*, Deans spit out his regulator and called to someone on deck that John was stuck in the hole and they had to get him out now. He put his regulator back in his mouth, descended the decompression line, and switched to the oxygen regulator while looking above him, all the time thinking, "Come on, guys, get someone down here!"

Deans hovered in the water at fifty feet thinking about what else he could do. He looked at his pressure gauge and saw he had about one thousand pounds, or about one-third of his air supply, left. He knew he had to go back down to the wreck to try one more time to help John, even though the situation looked hopeless, or he could never live with himself.

Rick Jaszyn, at his thirty-foot hang, saw Deans down below him. He vividly remembers how Billy punched the palm of his hand in frustration. Then Rick saw something that was a revelation.

"He was ten to twenty feet below me, and I saw the wire hanging off the manifold of his tanks. I put two and two together. I had seen that spaghetti nest of wire in the hole, and I realized that Billy and one of his buddies must have gotten tangled up in it."

Deans was back at John's side in minutes, but he saw no more air bubbling from the exhaust ports of the regulator. John Ormsby was not going to make it out alive.

On the anchor line at their first decompression stop at forty feet. Sally had tried to make Gary understand what happened via sign language. Gary recalled that he was never aware that Sally had disappeared. Engrossed in his digging and engulfed in a cloud of blinding silt from the effort, he thought she was beside him until near departure time, when he checked his gauges and noticed Sally was not there. That didn't particularly worry him since they had agreed beforehand that if one got "weirded out" or narced (suffered nitrogen narcosis), he or she would exit and wait at the entrance to the hole. On the anchor line he was trying to figure out what Sally was telling him.

At the stop Sally and Gary were surprised to see Billy Deans swim up to them with a writing slate. Then Sally realized what had happened. What had slammed into her was John Ormsby, and now he was trapped inside Gimbel's Hole, two hundred feet beneath the surface.

Gary Gilligan grabbed the slate and swam up another ten feet. He got fellow crew member Craig Stemitez's attention. Craig was just finishing up his last decompression and most critical stop at the ten-foot mark. Craig swam down and read the slate. Realizing the gravity of the situation, Craig took the slate and broke off his last stop, risked getting bent, and headed for the surface to get help from the *Wahoo*. Stemitez was unaware that the *Wahoo* had already been alerted by Deans, who had totally blown off his decompression to get word topside of his buddy's predicament.

Aboard the *Wahoo*, Gary Gentile had his tanks rigged and ready to go for his second dive of the day. As soon as word reached him that someone was stuck in Gimbel's Hole, Gentile jumped into his suit and quickly strapped on his tanks. Gentile remembers that Janet Bieser was like a pit-crew chief and took charge of getting Gary into the water as quickly as possible. Captain Janet zipped up his suit, snapped on his light, handed him equipment, stuffed his hands in his gloves, hooked up his inflator hose to his dry suit, and helped him on with his neoprene hood.

All set to go, Gary had just made it to the rail to make his entry when Steve Bielenda pressed a tank and a regulator under his arm. Gentile had been so focused on getting ready and into the water that he was unaware Bielenda had together a rig to be passed to Ormsby.

Bielenda told Gentile to remember to pass the tank to Ormsby butt end first. The *Wahoo*'s skipper did not want a grasping panic-stricken diver taking another one with him. Within six minutes of getting word of Ormsby's predicament, Gentile was furiously swimming down to the wreck.

Once again Sally Wahrmann and Gary Gilligan saw another diver fly by them. But this time it was an act of heroics and not one of greed. Ironically, however, the two were linked.

Gentile shot down the line faster than he had ever done before. Fortunately the visibility was excellent, with no current to battle and the *Wahoo* tied off within sight of the hole. In one sweeping movement Gentile was over the hole and dropping in. His first thought upon entering the hole was "Where am I going?" In the pandemonium aboard the *Wahoo*, neither Gentile nor anyone else had considered where Ormsby was in the long, wide, gaping labyrinth.

Since it was midday and the bright July sun was high overhead, plenty of light was streaming down into the depths, illuminating the entrance to the hole more than usual. Still, overhangs and collapsed bulkheads and hanging cables obstructed the light. Letting his negative buoyancy carry him deeper into the hole, Gary followed his sweeping light. Almost immediately he caught a flash, a glimmer of light below him and to his right. His searching light caught some shiny metal. Pointing his powerful beam in the direction of the flash, Gentile saw the now upside-down body of John Ormsby. His light also caught the figure of the hovering Billy Deans.

"I saw Billy—and this is the spooky thing," Gentile later remembered. "He pushed away from Ormsby, and Ormsby's arms reached out to clutch at him. Billy backed up and I dropped in between them. Billy was out of time and low on air. He gave me a signal that he was out of there. But seeing that movement by Ormsby, I thought he was still alive. Of course later I realized he was already dead. Seeing him hanging in that awkward position should have been the tip-off. An alive and conscious diver would have been upright."

By this time Ormsby's regulator had slipped out of his mouth. Gentile shoved the regulator from the spare tank that Bielenda had given him into Ormsby's vacant mouth. Ormsby did not take a breath. Gentile pushed the purge button on the regulator forcing air into Ormsby's mouth and began punching his chest trying to get him to breath. The air just bubbled out around his lips. Gentile then held the back of Ormsby's head in one hand and the regulator in the other and repeated the purging process. Here, fifty feet inside the hole, it was pitch-black. In his efforts to revive the lifeless diver, Gary's light had dropped from his grip and hung limply from his wrist lanyard and spun in the water, giving a strobe effect to the already eerie scene.

After about two minutes of futilely trying to get Ormsby to breathe, Gary Gentile realized that there was no hope for him. The arm movement had just been a reflex motion when Deans pushed off. Since he had almost twenty minutes more of bottom time, Gary decided he would retrieve the body. Taking out his knife, he started to slice away at the one-inch cables. He managed to cut a couple away but quickly realized the knife would not suffice. Gentile had another idea. He removed a hundred-pound lift bag from Ormsby's harness, filled it with air, then watched as the bag struggled to lift Ormsby. The body did not budge.

Gentile then began to contemplate his own situation. This was his second dive of the day, and he could only guess at his surface interval, which was certainly not long enough to stave off the problem of residual nitrogen in his system. Prior to the emergency dive to rescue Ormsby, Gary had judiciously planned for a dive three hours later than his unexpected rescue dive.

He made his escape from the hole and began the long ascent back up the anchor line. Only then did he realize that in his haste to enter the water he had not put on his thermal underwear under his dry suit. The forty-degree waters began to take their toll. Gary remembered shivering violently on his long decompression hangs.

On his hang, another diver came down the line. He shoved a slate in front of Gary's faceplate: "What do we do now?" Gary took the slate and wrote, "Get hacksaws." The other diver read it and apparently did not comprehend what it meant and quickly scribbled, "Is he alive?" Gary just shook his head.

Collapsing on the deck of the *Wahoo* under the weight of all his gear and thoroughly exhausted from the ordeal and depleted of adrenaline, Gentile was now also hypothermic.

• • •

Sally Wahrmann had made an unplanned visit to the very bottom. The *Doria* lay in 235 feet, but because the mammoth hull had settled deep into the sand, another eighteen feet of her lay beneath the bottom. Sally could only guess what her decompression stops should be. Pushing her air supply, Sally spent over two hours hanging at depths of forty, thirty, twenty, and ten feet. Dehydrated, numbed by the cold water, and exhausted by the harrowing experience of near death, she climbed aboard the *Wahoo* and into the waiting arms of Captain Bielenda.

Everybody aboard the boat was concerned about her and her unexplained long hangs, not knowing that the collision with Ormsby had sent her to the bottom, thereby forcing her to extend her decompression stops.

Bielenda asked if she was upset by Ormsby's death. Sally replied, "Steve, if he was alive on this boat now, I'd stab the son of a bitch with my knife."

A diver usually enters Gimbel's Hole feetfirst, slowly dropping in. Ormsby must have gone in headfirst. Apparently he did not have enough buoyancy to sustain a slow and safe penetration. Speeding down the corridor, Ormsby must have aimed for a protruding bulkhead to grab something to stop himself. What he got was a handful of electrical cables. But the cables pulled loose and cascaded on top of him, adding to his weight. Ormsby plummeted down to his collision with the unsuspecting Wahrmann.

After sending Sally Wahrmann to the bottom, Ormsby managed to swim, despite being ensnared by cable, up from the 223-foot depth to 206 feet. But then he was hopelessly snared.

Gilligan and Wahrmann never saw the struggling or unconscious Ormsby when they exited the dark and silted corridor. By the time Deans and Delotto arrived at Gimbel's Hole, Gary and Sally were already making their slow ascent up the anchor line.

• • •

Back aboard the *Wahoo,* Ormsby's death cast a pall over the expedition. Bielenda notified the U.S. Coast Guard about the fatality. If someone was hurt or lost, the Coast Guard would have dispatched a chopper or cutter, but since the death was confirmed, there was no need for an emergency trip far out into the ocean at the taxpayers' expense. The *Wahoo* was instructed to recover the body.

Bielenda was unwilling to risk a nighttime recovery of the body. As Captain Janet Bieser said, "You never send live marines up the hill to get the dead ones." Divers Rick Jaszyn and Gary Gentile were given the grim task of recovering Ormsby's body from the hold of the *Doria* the next day.

In his panic-stricken struggle to free himself from the jungle of wires and cable, Ormsby had wrapped himself cocoonlike in solid-core wire. Knives were useless. Fortunately, a pair of heavy-duty bolt cutters was aboard the *Wahoo.*

When Jaszyn and Gentile got to the bottom, they secured a seventy-five-foot line to the anchor line with a carabiner and took the free end into the hole with them. Reaching Ormsby's body, they slipped the free end onto one of his D rings on his harness, so that once his body was cut free, it would be tethered to the anchor line.

Jaszyn and Gentile began to cut away at the cables on either side of the body. A few minutes into the effort Gary felt a tug on his tanks. He knew immediately he was snagged in the cables. He froze and started to flash his light at his dive buddy. Rick looked over and seeing Gary pointing his thumb to his back, quickly understood the predicament. Rick swam over and freed Gary.

"It was a scary couple of minutes for me," Gentile would later relate, "but one thing you learn in wreck diving, when you get tangled, you have to remain calm, because twisting and fighting will only make it worse. When you have a buddy there, you let him do the work."

Gentile and Jaszyn created a cloud of silt in their effort to free the body. Jaszyn was amazed how tightly Ormsby was wrapped in the cable. He could not even get his finger between the cable and

Ormsby's dry suit, so he had to cut the suit to get at the cable. While he worked to free the body, Ormsby's face was never more than six inches away from his. He and Ormsby were the same age and had been friends. It was hard for Rick to set aside his emotions. It was a "shitty job," but John Ormsby had a family, Jaszyn had to remind himself, and they could not just leave John behind like that.

Once they had gotten most of the cables cut free, Gentile snapped another lift bag to a D ring on the body and inflated it, figuring they could now raise the body out of the hole. They couldn't.

Gentile then noticed that a cable had been snagged by a brass spring-gated clip, or "suicide clip," that Ormsby had rigged to his harness to hang tools from. It was a telling moment for Gentile. He now knew what had happened to Ormsby. The cable that snaked up his leg to his back must have prevented Ormsby from escaping, causing him to struggle and entangle himself even more.

Gentile cut that last cable loose, and the body immediately began to rise. The body was not precisely under the hole opening and came up on the wrong side of a protruding bulkhead. The body and the lift bag got lodged in the ceiling. Both divers were exhausted from their efforts, and Gentile remembers how he was overbreathing his regulator and he got "real scared." Gentile and Jaszyn threw their hands up and exited the hole.

Both men lay back on the flat side of the wreck and tried to catch their breath. Gentile was gasping. Jaszyn gave his buddy the palms-down relax signal. After resting on the hull of the ship for about two minutes, they finally regained their composure. Looking at each other, they knew what they had to do. They reentered the wreck.

Gentile deflated the lift bag enough so the body began to drop. They then pulled it over from under the bulkhead, put more air in the bag, and as Gentile recalled, "the body went up and just sailed away."

Emerging from the hole, Jaszyn and Gentile reached the anchor line to see the carabiner-tethered line sliding up the anchor line. At the other end was John Ormsby's body. The two divers knew their job was done.

Crewmates Donny Schnell and Craig Stemitez fired up the inflat-

Ormsby's body bobs on the surface.
(Photo © Steve Bielenda)

able boat and sped out to the bobbing lift bag that served as a watery tombstone for the Florida diver. Ormsby had been underwater for more than a day, and rigor mortis had set in. Stemitez grabbed the lift bag and dragged it over to the boat. One of Ormsby's gloved hands popped out of the water and smacked Stemitez in the face. The shocked Stemitez let go of the lift bag, its snap broke, and the body plummeted back down to the bottom.

A diver sent back down found the tether and hauled the body back up. If the body had not been secured to the anchor line by Gentile and Jaszyn, it would have been lost to the sea forever.

Bielenda sent the crew and clients all forward to the bow once the body was on deck and asked Neal Watson to assist. Gary Gilligan remembers the rest all watched from afar while Bielenda and Watson struggled to pull the gear-laden body out of the water from the dive platform onto the open stern area of the *Wahoo*.

They removed only the tanks. Bielenda had been through body recoveries before and knew the less tampering with the body the better, knowing full well investigators would want to see the body as found.

Ormsby's legs were still wrapped in cable. His arms were fully extended in the rigor mortis pose. Bielenda conferred with a diver who was a veterinarian, who told him the arms could be bent then tied to the torso. Blood was in Ormby's mask, and a bloody froth was coming from his mouth. Once the body was stuffed into a sleeping bag and the deck washed of blood, everyone relaxed. All aboard made more dives on the wreck, including Deans and Delotto.

The Coast Guard instructed the *Wahoo* that once their dive operations were complete, they were to proceed to New Harbor, Block Island.

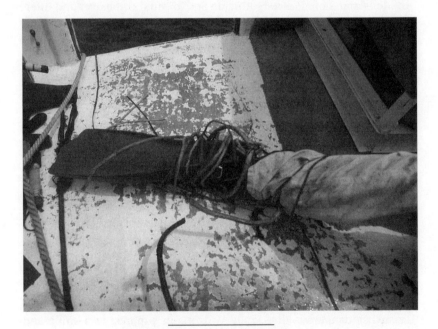

Cable wrapped around Ormsby's corpse.
(Photo © Steve Bielenda)

When they arrived at midnight at the Block Island Coast Guard Station, a cutter out of Point Judith, Rhode Island, was waiting. The body was placed in a body bag and removed to the cutter. The commander of the station was called in, apparently not pleased at having being summoned from bed.

"He was ticked off," Bielenda recalled, "and came in barking orders. First he wanted a detailed report from Billy Deans and Lou Delotto. As master of the boat, I told them to make it in a few sentences because I did not want them to get diarrhea of the mouth and start speculating."

To the continued irritation of the Coast Guard officer, Bielenda reviewed the statement. The *Wahoo* then lay up at the ferry dock. Two hours later another Coast Guard officer came aboard and told Bielenda that they were to stay put until an investigator from the Rhode Island State Police Homicide Squad could come over and interview the crew and divers.

In the wee hours of the morning, the crew was questioned one by one about the accident by a detective in the cabin of the *Wahoo*. According to Bielenda, the detective had an "attitude." He was a diver who believed that sport divers had no business diving below the accepted limit of 130 feet, and that this is what happened when they failed to observe those limits.

Bielenda was interviewed first. The detective then dismissed him and called in Janet Bieser. Bielenda said he had no intention of leaving since he was captain of the *Wahoo* and had the right to hear everything that everyone had to say aboard his vessel. After a heated exchange the Rhode Island detective relented and Bielenda sat through all the ensuing interviews.

When Sally's turn came, she was surprised when the detectives asked if she had read Ormsby's log, checking to see if he was qualified for such a dangerous dive. Sally Wahrmann suppressed a smile and answered yes, she had indeed read his log. She didn't add that it was the only one she had read and that she had studied it "just to bust his balls."

After three hours, the detective concluded his official business. As he walked away from the boat, Bielenda could not contain his curiosity. He called after him, asking what would happen next in the investigation. The detective stopped, quietly walked back a few steps, and solemnly looking at Bielenda said, "This is the last time you'll hear from me." The detective spun on his heels and strode off, disappearing into the early-morning crowd of tourists who flocked to the docks in search of nautical ambience on the resort island.

Upon returning to Long Island, Bielenda did, however, get one more call from the authorities regarding the demise of John Ormsby. The Rhode Island coroner wanted to know why John Ormsby's arms were suspiciously bound to his torso by rope.

In July 1985 it had been twenty-nine years since the disastrous sinking of the *Andrea Doria*, yet the "Mount Everest of wreck diving" had claimed yet another victim. John Ormsby was not the first diver to perish on her, and he would not be the last. As Captain Steve Bielenda and Billy Deans both remarked, it was the first death in which greed, or "china fever," was a factor. Such china fever would form a troubling pattern in *Andrea Doria* diving deaths, which would reach their tragic peak thirteen years later.

TWO

THE WRECK OF THE
ANDREA DORIA

*Despite all the safety gadgets, the mind is supreme
and the mind is fallible.*
—Captain Harry Manning, SS *United States*

The western and central section of New York's Long Island is a myriad of expressways, parkways, and turnpikes, the kind of urban sprawl that enlightened city planners love to point to as the epitome of poor vision. You have to look no further than the Jericho Turnpike to understand their thinking. Flanking this multilaned blacktop, whose serpentine path winds eastward to the more benign and pastoral stretches of eastern Long Island, is a seemingly unending string of fast-food restaurants, auto-body and muffler shops, and gas stations. Then smack-dab in the middle of the concrete morass in the town of Syosset, there is the Caracalla Restaurant.

The Caracalla's faux Italian Renaissance decor may strike some as kitschy, but it is a welcome visual respite from the glut of indistinguishable architecture that greets the eye on the Jericho Turnpike. The

freestanding building is overseen by chef Vincenzo Della Torre, surviving first-class sous-chef of the *Andrea Doria*.

Vincenzo is a little man, not more than five feet four. He is sixty-
six years old and spry for his age. He has that debonair European
demeanor and the Italian propensity for wrapping his arms around
perfect strangers. On my first visit he escorted me to the bar and without sparing a word asked me, "Who do you think was responsible?"

I had come to talk to him about his experiences aboard the
Doria and what had happened that night. I was not ready to render
a decision about where to lay blame. But in his embrace and under
his piercing stare I uttered, more out of intimidation than anything
else, that it must have been the *Stockholm*'s fault for sending the
ship to the bottom. It did, after all, I reasoned, breach the Italian
beauty's vitals with its ice-breaking bow, analogous to broadsiding
another automobile at an intersection after running a red light. He
smiled and patted me on the back. It was the answer he wanted to
hear.

Dressed in his kitchen whites, with a kerchief nattily tied around
his neck and a balding pate ribboned by a wisp of graying hair and a
goatee impeccably maintained, I could envision him hard at work over
a stove on the flagship of the Italia Line almost a half century ago.

Vincenzo hosts a yearly party for *Doria* survivors at his restaurant
on the anniversary of the sinking. "It was the best ship in the world,"
he told me as he tells anyone who asks, "but everybody know that. But
the thing is, when you write this book, you got to tell the truth about
what happen. Captain Calamai was right."

A natural response for the aggrieved, one might suppose.
Vincenzo Della Torre was no sailor. He was a twenty-two-year-old
cook aboard a luxurious ocean liner and knew little about the intricacies of maritime right-of-way, but who was to blame for the sinking of
a pride of a nation is serious business to people like Della Torre. And
rightly so. The *Andrea Doria* was not only a magnificent ship, she was
emblematic of the times, and most of all she was the product of a

proud people from a struggling nation who wanted the world to see that it was still capable of producing a masterpiece.

Genoa has always been Italy's window to the sea. Once a mighty city-state that rivaled Venice for power and prestige in the Mediterranean, Genoa produced Italy's two greatest mariners, Christopher Columbus and Andrea Doria (1466–1560). While Columbus's name is more recognized around the world, Andrea Doria had the more swashbuckling career.

Doria was captain general of the Genoese navy from 1512 until the city was taken over by the Spaniards in 1522. By 1528, he had helped restore its independence in allegiance with the Holy Roman Emperor Charles V. Doria went on to lead the sea battles in the bloody wars against the French and the Barbary pirates. Andrea Doria also helped Charles V capture Tunis and saved the Holy Roman Empire from a disastrous expedition against the North African city of Algiers in 1541. As a statesman, he was not above immersing himself in the bloody Genoese feuds and conspiracies. Much like his American counterpart George Washington, Andrea Doria is often referred to as "the father of his country." Doria is also credited for being the first mariner to devise a method for sailing a ship against the wind.

After a distinguished career, Andrea Doria retired to a monastery at eighty-seven. Such monastic retreats were the reward for exemplary public service, but his contributions to his city were not over. When France tried to annex the nearby island of Corsica, Doria was recalled to duty and once again led the fleet to victory. Andrea Doria finally died at ninety-three, an extraordinarily long life span at the time.

None too surprisingly, the name *Andrea Doria* would grace the transom of many an Italian ship. A brig called the *Andrea Doria* had the honor of being the first foreign ship saluted by the independent United States.

In 1949, Italy was still struggling to raise herself from the ruins of World War II. World tourism was blossoming and bringing incredible

wealth to many nations. Italy had many cultural and architectural treasures to lure tourists to her shores. The reconstructed country turned to
Genoa to provide a vessel to bring hordes of dollar-laden tourists to Italy.

There was plenty of competition for transatlantic tourism:
England, France, the Nordic countries, and the United States all had
stately ships to entice travelers. Not to be outdone, the world-famous
Ansaldo shipyards in the Genoese suburb of Sestri laid the keel for
what was to be the most elegant ship of her time, to be named after the
naval hero, statesman, and innovator Andrea Doria. On May 22, 1950,
to the cheers of the proud Genoese, the newly christened *Andrea Doria*
slipped into the shimmering waters of the Ligurian Sea.

It took another eighteen months for the ship to be outfitted for
transatlantic service. The owners of the ship, the Società da Navigazione
Italia (Italia Line), decided against competing with the British and the
Americans in building the largest and fastest of ships. Instead the Italia
Line wanted to entice their passengers with luxury and art and built
what was to later be described as a "floating art palace." They also
wanted their ship to incorporate the latest techniques in shipbuilding
and spared no expense.

The *Andrea Doria* had a revolutionary design: the forebody incorporated a radical flare, which terminated forward in a knuckle and a
bulbous bow—a feature designed to reduce drag and increase speed.
The stern allowed for a free flow of water over the propellers, with the
propeller shafts fully enclosed.

The Ansaldo yards used a new technique of prefabrication with
electronic welding, with some assemblies weighing in at twenty-seven
tons. The hull was divided into eleven watertight compartments by
transverse bulkheads extending to the main deck, with a collision
bulkhead carried to the Upper-Deck level. The bulkheads were distrib-
uted so that the ship would float with even two compartments flooded.
The hull contained seven decks; the superstructure had four and rose
over a hundred feet above the waterline. The *Andrea Doria* also had a
double bottom extending almost the entire 697'2" of the ship.

The power and speed of the ship were mind-boggling. Her massive twin-turbine engines were fired by high-compression steam generated by four main water-tube boilers and two auxiliary boilers. She cranked out thirty-five thousand horsepower and could maintain an average speed of twenty-three knots for the duration of her Atlantic crossing, burning ten to eleven tons of fuel oil an hour.

The *Andrea Doria* sailed with a complement of 575 officers and crew, a one to three ratio in crew to passengers. Shipbuilders had not liked to use the term *unsinkable* since the *Titanic* disaster forty years before, but the term, in an echo of history, got bandied about nevertheless.

In event of a maritime accident, her Italian builders spared no expense in safety equipment. Twenty lifeboats accommodated over two thousand passengers, or more than the ship carried. She had thirty-three fire-safety zones. Each one of them could be sealed off in case of a fire within. In an age before they were required, the *Andrea Doria* had an automatic sprinkler system and a carbon-dioxide fire-smothering system. The ship even had its own hook-and-ladder fire-fighting company.

As far as creature comforts, the *Andrea Doria* was without equal. Antiques and modern art by Salvatore Fiume, Luzzatie, and Ratti were everywhere. Paintings, murals, mirrors, ceramics, and crystals adorned the walls of the massive ship. The thirty-one public rooms provided an average of forty square feet of recreational space for each of the 1,290 passengers that the ship could comfortably accommodate.

For the moneyed elite, the Italia Line provided four unique deluxe suites designed by Italy's top artist-designers, each consisting of a bedroom, sitting room, powder room, and bath.

As for the rest of the ship, luxury was broken down into three classes, first class, cabin class (second class), and tourist class (third class). First class could accommodate 207 passengers, cabin class 376, and tourist class 707. All first-class and cabin-class staterooms had private showers and toilets. The entire ship was air-conditioned, and each class had its own dining room, bar, lounge, movie theater, recreational area, and swimming pool. The three swimming pools sat terraced in the stern section of the ship, as one contemporary account described, "in country club settings of tables, sun umbrellas, pool bars, and white-waistcoated waiters." Construction costs for hull and machinery alone reached $30 million, and the art and furnishings equaled that.

Perhaps the most striking thing about the *Andrea Doria* was not her detail, her machinery, or even her inboard treasures, but the image she struck steaming across the horizon in her full glory. I was a witness to that very vision on more than one occasion.

I grew up in the Rockaways, a sandy spit of land extending out from the western end of Long Island. Sitting on the jetty-girded beaches of the Rockaways, I witnessed many of the glorious entrances of the proud ocean liners, now long since gone.

The Cunard's *Queen Mary* and *Queen Elizabeth,* the French *Ile de France,* and the SS *United States,* and *America* all fell under my spellbound view sitting there on the ocean's edge. But it was the *Andrea Doria* that took my breath away. Her jet-black hull and the gleaming white superstructure, the rakish single smokestack emblazoned in Italy's colors of green, white, and red, made for as entrancing a sight as I had ever seen. Those long, elegant, sweeping lines would forever characterize Italian design for me.

Sitting on that Rockaway beach so many years ago, I never dreamed that I would visit that exquisite ship, half a lifetime later, in her grave at the bottom of the Atlantic.

At fifty-eight, Superior Captain Piero Calamai had spent thirty-nine years of his life at sea. A merchant marine cadet, he was awarded the Italian War Cross for military valor during World War I when he was only eighteen years old. As a reserve lieutenant commander during World War II, he was again awarded the War Cross for valor. Over his career he served as an officer aboard twenty-seven ships in

Glamour shot of the *Andrea Doria*.
(Photo courtesy of the Mariners Museum)

the Italian merchant marine before being rewarded with the command of the pride of the Italia Line—the newly launched *Andrea Doria*.

Captain Calamai was not gregarious. "Dignified but distant" was how his senior chief officer, Luigi Oneto, described him. Calamai found the social obligations aboard a luxury ocean liner distasteful. Shy, introverted, a teetotaler, he preferred sharing meals with his officers in their private dining area to the ostentatious soirees in the passenger dining rooms that had become obligatory for any ocean-liner master. Ever the proud captain, however, he was always willing to give tours to those interested in the mechanisms of navigating an immense floating city, from his command center on the bridge.

Calamai was revered by his subordinates. He was always discreet enough to take a man aside and advise him of his mistakes rather than humiliate him in front of his peers. He had the aristocratic demeanor of a polished, concerned, and educated man. His swarthy, sea-weathered countenance was a habitual presence on the bridge of the *Andrea Doria*, and he rarely took refuge in his comfortable captain's quarters.

After weighing anchor at Genoa on July 17, 1956, the *Andrea Doria* made three scheduled stops at Cannes, Naples, and Gibraltar. At precisely 12:30 P.M. Friday, July 20, the *Doria* bid adieu to Europe with 1,134 passengers and 401 tons of freight. Among the cargo was a special automobile, the Norseman, an experimental prototype designed and constructed by the Ghia plant in Turin for the Chrysler Corporation. It represented an investment for the Detroit automobile giant of $100,000, and they were anxiously awaiting its arrival stateside.

Captain Calamai piloted his ship on what was called the great-circle route. After skirting the Azores to the northwest, the *Andrea Doria* steered a course due west for the Nantucket Lightship, the welcoming beacon to the New World.

Captains of ocean liners were always under tremendous pressure to arrive at port on time. Arrival times were carefully calculated with the ship at full speed, and any delays meant cost overruns. The additional costs were for fuel, meals for passengers, and two-hundred longshoremen who were hired for the day and who had to be paid. If the ship arrived at dock late, there was also the public relations nightmare of irate passengers late for connections. Such were Captain Calamai's concerns on the evening of July 25.

One hundred and sixty miles east of the Nantucket Shoals the *Andrea Doria* began to run into light, patchy fog. Calamai had seen the conditions deteriorate for himself from the exposed bridge wings that extended out from the bridge. The captain knew conditions would worsen once the ship approached the Nantucket Lightship, which was anchored on the southern tip of the shoals. The shoals were infamous for their hazardous fog conditions during July, when the warm, moisture-saturated southwestern breeze blew over the frigid Labrador currents emanating from the North Atlantic. Although Captain Calamai had encountered them before, he was always a worrier. Unlike many other ship masters, he did not leave fog watch to junior officers. He remained on the bridge.

Earlier that day, some three hundred miles away, the Swedish-American Line's *Stockholm* had departed from the Fifty-seventh Street Pier on the west side of Manhattan at 11:31 A.M. on a hot and muggy summer day. The *Stockholm* was not in a class with the *Andrea Doria*. Built in 1948, the stark white *Stockholm*, with its single, yellow smokestack, was 525 feet long, and her top speed was a respectable eighteen to nineteen knots. Her sharply pointed bow was reinforced for following icebreakers, a necessity for the northerly routes she had to take to reach her Nordic destinations.

The *Stockholm*, a compact ship, was a testament to the frugal ways of the Swedes. She carried only 534 passengers, spread out over her efficiently laid-out seven decks. Her passenger quarters were comfort-

Glamour shot of the *Stockholm*.
(Photo courtesy of the Mariners Museum)

able but certainly not luxurious. Because of her unique design—she resembled a large yacht as opposed to an ocean liner—her cabins for passengers and crew alike all had portals to the sea. The *Stockholm* had only one indoor swimming pool and just the necessary number of public rooms for her passengers. Overseeing the ship with typical Swedish-American Line efficiency was the austere Captain H. Gunnar Nordenson.

Captain Nordenson, sixty-three years old and a veteran of forty-six years at sea, was a taskmaster. Fraternization between officers and crew was forbidden, as was smoking and coffee drinking while on duty on the bridge. The only words heard in the nerve center of the *Stockholm* were the orders of the officers and the requisite responses from crew.

The *Stockholm* followed the *Ile de France* down the Hudson River. The 793-foot *Ile de France* was one of the more storied ocean liners of the century. Though an aging lady of the sea and a behemoth by any-one's standards, the much faster French ocean liner left the *Stockholm* in her dissipating wake. By the time the *Stockholm* had reached the Ambrose Lightship, outside of the New York Harbor entrance, the *Ile* had already disappeared over the horizon. Full speed ahead, the next stop for the *Stockholm* was Copenhagen, Denmark, then on to her home port of Gothenburg, Sweden.

The Swedish-American Line was one of the few transatlantic lines that only required one officer to stand watch while the ship was under way. Most ocean liners had two on duty. The frugal-minded Swedes felt their officers could discharge their duties without redundancy. Seven hours and 130 miles out from Ambrose Lightship, Third Officer Johan-Ernst Carstens-Johannsen relieved Senior Second Officer Lars Enestrom for his four-hour watch.

Seeing to the passengers' needs prior to departure and the loading of cargo and then negotiating the tricky narrows of New York Harbor had worn out all the officers aboard the *Stockholm*. Captain Nordenson had already retired to his quarters for some paperwork but continued to make unannounced visits to the bridge to check on the ship's head-ing and scan weather reports.

Carstens-Johannsen, or simply Carstens to his shipmates, had been revived by a few hours of rest, a filling meal, and a steam bath. Before joining the helmsman, lookout, and standby lookout on the bridge, he had checked out the navigational chart spread in the chart-room just behind the bridge. He also noted the weather forecasts and was not surprised to learn that heavy fog could be expected ahead. Surveying the empty ocean in front of him, Carstens settled into a rou-tine he relished. The tall, robust twenty-six-year-old expected his first turn as commander of the *Stockholm* for the voyage eastward to be uneventful.

Twenty-year-old Ingemar Bjorkman manned the wheel of the *Stockholm*. In front of him, past the windows of the bridge, was the twilight gloom of the open seas. Bjorkman, who had only three years of sea experience, glanced regularly at the gyrocompass, making sure the course was true to the ninety degrees indicated by the course box, which contained three wooden cubes that resembled oversize dice and read "090."

At 9:40 P.M. Captain Nordenson arrived on the bridge and without ceremony ordered Carstens to change course to eighty-seven degrees. Carstens immediately arranged the wooden cubes to read "087." Bjorkman turned the wheel so the gyroscope headings coincided with the numbers in the course box. Carstens did not question his captain's change of course. He assumed he wanted to cut closer to the Nantucket Lightship before heading east into the open Atlantic.

Approaching the lightship that close was against the 1948 International Convention for the Safety of Life at Sea. However, the Swedish-American Line was not a signer of that convention, nor was the Italia Line. The convention would have dictated a course twenty miles farther south.

Carstens switched his radar scope's range from fifteen to fifty miles. The *Stockholm* was now plying one of the busiest sea-lanes in the world. After a few minutes, with just a few blips on his radar screen, he switched it back to the fifteen-mile range. He checked the helmsman's gyrocompass, then returned his gaze to the featureless sea in front of him, wondering when they could expect the curtain of fog to fall on them.

Captain Nordenson once again left the bridge, but not before telling Carstens that the captain was to be notified once the lightship was sighted. Carstens took a reading of the ship's position by dead reckoning. Ascertaining the position of the ship by dead reckoning was a reasonably accurate and common navigational practice aboard ships at the time—loran was still new and not totally trusted and GPS (global positioning system) unheard of. In dead reckoning, the present position was determined by the distance traveled in relation to the last known position. Carstens calculated that the *Stockholm* was over two miles north of their desired position, due, no doubt, to tidal drift.

The *Stockholm* was now in a deep fog bank. At 10:04 P.M. Carstens compensated for the drift north by changing the course to eighty-nine degrees, turning the ship in effect more to the south, or to the right. By this time Peder Larsen had exchanged his lookout post for Bjorkman's post at the wheel. This was the young Larsen's first voyage aboard the *Stockholm*. At 10:30 P.M. after a position determination from the lightship's radio beacon, Carstens adjusted the ship's course to ninety-one degrees since he thought the *Stockholm* would be approaching the lightship within the two-mile safety range. With almost zero visibility, the radar, foghorn, and navigational lights would have to compensate. Glancing at his radar scope, still set at the fifteen-mile range, Carstens noticed a blip on the screen.

Aboard the *Andrea Doria*, Captain Calamai still paced his bridge. The heavy cloud of water particles clinging to the ocean's surface had forced Captain Calamai to order his lookout down from the mast's crow's nest to the bowsprit so he would have a better view of what lay ahead. The fog whistle was set to boom its warning every hundred seconds. From a control panel on the bridge, all eleven watertight compartments were shut.

The speed of the ship was slowed down to twenty-one knots from twenty-three knots, not enough of a reduction to satisfy the Regulations for Preventing Collisions at Sea, an internationally recognized agreement. The regulations were somewhat nebulous about the reduction of speed since they simply stated that the ship should slow to a "reasonable speed." The general rule of thumb was a ship should slow to a speed where it could stop within half the distance of its visibility. But visibility was virtually nil, which meant if the rule of thumb was to be followed to the letter, the *Doria* would have to had come to a complete stop. That, of course, was unthinkable. The *Andrea Doria* was already a projected hour behind its 9 A.M. scheduled arrival. The minimal reduction of speed, nevertheless, was a compromise of safety that would later haunt Captain Calamai.

Fourteen miles east of the Nantucket Lightship, Captain Calamai

47

ordered his helmsman, fifty-nine-year-old Carlo Domenchini, to follow a course of 261 degrees, which brought them abeam of the lightship one mile south of it at 10:20 P.M. Calamai then changed the
course to 268 degrees, on a direct line to the Ambrose Lightship, now
only two-hundred miles away.

At approximately 10:40 P.M. Second Officer Curzio Franchini
noticed a blip on his radar scope. He alerted Captain Calamai of the
position of the unknown ship, which was four degrees to starboard
and seventeen miles away and closing. No officer on the bridge of the
Andrea Doria was alarmed since a single ship in front of them—even a
ship on a parallel course—posed no serious threat.

The "rules of the road," maritime right-of-way, called for ships on
head-on courses to turn right for a port-to-port (left-to-left) passing.
Captain Calamai determined there was ample distance between the
ships, so he continued on his course, which veered left, or out to open
sea. The Andrea Doria's master might have acted differently had he
known the ship bearing down on his was not a small fishing vessel, as
he was led to believe, but another fast-moving ocean liner also intent
on keeping to a tight schedule.

Second Officer Franchini switched his radar scope from a twenty-
mile to a seven-mile radius. Surprised at what he saw, he informed his
captain that the ship was bigger and moving faster then they had initially surmised. Still, the second officer projected that they would pass
each other a mile apart. Helmsman Domenchini was relieved at the
wheel by seaman Giulio Visciano. Calamai then made a critical decision.

Calamai instructed Visciano to turn four more degrees to the left,
"and nothing to the right." That meant helmsman Visciano was to execute a slow, even turn to the left. Such a maneuver was a fuel-saving
and smoother turn, but it was also harder to decipher on radar by
another ship.

Informed by Officer Franchini that the approaching ship was only
two miles away and still on a parallel course, Calamai and Third

Officer Eugenio Giannini made their way to the wing bridge to see if they could see the ship or hear its fog whistle. Giannini caught sight of its masthead lights. Moments later, the lower forward masthead light and the aft higher masthead light on the *Stockholm* appeared to reverse themselves. Adding to his horror, Giannini saw the red light affixed to the port side.

The *Stockholm* was turning directly into the path of the *Andrea Doria!*

Giannini cried out, "She is turning, she is turning. She is showing the red light! She is coming toward us!"

Captain Calamai ordered his helmsman a *"Tutto sinistra"* (all left). Visciano frantically turned the wheel hard left. Hoping to outrace the oncoming vessel, Calamai opted not to attempt to stop the ship or reduce speed, knowing it would take at least three miles to do so. In a split-second decision, he also decided against the accepted turn toward the oncoming ship, or turning to his right. Such a seemingly dangerous maneuver was considered preferable when collision was imminent: better to chance a bow-to-bow glancing strike than a potential mortal blow to the ship's flank.

Because of her mass and forward motion, it took half a mile before the *Andrea Doria* began to respond to the radical course change. The white-knuckled crew on the bridge of the Italian ship watched in horror as the sharply raked bow of the *Stockholm* appeared out of the fog. All that was left for them to do was to brace themselves. The *Stockholm* knifed into the Doria, directly under the right wing of the bridge, with a sickening, jolting crunch.

Vincenzo Della Torre was relaxing, puffing on a cigarette as he leaned over the ship's port-side railing, staring out into fog. His kitchen duties had ended fifteen minutes earlier. He recalled that night from the comfort of his own restaurant and from forty-three years of hindsight.

"I was thrown by the tremendous impact and ran to the opposite

The stricken *Andrea Doria*.
(© Harry Trask / Mariners Museum)

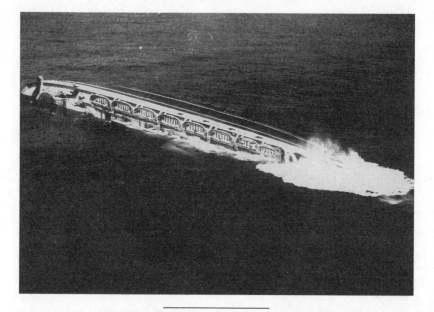

Top: The *Andrea Doria* heels over. *(© Harry Trask / Mariners Museum)*
Bottom: The *Andrea Doria* succumbs to the depths.
(Photo courtesy of the Mariners Museum)

side of the ship where we were hit," he told the *New York Times*. "Fog was heavy. At first I saw nothing, but then I could make out the *Stockholm's* bow stuck deep in our side. People were rushing onto the deck from inside, panicking and screaming in Italian. 'Calmatevi! Calmatevi!' I hollered. 'Be calm! Be calm! I was wearing my white kitchen jacket and they could see I was crew. Most obeyed me. But, to tell the truth, I was just as scared and panicky as they were."

The memories of that night were still vivid forty-four years later in the mind of Pat Mastrincola, of West Milford, New Jersey. The nine-year-old, with his mother, was watching a movie in the tourist-class theater that had earlier served as their dining room. "All of a sudden, the ship made a tremendously hard turn. We all knew something was wrong. The movie screen and projector tumbled over. Dinnerware on shelves behind us avalanched down. The whole audience broke into a panic."

The young boy and his mother scrambled for the exit and through crowds of panicked passengers back to their cabin, at the other end of the ship, where Pat's younger sister had been left to sleep. Smoke and white powder from the burning insulation ignited by the friction of steel against steel filled the corridors. Amazed, they found the little girl still asleep, even thought she had been thrown from her bed. Because of the severe list of the ship she was sleeping against a tilting cabin wall.

"Eventually, my mom, sister, and I worked our way out to the ship's fantail. Then the ship dipped further, to twenty-five degrees. B and C Decks were completely flooded. That's when terror really set in. Mother, sister, and I clung to the ship's high side. The interior was filled with smoke. Splintered steel and lumber were everywhere. There was nowhere to go. It was foggy and dark. Visibility was zero. There was no sign of help."

Walter G. Carlin, a retired lawyer from Brooklyn, was getting ready for bed in first-class cabin No. 46, located on the starboard Upper Deck. He had just entered the private bathroom to brush his teeth. His wife was propped up in bed reading a book. The next thing he knew he was sent sprawling to the floor. Staggering back into the stateroom, he found his wife, her bed, and her night table all gone. In horror he stared out of the gaping hole where his wife had been, into the black void of night air, fog, and sea.

Several doors down, Thure Peterson, a chiropractor from New York, had just fallen off to sleep in his cabin when the *Stockholm* struck. He was awoken by a "tremendous thud, the sound of ripping steel." Then he saw a mass of white steel brush by him. He felt as if he were flying through space. He then lost consciousness.

Aboard the *Stockholm*, Captain Nordenson with his officers surveyed the damage to his now idle ship. Stunned to wordlessness, they found that seventy-five feet of the bow had been reduced to a jumble of twisted and broken steel. Ten crewmen had been asleep in their forward quarters. The ones who were not crushed to death in the accordioned bow had been plucked from their bunks and swallowed up by the sea. In the crush, the *Stockholm* had lost her anchor chains, spilling all seven hundred feet of the heavy links onto the ocean floor. The anchor winches were obliterated in the collision.

The Swedish sailors then made a shocking discovery. Hearing a plaintive voice calling out in a strange language from the wreckage of the bow, they found a young girl wearing tattered pajamas. No one knew who she was; her name was nowhere to be found on the passenger roster. Fourteen-year-old Linda Morgan had been traveling with her mother, stepfather and sister aboard the *Andrea Doria!* The teenager had been catapulted by the bow of the *Stockholm* at impact, then withdrawing wreckage of the bow had somehow scooped the girl up. She was found some eighty feet from what had been the peak of the bow, huddled behind a sea breaker wall. Her younger sister and stepfather perished in the collision. The New York tabloids christened Linda Morgan the "miracle girl."

Under her own power, the Swedish ship eventually limped back to New York with hundreds of survivors from the *Andrea Doria*.

Although Thure Peterson regained consciousness and managed to free himself from under the debris of what remained of his cabin, forty-three passengers on the "unsinkable" Italian ship died. With its ice-breaking bow the *Stockholm* struck deep into the heart of the *Andrea Doria*. All seven lower decks had been exposed to the sea in the shape of a *V* below the wheelhouse. The bulkhead deck, or A Deck, was where the bulkheads separating the ship into the eleven watertight compartments ended. The steel cap at the A Deck was suffused with seventeen stairways to accommodate passengers. On a military ship, small hatches could quickly be battened down. But the seventeen cavernous stairways of the Doria became conduits for the rush of water and oil from ruptured tanks, flooding neighboring watertight compartments on the listing ship. The *Andrea Doria* had been built to survive the flooding of only two of the eleven watertight compartments.

Hollywood movie star Ruth Roman was dancing in the first-class ballroom on the Belvedere Deck, the very top of the ship. She later told a reporter from The *New York Times* that without warning "we heard a big explosion like a firecracker." Seeing smoke, she left the dance floor in her nylon-stockinged feet and rushed aft to her cabin, where her three-year-old son, Dickie, slept. Awakening the little boy, she told him they were "going on a picnic." In the crush of panicked passengers she got separated from her son. Only when she arrived in New York the next day, exhausted and hysterical with worry, was she reunited with the boy.

Ruth Roman's escape from the stricken ship was far easier than that of the poor souls in the cheaper cabins belowdecks. In the bowels of the ship, passengers in B and C Decks had to fight their way up pitch-black, narrow staircases filled with their terrified neighbors. Cold seawater, fouled by engine oil, cascaded down the stairs and passageways, forcing them to pull themselves hand over hand across slippery steel rises up to the Boat Deck of the ship. The horrible ordeal took many of them over a hour to complete. It was on A, B, and C Decks that the majority of the forty-three victims perished. Most were poor immigrants dreaming of a new life in America; some were nuns returning from a pilgrimage to Rome.

The last person to leave the *Andrea Doria* was not an officer or the captain as was thought on the morning of July 26. That dubious honor went to an American seaman by the name of Robert Hudson.

The thirty-five-year-old sailor had been injured in an accident aboard a freighter en route to Europe. He had been taken aboard the *Doria* at Gibraltar and quartered in the ship's hospital for his trip home. Without telling the ship's hospital staff Hudson had taken a more comfortable bunk abutting the ship's hospital and had fallen into a heavily sedated sleep.

Hudson's slumber was not disturbed by the collision or the pandemonium aboard his comfortable seagoing ambulance. When he awoke early the next morning, he was alone on the severely listing ship. He struggled with his debilitating injuries for over an hour to reach the stern.

A lifeboat dispatched by the late-arriving tanker *Robert E. Hopkins* to search for survivors spotted Hudson. The seamen manning the boat were afraid to approach the sinking ship for fear that if the Doria capsized, they would be sucked under with it. Hudson alternated between begging for help and cursing his would-be rescuers for an hour and a half. Finally spurred to action, the lifeboat plucked the injured Hudson from the dying *Doria* and escaped its suction by some ferocious rowing. It was 7:30 A.M. The *Andrea Doria* was now a ghost ship waiting to be received by the ocean bottom.

What was later described as a billion-to-one-chance accident was the first collision between two ocean liners in history. The rescue of the surviving twelve hundred passengers and the crew from the doomed ship is considered the greatest peacetime sea rescue of all time. Besides the *Stockholm*, four other ships answered the *Andrea Doria*'s distress call. One of those ships was the *Ile de France*. She raced from her position forty-four miles away to help in the heroic rescue mission.

The damaged *Stockholm* arrives in New York.
(Photo courtesy of the Mariners Museum)

There is still some mystery today as to how these two huge ships managed to collide. The collision would never have occurred had the Swedish-American Line subscribed to the Convention for the Safety of Life at Sea. As William Hoffer said in his book *Saved!*: "The *Stockholm* was, in effect, legally driving in the opposite direction on a wide, but potentially dangerous, one-way street. Had they [the Swedish-American Line] followed the 1948 Convention, the *Stockholm* and the *Andrea*

56

Doria would have passed each other safely at a distance of twenty miles." After a lengthy litigation in a New York court in 1957, the Italia and Swedish-American Lines agreed to an out-of-court settlement, but the controversy continues to this day.

Some maritime experts blame the Italian captain for excessive speed in less than optimum conditions and for failing to execute the port-to-port passing. Captain Robert Meurn, a professor at the United States Merchant Marine Academy in Kings Point, New York, takes a different view. Captain Meurn is a recognized authority on the *Andrea Doria–Stockholm* collision. He teaches a course in bridge simulation training at the Merchant Marine Academy, and he says the *Andrea Doria* sinking is a textbook example about what can go wrong when two ships are on a collision course. Meurn is of Swedish descent, and his grandfather taught at the Swedish Merchant Marine Academy. As a boy in Sweden, Meurn even met the *Stockholm's* Captain Nordenson. He says he had all the built-in pro-Swedish prejudices when he began to examine the accident. Still, he came away with a surprising conclusion: "The majority of the blame I attribute to Carstens-Johannsen."

Meurn has inputted all the data from both ships into the ship's-bridge-simulator computer at the Merchant Marine Academy. The computer projects images onto a screen, and the two ships were put at the distances apart and the times that both the Italia and Swedish-American Lines concurred on. Carstens's testimony at the inquiry, according to Meurn, did not jibe with the facts.

Meurn explains that Carstens had initially claimed he saw the blip of the *Andrea Doria* at twelve miles, when it was actually only four miles away. In 1956 radar scopes had range scales, which were adjusted by turning a knob. You needed a flashlight to see what scale you were on in a darkened bridge. Carstens, in testimony given at the official inquiry, said he picked up the *Andrea Doria* on the fourth range ring from the center of the scope. Meurn says Carstens wrongly assumed he was on the fifteen-mile scale where the fourth ring would have indicated the blip was twelve miles away, when in actuality it was on the five-mile scale, making the fourth ring just four miles away.

In accordance with the rules of the seas, Carstens testified, he then came about right at 23:05 (11:05 P.M.) at the supposedly twelve-mile mark when he realized the ships were on reciprocal courses. Captain Calamai had the *Stockholm* correctly plotted from as far away as seventeen miles and rightly assumed, if the courses were held, the two ships would safely pass each other starboard to starboard three-quarters of a mile apart. Still the Italian captain came left to increase the distance between the two ships.

As to the charge the *Andrea Doria* did not reduce speed significantly in fog conditions, Captain Meurn has only to point to the SS *United States*. In 1952 the American ship set a transatlantic record with an average speed of 35.59 knots even though the ship was in heavy fog half of the time that she took to cross the Atlantic. Captain Meurn explained, "In those days they all went at full speed through the fog. If they [ocean liners] slowed down every time they encountered fog, they [ship captains] would have been relieved of duty. They had schedules to maintain."

Five minutes before the collision, the *Stockholm* had changed position and came right toward the *Andrea Doria* without signaling with the two sharp blasts of the fog whistle as required. According to Captain Meurn, at that very moment the *Andrea Doria*'s fate was sealed.

Meurn also believes Carstens was afraid to call the captain when the blip of the *Doria* was first seen. Meurn describes Nordenson as having an intimidating presence. Carstens, a third officer, should not have been alone on the bridge under such conditions with another ship rapidly approaching it from the opposite direction.

According to Meurn, Carstens's account of seeing the *Andrea Doria*'s red light (on the port side) when he made his last desperate turn to starboard minutes before the violent encounter is not plausible. The computer simulator proves that the turn was made later, some thirty seconds before impact, much too late to avoid it.

Meurn believes that some good came out of the tragedy. An agreement by all ocean lines shortly after the accident required two officers on the bridge during a watch, and VHF radio contact between ships was established.

Hearing of Captain Meurn's conclusions brought a sad smile to the face of Vincenzo Della Torre. As with any tragic mishap or senseless act of violence, there is only the term *closure* for the victims. But for Della Torre there is some satisfaction in knowing the love of his young life was not responsible for her untimely end. Nevertheless, the thought that the sea is now her grave is unbearably sad for the Italian expatriate. He still grieves over the loss.

For those of us who love the sea, the loss of human life is tragic, but there is no disgrace in an oceangoing vessel's finding rest under the waters. Had the *Andrea Doria* been able to avoid the bow of the *Stockholm,* she would certainly have gone on to serve transatlantic passengers for many more years. They would have been wowed by her structural beauty, her service, her elegance, and her artworks. But eventually her utility would have come to an ignominious end, as it does for all successful ships. If not the jet airliner, it would have been age that would have done the grande dame in. Had the whims of fate not interfered, the *Andrea Doria* would have been stripped of her artistic trappings soon enough and her hull would have been scrapped— the ultimate indignity for any proud ship.

To divers like me, the *Andrea Doria* still lives. It is just that her life goes on many fathoms under the sea where only an intrepid few get the chance to relive her charms.

THREE

MY FIRST DESCENT

Fortune favors those who dare.

—Virgil, *The Aeneid*

I was destined to dive the *Doria*.

In June 1990 I wrote an article on shark diving for *Compass Readings*, the in-flight magazine for Northwest Airlines. The article was the kind of adventure-immersion story that was gaining favor with travel publications. The piece was about Bob Cranston, a California diving outfitter who was chumming for sharks in the waters off San Diego, then dropping divers in shark cages in the midst of the ensuing feeding frenzy.

The publisher of *Compass Readings*, Skies America, had recently taken on the job of producing the magazine for the Minneapolis-based air carrier. Skies America was desperate to acquire more stories for their monthly travel/adventure column. Editor in chief Terri Wallo called me from Portland, Oregon, and asked if I had any other ideas for the column. Yes, I responded, I wanted to dive the *Doria*.

At that point I had been diving for over twenty-two years. Fascinated by Lloyd Bridges's TV program, I had watched his underwater exploits on our black-and-white set as a kid. When I was eighteen, I had enrolled in a scuba-diving class at Central Skindivers in nearby Brooklyn, against my father's wishes.

My father always said I could swim before I could walk, and I don't recall ever taking a swimming lesson. The beach was at the end of our street in Belle Harbor, Rockaway. Bobbing in the surf, bodysurfing, and beachcombing—that was how my friends and I spent our summer days. My high school swim-team competitions later evolved into participating in triathlons and three finishes in the 28.5-mile marathon swim around Manhattan Island.

"Honest Archie" at Central Skindivers sold diving gear. They had a pool on Utica Avenue just off Flatbush in which they gave scuba instructions. The course, tank, regulator, mask, snorkel, fins, and a "shorty" wet suit set me back $150, which was more than a week's wages from my summer job at the New York City Department of Parks.

By the summer of 1968 everybody was talking about the growing conflict in Southeast Asia, but my buddies and I still focused our attention on diving. Every chance we got, we filled up our tanks for a dollar at Central Skindivers and headed down to Beach 8th Street in Far Rockaway. Spearguns in hands, we would take the plunge off the jetty into the Rockaway Inlet and hunt for striped bass, fluke, and bluefish under the Atlantic Beach Bridge. We discovered that eels sprouted like weeds from the rocky bottom of the inlet. They were easy pickings for our trident-headed hand spears. Since the slimy creatures rarely took a hook, we had the Italian fishermen—who considered eel a delicacy—green with envy. We would emerge with dozens of them and get two bucks apiece for them. It paid for our diving and gas for our vehicles and also covered many rounds of beers at the Belle Harbor Tavern.

After college, like many of my generation, I moved out to California. The Golden State was North America's hotbed of diving. Securing a reputable agency's certification from the Los Angeles County Aquatics Division, I got a taste for abalone and lobsters caught in the chill Pacific waters and kelp beds off the Santa Barbara Channel Islands and Santa Catalina Island. There were half a million certified divers in California then, more than in the rest of the entire country. There was another telling statistic. In one year, 1972, all twenty-four recorded drowning deaths on the vast stretches of southern-California coastline were scuba-related. Scuba was not a pursuit of the recreationally minded; it was one of the first extreme sports.

By the mid-1970s I had drifted back to my old East Coast haunts, in the meantime picking up another avocation—writing. I tackled the subject of adventure travel, mostly about scuba diving and mostly for low-paying niche publications such as *Skin Diver* and *Underwater USA*. Occasionally I would break into mainstream publications; getting my foot in the door at Skies America with the shark-diving story was a godsend. The assignment to write about the *Andrea Doria* was my chance to revisit an old friend. I had seen the *Doria* in her prime, but there were other bonds.

My parents were in Europe that summer of 1956, and they had tried to book return passage on the *Andrea Doria*. For some forgotten reason they were unable to do so. Never one to let the facts interfere with a good story, I fabricated a fantastic tale of their escape from the sinking ship to impress my friends. I had forged a link, however bogus, to the Italian liner.

In the headlines in the faded, yellowed local newspapers and the *Life* magazine cover story in 1956, I uncovered in my research some long-forgotten memories. I was only six years old at the time, but this sea catastrophe—like many dramatic events in a young person's life—lay there smothered under layers of recollections and musings piled on by the years. The last voyage of the *Andrea Doria* and my planned deep descent to her grave was to be a voyage of introspection for me as well as a physical challenge.

I was vaguely aware of the sunken ship's appeal to wreck divers. I knew it was far deeper than I had ever gone before, and dangerous, and that it was somewhere out in the Atlantic off the coast of Massachusetts. By that point I had made a multitude of wreck dives, but they were mostly in shallow coastal waters, tame stuff compared to a deep-ocean dive on the *Doria*.

Then my brother and I met Richie Maranda, a law enforcement officer for the waterways of Long Island's southern shores. Maranda was one of the old-timers of Long Island diving, one of the first to explore the interior of the underwater hulk of the USS *San Diego*, twelve miles out in the Fire Island Inlet. Maranda even got lost inside the 504-foot heavy cruiser and wrote a riveting account of his escape for *Reader's Digest*. He told me there was only one boat I should be on if I wanted to dive the *Doria*: Steve Bielenda's *Wahoo*.

A dive boat is more than just a bus to a wreck site. Getting to the wreck safely on a seaworthy boat with the latest in oceangoing electronics and navigated by a competent captain is important, and a good dive-boat skipper has the knowledge and experience to put you on the desired portion of the wreck securely. A capable crew is necessary to help a gear-laden diver in and out of the water. But the most important consideration of all is the boat captain's intuitive and judgmental skills. The captain is the final arbiter of who will—and will not—make the dive. The boat captain has a serious responsibility to the diver's family, and to the divers. Putting an unqualified person in depths that are beyond his skill jeopardizes the diver's safety and the success of the trip. Diving accidents cast a terrible pall over an expedition.

Bielenda agreed over the phone to discuss the possibility of taking me on one of his expeditions out to the *Doria* that summer of 1990. He told me to meet him on his boat at Captree Boat Basin, at the extreme east end of Jones Beach Island, just inside the Fire Island Inlet. And so on a violently rainy and windblown April evening, I drove down for the rendezvous.

I had done my research on Steve Bielenda, called by Long Island's Pulitzer Prize–winning newspaper *Newsday* "the king of the deep." Bielenda, the grandson of Polish immigrants, was born in Harlem and raised in Brooklyn, where his father had worked in the navy yard. Fascinated by pulp stories and movies of the navy frogmen, he was one of the first students when Central Skindivers opened up in 1959. Two years later he became an instructor and gained a reputation as an underwater salvor; most of his work was in lifting small boats from the bottom and finding lost outboard engines, anchors, and personal belongings. Occasionally he also found a body. His underwater experiences led to larger undertakings, and by the 1970s he was so busy with his underwater salvage business that he sold his three service stations and focused full-time on what the seas offered up. But Bielenda wanted to own and captain the ultimate dive boat, and in 1980 he commissioned the building of the research vessel *Wahoo*.

My drive down to the barrier island that rainy April was unnerving. The southern coast of Long Island was being pounded by high winds and seas, and in the drive along the pitch-black shoreline I had not seen one other car in either direction. Was I the only fool out in this weather?

At Captree Boat Basin, I carefully walked the gangplank onto the rocking *Wahoo* toward the faint glow of light coming from the enclosed cabin. The moonlight illuminated the froth of the whitecaps that churned in the channel, and there was Steve Bielenda sitting at the table in the boat's galley patiently awaiting my arrival.

He was fifty-five years old at the time, short, burly, and barrel-chested, obviously a man who made his living doing hard physical labor. With the squint of a man who spent a lot of time at sea, he watched and listened intently while I rattled off my diving credentials. I told him what I had hoped to achieve on the *Doria* and what I wanted to write about. Bielenda, I quickly learned, did not beat around the bush.

His first comment after sizing me up was "you're no kid," the implication being that I was a little old to be taking up new and dangerous pursuits. Yeah, he said in his Brooklyn patois, my diving career was long and varied, but I had never been down that "fucking deep."

But Bielenda was also a good businessman, and I knew it was tough making a buck catering to a small, hard-core group of wreck divers. A feature piece in a magazine read by four hundred thousand people would be good media exposure. Bielenda was also eager to trumpet the adventure of wreck diving. He agreed to take me under one condition: I had to first make several dives from the *Wahoo* on some shallower wrecks, so he could take a measure of my diving skills. If I passed muster, I would be welcome aboard the *Wahoo* for the second trip out to the *Doria* in July.

Imagine walking into the locker room of any major league team, and you will have some idea of what it was like for me to step aboard the *Wahoo* for my first dive. With my single tank, my wet suit, and my twenty-year-old regulator, I was surrounded by the elite of the sport with double tanks with ponies (small reserve tanks), multirigged regulators, monster dive lights, crowbars and hammers, dive computers, and dry suits amounting to thousands of dollars of gear. I looked and felt like a rank amateur.

After a two-hour boat ride from Captree, we were floating sixty-eight feet above the hull of an old ship from the World War I era. The *San Diego* was a perfect example of what wreck diving was all about.

On July 8, 1918, the former flagship of the Pacific Fleet had just replenished her coal supply in Portsmouth, New Hampshire, and was on her way to New York to take up escort duty for a convoy to Europe. Hugging the East Coast shoreline, steaming south, the heavy cruiser was following a routine zigzagging course to confound enemy submarines. On a hot July afternoon just a few hours from New York Harbor, the ship, which had been part of Teddy Roosevelt's Great White Fleet, struck a mine within sight of land. Normally the massive iron ship would have withstood the blast of a single mine, but this one struck amidships on her port side just outside the ship's well-stocked magazine. A secondary explosion ripped a huge hole in the *San Diego* and she sank in just twenty-eight minutes, taking six sailors with her.

The rest of her eleven hundred crew escaped, with some of them rowing some ten miles to Fire Island. The mine, it is believed, was laid by the German submarine U-156, which ironically sank in midocean during her escape, a victim herself of a US-laid mine.

The *San Diego* is a striking sight lying on the stark sandy bottom. Three- and six-inch guns still protrude from her flanks, seemingly still poised to fire at anything that resembles a periscope, something that according to legend she did as she was sinking. The partial remains of her crushed superstructure and her radio tower rest beside her. Like all wrecks in the region, she is covered from stem to stern in anemones and cruised by game fish and an occasional pelagic shark. Her crumbling carcass is also well-known as a lair to legions of lobster.

The *San Diego* is touted by some as a good "beginner wreck dive." It is not. Yes, you can touch her at only sixty-eight feet and it bottoms out at one hundred ten feet, well within "safe diving limits," but the *San Diego*'s charms have barbs.

In 1989 the New York tabloids labeled the *San Diego* the "ghost ship" after she took four lives in just twelve months. That summer Gregory Bryson and Jeffery Springer were two of the fatalities. The two buddies were making their first dive ever on the *San Diego* from Captain Howard Klein's *Eagle's Nest* out of Point Lookout, Long Island. It appears that they got lost in the vicinity of the ship's infirmary and could not find their way out and drowned. Three crewmates aboard the *Wahoo*, Sally Wahrmann, Gary Gilligan, and Hank Garvin, recovered their bodies the next day. The trio's story of finding them and how the abject fear was still frozen on the corpses' faces has sent many a shudder down a first-time diver's spine just listening to the tale. I know that shudder well.

Visibility on the *San Diego* can be excellent for North Atlantic waters, sometimes well in excess of fifty feet. But the upside-down hull of the ship is notorious for the swift currents that sweep across her, making it extremely difficult for a diver to navigate the hulk.

Holes opened by the corrosive action of the sea have tempted many a curious diver, but like the unfortunate duo of Bryson and Springer, some never get out alive. Steve Bielenda had his own harrowing story on getting lost inside the *San Diego*. In 1978 Bielenda and his close friends and dive buddies Ray Ferrari and Hank Keats were making one of their weekly dives down to the navy cruiser. Visibility had been excellent, so the trio decided to penetrate the wreck. Bielenda had not brought along a penetration reel, but the inside of the wreck was not mucked up, and once inside he could clearly see escape holes in the iron walls around him. They went deeper inside.

Something bright then caught Bielenda's eye on a partially collapsed deck below. Down in the darkness a piece of metal had reflected the beam of his dive light. He looked harder and immediately recognized it as a brass-star muzzle cover to one of the six-inch guns, a coveted prize to an artifact collector. Ferrari and Keats were busy wrestling a brass valve off a pipe. Bielenda, without indicating to his buddies his intentions, dropped down and swam along the corridor to the glittering metal. He snatched the muzzle cover from its sixty-year-old bed of silt and carefully placed it in his goodie bag. Suddenly, silt stirred up by Keats and Ferrari and carried by the current fell on Bielenda like a shroud, obscuring all ambient light. Swallowed up by the darkness and without a penetration line as an escape route, Bielenda felt a twinge of panic in his gut.

He knew he was near a bulkhead and frantically reached out with his neoprene-gloved hand, hoping to feel the iron wall so he would not lose his orientation, and almost instinctively, he froze his movements, giving time for the silt to settle. A minute should have done it, but a minute deep underwater, inside a metal hull in pitch-blackness, can seem like a lifetime. Bielenda willed himself to breathe shallowly, conserving his precious air supply. He checked his pressure gauge by sticking the illuminated dials right up against his faceplate and saw that he still had half his air supply. Bielenda remembered wondering if this was the way he was going to die.

His two buddies, unaware of his predicament, had momentarily halted their efforts, so the silt stopped billowing down on Bielenda. Visibility improved, but not much, and he was still disoriented. The ship is upside down and lies at an almost imperceptible eight-degree pitch. A diver could swim straight and level and still pass between collapsed decks and get lost without being aware of it. Bielenda made a slow, tentative probe ahead.

He swam along a confining corridor until he found a small hole above him. Poking his head up, he could see the fins of one of his working buddies. But the hole was too small to pull himself through with the double tanks strapped to his back, and the fins were beyond his reach. Adrenaline pumping, he tried to stifle the panic that was now welling in his throat. He purposely swam slowly down the corridor, searching with his light for a hole large enough to squeeze through. Ahead of him he spied a hatchway. Realizing his desperate situation, he felt he had no choice. Swimming through the narrow opening, he blundered into another room. The green light of the sun, filtered through a hundred feet of water, streamed in through a hole large enough to drive a truck through. He gave thanks to his God and at the same time cursed himself for his stupidity.

Bielenda put the experience into his "bag of tricks," a veritable cornucopia of diving experiences he could fall back on if a similar situation arose in the future. But he also has the brass-star muzzle cover, which now rests prominently on his mantelpiece, always there to remind him of his foolishness and the near-death experience.

Steve Bielenda also required me to visit another relic of the past. The *Oregon*, a Cunard liner, sank on March 14, 1886, after a collision with a smaller vessel a few miles past the grave of the *San Diego*. Because it was deeper—130 feet to the bottom—the *Oregon* was considered a good warm-up dive for the *Doria*. A dive of any length on the old steamship required several decompression stops.

Being much older than the *San Diego*, the *Oregon* is less recognizable as a shipwreck. Portions of the hull and her boilers are the only remnants of the once proud liner. Some of the elegance of her Victorian glory still clings to her skeletal remains—even if mostly in the imagination of her visitors. She has also been generous in yielding up of some of her china and silverware treasures.

The *Oregon* evokes a mystery and an era long gone, now enjoyed only by the few willing to assume the risks of deep diving. For some of those divers, it was not worth it. A year after his dive buddy Bielenda's brush with death on the *San Diego*, Ray Ferrari ran tragically afoul on the 518-foot Cunard ship.

On their first dive down to the wreck, Ferrari's tank valve malfunctioned. Bielenda had to share his air with Ferrari to get him safely to the surface 130 feet above. Ferrari tinkered with the valve back aboard the boat while Bielenda teamed up with another buddy for a second dive. Ferrari got the valve to work, slipped it on, and made his entry, believing he could catch up with the pair. Apparently the valve malfunctioned once again, and his air supply was lost. This time Ferrari did not have a buddy to save him. Minutes later he popped up to the surface unconscious. He was hauled aboard the boat and given cardiopulmonary resuscitation, but he never responded. Bielenda attended his funeral, neither the first nor the last friend he would lose to diving.

As recently as the 1998 dive season, Harvey Leonard's luck finally ran out on the *Oregon*. Harvey was a legendary figure in the dive industry and in the Northeast wreck-diving community. He owned and operated Harvey's Dive Shop in Brooklyn's Sheepshead Bay for thirty-eight years. The shop was a magnet for wreck divers and bargain hunters since Harvey was famous for discounting dive gear, an unheard-of practice given diving's limited market and razor-thin profit margins.

Despite his sixty-three years, he was a regular on the dive boats that visited the wrecks off Long Island and New Jersey. Harvey was notorious for ignoring decompression tables to fit his eccentric modus operandi while deep diving. A wiry little guy, he had a running bet that no one would pull a bigger lobster off a wreck during a season. He never lost that bet, even on his fatal dive.

On July 10, 1998, Harvey was on one of his weekly *Oregon* dives aboard the *Sea Hunter III* out of Freeport, Long Island, looking to bag some lobsters. Harvey was breathing 32 percent oxygen and had slung a bottle under his right arm containing 50 percent oxygen mix for decompression and had a 100 percent oxygen bottle to hit on in between dives.

After he completed his first dive, he spent two hours on the *Sea Hunter* and then reentered the water alone. Eighteen minutes later, another diver found Harvey Leonard lying faceup on the wreck with no regulator in his mouth just a few kicks from the anchor line. The diver tried to reinsert the regulator in Harvey's mouth, but it was hopeless at that point. Realizing he could do nothing more for him, the driver attached a lift bag to Harvey's body and sent it to the surface. Efforts to revive Harvey aboard the *Sea Hunter* were fruitless. But back on the bottom, his weight belt and goody bag were recovered—with his three lobsters inside.

Although his death was officially listed as a drowning, it was widely suspected among wreck divers that Harvey had "toxed out." He was known to blend his mixes "heavy," or high in oxygen (to lessen time for decompression stops), making an oxygen-toxicity hit the likely suspect in his demise.

I was on the *Wahoo* every weekend during the months of May and June 1990, logging dozens of dives on the *San Diego* and the *Oregon*. Besides bringing my dive skills up several notches, I also upgraded my dive gear. As the July expedition date approached, I felt I was ready for the *Doria,* and so did Captain Bielenda.

If there were any doubts about what I was getting myself into, they were dispelled when I read the waiver of risk for an *Andrea Doria* expedition. Three pages long, it plainly states that diving the *Doria* is extremely dangerous and that serious injury and even death may result. The waiver not only required my signature but also those of my wife and a notary public.

Because of his many visits to civil court, Bielenda was now a careful man. I could imagine what an impression a grieving widow could make on a sympathetic jury. Just because her husband was a jerk and risked his life and lost, that did not necessarily mean the wife and family should suffer as a result. Only her own signature on the legal form could swiftly switch sympathy to the defendant.

I was the first paying customer on the boat the day of departure for the *Doria*. Normally I was imune to the ravages of mal de mer, but I had been warned that the eighteen-hour trip out might be rough. Seasickness can be psychologically induced. If you expect the worst in sea conditions, anxiety inevitably creeps in. The underlying fear about the dive adds to your psychological terror, and the body responds in kind. I could detect the rumblings in my stomach before leaving the dock, so I popped a Dramamine.

The trip out lived up to my worst nightmares. Nine-foot swells greeted us as we left the protection of the inlet for the open ocean at 9 P.M. that evening. I spent little time topside with my fellow adventurers, seeking refuge instead in my sleeping bag.

For two hours Captains Bieser and Bielenda tried to make some headway through the pounding waves. The boat would climb a wave, only to drop again into a trough with a crash. The frigid water came leaking through the "watertight" hatches and seams above me, and I quickly became soaked. Just hours into the trip, I was already miserable and found myself muttering to no one, "What have I gotten myself into?" My only solace was seeing that Hal Watts, an elite Florida diver who was known as Mr. Scuba, was suffering every bit as much as I was. His perpetual smile was now a grimace, and his entire wardrobe of flashy after-dive attire was sopping wet with seawater.

After several hours, I thought I had detected a bit of a calm, but

Rough seas on a *Doria* expedition.
(Photo courtesy Jon Hulburt)

the *Wahoo* had given up its battle with the raging seas and high-tailed it back to its slip in Captree. The calm was from our reentry into the protection of the inlet. We were all informed another attempt would be made in the morning. I got a fitful few hours of sleep at the boat slip despite a wet sleeping bag and the snoring of my cabin mates.

In the morning the seas had subsided somewhat. Instead of making a beeline to the wreck site 160 miles due east from the Fire Island Inlet, the *Wahoo* hugged the southern coast of Long Island all the way out to distant Montauk Point. But the seas got worse once we were out of the lee of Long Island. The very real possibility that the expedition would be aborted was the topic of conversation for all twenty-four aboard.

Captains Bieser and Bielenda decided to make a run for New Harbor on Block Island, hole up, and pray for better weather, so that in the early-morning hours we would make a mad dash to the *Doria* site and get some diving in. I went over my navy dive tables, studied the *Doria*'s ship plans, and made small talk with the other divers, but my main focus was keeping my lunch down and staring at the bouncing horizon to maintain some semblance of equilibrium. My wife's last words to me before departing still rang in my ears: "Don't get killed, asshole."

I began to hope secretly that the trip would indeed be aborted since I could not imagine the seas acquiescing. The *Wahoo* left New Harbor in the wee hours of the morning, and I was only vaguely aware of the boat's movement, having finally drifted off to sleep. At 5 A.M., the word made its way through the tight quarters: we were there.

Out on the wide expanse of the open ocean, dawn does not creep up—it bursts spectacularly. By the time I emerged from belowdecks, the sun was a large orange disk on the eastern horizon. There was not a cloud in the sky, and the ocean had not even a ripple on it. The *Wahoo* hummed in neutral gear. Captain Bieser hollered down from the wheelhouse that she had the wreck on her depth finder and ordered the crew forward to get the grappling hook ready. As if on cue, divers scrambled to their gear, dragging tanks across the deck, methodically rigging regulators, opening valves, and pulling masks, fins, and dry suits from gear bags.

I held back, having no desire to be the first in the water. I planned to make just one dive a day so I would not have to deal with surface intervals and multidive plans. I was going to play tourist—touch the wreck and swim around and take in the scenery. Bielenda took note of my bystanding and smiled at me. He knew I did not have the "fever" and no doubt was thankful that he didn't have to worry about one more rookie getting lost inside the mammoth ship.

My attention was drawn to a splash near a piece of driftwood floating twenty yards astern of the boat. Then I saw the dorsal fin. The cobalt blue color and the protruding caudal fin some six feet behind it meant only one thing: a blue shark, a fairly common variety of shark found in deep waters. Blues were known to attack man, but even the large ones were

74

Above: Shark gets manhandled by diver off the *Wahoo*.
Below: Boated shark on the *Wahoo*.
(Photos © Steve Bielenda)

easily dissuaded in their quest for a snack by a well-placed blow to the snout. *Doria* divers considered blue sharks more a nuisance than a threat. Still, one had to remember that none of the forty-three victims' bodies that went down with the *Andrea Doria* were ever recovered: blue sharks, the jackals of the deep, had a taste for human flesh.

Transfixed, I watched the torpedo-like form playfully nudge the driftwood. The shark finally lifted its jaws out of the water and snapped at the flotsam. Bielenda followed my line of sight, turned to me, and deadpanned, "He's getting hungry waiting for you guys."

Gary Gentile and Gary Gilligan were given the chore of securing the grappling hook to the wreck with a shackle. The buzz aboard the boat was that the two experienced *Doria* divers would then enter the wreck via Gimbel's Hole, drop down to the first-class gift shop and dig there for artifacts. They would pass by where John Ormsby's body had been found. I wondered what horrible memories that would bring back to them.

After their entries, several aboard including myself watched from

Gary Gentile and Gary Gilligan await the go-ahead for setting the hook to the *Doria*.
(Photo © Kevin McMurray)

Captain Bielenda ready to assist Gentile and Gilligan into the water.
(Photo © Kevin McMurray)

the bow of the boat for the signal that the *Wahoo* was securely tied in. The signal would be two styrofoam cups. The gas-impregnated foam would expand when jettisoned, shooting the cups to the surface in just seconds. Ten minutes after their entry, the cups bubbled to the surface on the port side of the *Wahoo*.

My dive buddy was Rob Stevenson from Greenwich, Connecticut. Rob had made the June expedition to the *Doria* and was intent on getting some china, but he was a firm believer in progressive penetration. Even though he had the fever, Rob wanted more external explorations with an occasional probe into the hull before he would attempt an entry into the wreck.

Rob, or Robert Louis Stevenson III, had an adventure streak bestowed on him by genetics. He is a descendant of the writer who penned *Treasure Island,* and on his mother's side he is related to the poet Hart Crane, who ended his life by leaping off a steamer returning to the United States from Cuba in 1932. Rob later showed another side true to his bloodlines when he wrote two works of fiction that borrowed heavily from his experiences diving the *Doria*.

I was the only one aboard the *Wahoo* wearing a wet suit. The water temperature at two hundred feet never rose much above forty-five degrees. In a wet suit you, of course, get wet. Upon immersion water quickly leaks into the suit and is heated by contact with the body, providing a warm thermal layer for its wearer. Wet suits work great in temperate waters, but in extended immersions in cold water where long, immobile decompression hangs are required, it is something short of torture. Another problem was the lack of buoyancy of wet suits at depths. The pressure of the depths squeezes the suit of its buoyancy, adding negative weight to the diver, making a wet suit akin to a suit of armor. On the bottom, I would have to blast additional air into the buoyancy compensator vest to offset the deadening weight. Upon ascent, there would be that much more air that I would have to purge to control my ascent and safely decompress as the suit reverted to its buoyant form. I would have loved the luxury of a dry suit, but the $1,000 price tag was more than I could afford.

Two crew members helped me get into my gear while I sat on the "doghouse," a raised compartment on the aft deck next to the entry slot on the gunwale. I slipped into my double eighty-cubic-foot tanks, which had a small pony tank containing emergency air wedged in between them. The crew members helped me arrange the three regulators so they dangled securely under my chin. On my wrist I wore a dive computer that I hoped would accurately interpolate my bottom times and tell me at what depths on ascent I should stop and how long I should decompress. In my vest pocket I had a slate with the stops and requisite times penciled in, in case the computer malfunctioned. I checked my wristwatch and noted the time.

I had a primary light tethered to my right wrist and a backup light stashed away in another vest pocket. Three knives, one strapped to my left leg, one to my right, and the other secured to my pressure-gauge hose would cut me loose—I hoped—if I got hung up on the wreck. My tank-pressure gauges were routed under my left arm by my handlers and secured with a Velcro strap to my vest. I slipped on my fins and extended my hands so the crewmates could pull on my neoprene gloves. Sally Wahrmann gave me a smile when she saw me tuck my mask strap under my hood. It was the practice that had saved her, and I did not want to leave anything to chance.

I tested each regulator one last time, gave the thumbs-up signal to my handlers and my buddy Rob, lifted myself and my cumbersome load, took two awkward steps to the railing and one giant step into the waiting Atlantic.

The strange thing about diving, at least for me, is that the most anxious moments are in the preparation. Once in the water the weight of the gear and the worries disappear. The water seeps into your wet suit and cools you. I am finally one with the ocean. I had now entered another world.

We dropped ten feet beneath the surface and pulled and kicked along the trail lines strung the length of the boat leading to the anchor line. Rob, who had made his entry before me, waited at the down line. He gave me the okay signal, which I returned. Dropping our shoulders and heads, we kicked for the distant bottom.

On most dives for the recreationally minded, the bottom is within sight upon entry. On this dive, all I could see below me was a blue-green void streaked by bolts of sunlight. I pulled myself down the line following Rob's bubbles, stopping only to purge my mask of leaking water and equalize the pressure in my ears by blowing hard through my nose. I strained mightily to see some kind of a man-made form below, but it would take a good four minutes until something materialized beneath me. When the ghostly form appeared, I glanced at my computer and noted the digital readout of 134 feet.

Nothing can ever prepare you either for the enormity of her size or for your emotions when you finally see the *Andrea Doria*. She stretches far beyond your field of vision. Fish are everywhere, totally unfazed by your presence. Occasionally one swims up to you, stares you in the face, then swims off, content in the knowledge that your slow-moving mass is no competition.

Sea anemones carpet the ship to such an extent that there is almost no exposed steel. The thousands of portholes that pock the hull are reminders that this behemoth was once a human habitat. I could imagine faces peering out of the portholes, and I found myself wondering what those faces saw that night of July 25, 1956, as the *Stockholm* tore loose from the gaping wound it had inflicted.

I stood unsteadily on the hull of the *Doria* and surveyed my surroundings. A gentle current was flowing, coming from the stern of the

Portholes on the *Andrea Doria*. (Photo © Bill Campbell)

ship. I was surprised to feel relatively warm in my thin skin of neoprene. Perhaps it was the effort of getting to the bottom that had warmed me or maybe it was just the excitement of where I was that made me numb to the cold, but I was grateful.

Visibility was good, sixty feet I guessed. I gave the shackle a hard tug, satisfying any misgivings I had regarding our lifeline to the surface. I was not carrying a penetration line, since I had no desire to drop into the wreck. Still, I knew how easy it was to get lost on the vast remains even with good visibility. I could be less than one hundred feet from the anchor line, a few seconds of swimming, and not see it. As a precaution I attached a strobe light to the anchor line a body's length above the shackle point. As we swam along the Promenade Deck, I constantly looked back, checking to see my flashing beacon. It eliminated to a degree my insecurity and let me focus on where I was and what I wanted to do.

The Promenade Deck was in effect the main street of the *Andrea Doria*. Forty-five years ago it was for strolling or for taking a respite in one of the many lounge chairs and inhaling the invigorating sea air. It ran almost the entire length of the ship, stopping just past the tourist-class pool and forward of the ship's transom. A pair of wing bridges marked its termination. The Promenade Deck was partially enclosed, open to the elements in the bow and stern areas. The enclosed portion of the deck had large sliding windows. After forty-five years underwater, the casings had rotted out and most of the windows had dropped inward, lying now on the walls of the deck, which had come to serve as the inverted ship's floor.

Rob and I nodded to each other and dropped into the deck through one of the large openings where a window had once been. The deck corridor was wide and relatively free of debris. Since most of the windows were gone, I did not feel that I was inside the ship, although technically I was. The fine teakwood of the deck was still intact, impervious to the corrosive action of the sea, also free of the ubiquitous sea anemone. I ran my gloved hand across the smooth wood and marveled how well this natural material had held up to the elements while all the man-made steel was crumbling around it.

We leisurely kicked along the corridor, pausing to peer into portholes with our lights. Rusting metal and disturbed fish were all I could see. Close to the fantail of the wreck, I let out a few short bursts of air from my buoyancy vest and slowly dropped down the deck until I came upon the tourist-class swimming pool.

On the night of the collision with the *Stockholm* the swimming-pool area was the muster station for tourist-class passengers, mostly poor Italian immigrants hoping for a better life in America. From this very same space on that night of July 25, as the *Doria* listed precipitously to her starboard side, screams from children in their orange life jackets and prayers from their parents beseeching divine intervention were shouted into the warm night air. A sudden chill made me shudder, but it was not because of the forty-degree water.

Flashing my light in a long, slow sweep, I entered the now vertical pool basin. The irony of the experience was not lost on me even though I was pleasantly narced by the compressed nitrogen flooding my brain.

I discovered during the dive that the narcosis heightened my paranoia. I dealt with it by systematically checking my gauges and reaching for the two other regulators and testing the air flow by pushing the purge button. The mechanics of the procedures soothed me. At 211 feet I glanced at my pressure gauge and calculated that I had exhausted a third of my air supply. I got Rob's attention and indicated I was ready to retrace our route back to the anchor line. He nodded his assent.

We made our first stop at forty feet and idled there for the required two minutes. At the thirty-foot stop the current hit us. I had just started to feel the elation of a successful dive to the infamous *Doria*, only to have the fear of death return with a current that had us flapping like pennants in a stiff wind on the anchor line. Clenching the anchor line tightly in my fist, I held on for dear life. If I got torn loose, I would have to make a crucial decision: either kick for the surface, which would blow off my decompression stops and possibly cause me to get bent, or try to maintain my stops while being carried off by the current to God knew where. I also began to shiver from the cold. I had pushed the limits of my wet suit's thermal properties and now I was paying the price.

Hanging there, I thought of the story of Billy Campbell, who the year before had come up under the *Wahoo* and got carried off before he could grab a trail line. By the time he reached the surface he was beyond shouting distance of the *Wahoo*, his minuscule bobbing head not visible to those aboard the boat. By the time his presence was missed he was over a half mile away. A Zodiac inflatable operated by Gary Gilligan and Dave Zubec was sent out by Bielenda into the fog to search for Campbell in the drift of the current. Guided by radar and in communication by radio with the *Wahoo*, Gilligan and Zubec found Campbell alive two hours later at dusk, with sharks bumping at him quizzically. He had dumped all his gear but his camera and light, ready to ride out the night lost at sea.

For another sixty-eight minutes at my thirty-, twenty-, and ten-foot stops, such thoughts preoccupied me. Not until I broke the surface and got my first lungfuls of warm, moist air did I know I was finally out of danger. The dive had been exhausting, both emotionally and physically. A touch of hypothermia brought on by my inadequate wet suit did not help matters.

The loot brought up from the depths by other divers was impressive: Gilligan and Gentile in particular were quite successful. They had enough cabin-class china to cater a large dinner party. There were also crystal martini glasses and demitasse cups and saucers. An assembled crowd of divers watched enviously as the artifacts were put out to dry on the doghouse of the *Wahoo*. I suddenly began to understand what "china fever" was all about. Covetousness is as powerful as it is disquieting.

The calm weather had held, and instead of sending the crashing waves of the previous days, the Atlantic gently rocked the *Wahoo*.

Above: Gilligan and Gentile with their haul.
Below, left: *Doria* dishes. Below, right: Tourist-class dishes.
(Photos © Kevin McMurray)

Before retiring below, I stood on the aft deck and scanned the moonlit darkness that engulfed our little vessel. I could make out ships' lights in the distance. I silently thanked the sea gods for the clear evening. Had it been a night like this on July 25, 1956, the *Andrea Doria* would not be resting directly below us now. I gave the sea around us another furtive glance and prayed our small profile was a blip on every ship radar scope in the area. Once I was snug in my still-damp sleeping

The *Wahoo* over the *Doria*.
(Photo © *Steve Bielenda*)

bag, I lost no time drifting off to sleep. It was the first full night of shut-eye I got in three days.

Our second dive of the trip followed the same route as the first, but this time we had agreed to drop all the way to the sandy bottom at 235 feet, where the *Doria*'s wounded starboard side rested.

Unlike the sunlit port side where the *Doria* met the bottom, the starboard side was dark and foreboding. Debris from the ship littered the bottom, and our dive lights illuminated only slivers of the wreck's detail. I also was well aware that I was narced out of my mind. I found myself shaking my head as if somehow I could by centrifugal force expel the fogginess from my brain. Realizing my impaired situation, I had the presence of mind to let Rob know that I had had enough.

Once I had lifted twenty feet from the bottom, my clarity of mind returned. The limitations of compressed air became all too real for me. I thought that I could never function with any sense of comfort deep in the bowels of the ship. Of course I wanted souvenirs to prove that I had been there, but was not about to risk my life for them.

This time our decompression hangs were uneventful. The ocean had given us a reprieve. Whatever self-congratulatory feelings I had felt back aboard the *Wahoo* were quickly dispelled when I watched as Gilligan and Gentile emptied their goodie bags from another successful penetration into the wreck.

Gentile, standing on the dive platform and still in his dry suit, was washing the muck from a collection of 78 rpm records liberated from the gift shop. They were still in their paper jackets. A howl of laughter from the circle of divers greeted his reading of one of the record labels: "Arrivederci Roma."

Gossip aboard the *Wahoo* had spread the word as to why I was there. Still, I was surprised when Gary Gentile approached me. In the wreck-diving community Gentile's reputation as a pioneer in diving the *Doria*, his success in locating precious artifacts, and his experiences in retriev-

Gentile recovered 78rpm albums from the first-class gift shop.
(Photo © Kevin McMurray)

ing bodies of those who had tried and failed placed him in an elite circle.
He was held in great awe by all deep divers.

The *Wahoo*'s somewhat less experienced crew resented Gentile to
a degree. Gary kept to himself, and when he was not diving, he could
usually be found in his bunk, sleeping, reading, or writing in his journal. He rarely socialized among the usually gregarious crowd that
made up wreck charters. By his own admission in his self-published
books, *The Lusitania Controversies I* and *II,* he was a tightwad. A free
berth and all the diving he could get in were incentive enough for Gary
to continue crewing aboard the *Wahoo.*

According to Bielenda, Gary considered the mundane chores of crewing beneath him. He felt his duties aboard the *Wahoo* were to secure the hook to the desired portion of the wreck and to bring aboard additional divers who wanted to rub shoulders with a legend. Bielenda enlisted him as a crew member for those very reasons, particularly the latter, since a few extra charterers could mean the difference between a profit and a loss on a *Doria* expedition.

Gentile had been alerted by Bielenda that I needed photographs, particularly underwater shots, to illustrate the article I had been commissioned to write. Having close to one hundred dives on the *Doria*, he had plenty to hawk.

We agreed he would supply some photos that would be considered; we shook hands and made small talk about the dives.

The trip back to Long Island was worse than the trip out to the wreck site. Captain Bieser had kept tabs on the weather forecasts and knew that stormy seas were heading our way. All afternoon dives were canceled, and everyone was informed that all gear was to be secured for a rough ride home. The *Wahoo* was just a few hours under way when the storm front caught up with us. It was unnerving to have mountainous waves lift the boat by the stern and propel it into troughs with an enormous force that only an angry sea could muster. The bow would disappear beneath the water, sending waves of it washing over the aft section of the boat. Many of the tanks broke loose, and bags of gear were ping-ponged all over the deck. No one dared to venture out on the deck to try to secure the loose equipment.

I tried to escape the weather by sleeping through it, but once again that tactic failed. After getting tossed from my upper bunk three times by the pitching of the boat, I gave up and pulled my sleeping bag back up to the main deck. It was dry there, but other divers had the same idea. We were packed in like sardines.

Some eighteen hours later, at 5 A.M., we motored into Captree. Utterly exhausted, I managed to throw my gear in my car, pour myself behind the wheel, and survive the two-hour drive home. I slept for a solid fifteen hours, but it took me two more days to get used to terra firma and not roll with imaginary waves.

Diving the *Doria* had been a heady experience. Not many people had accomplished what I had—fewer than a hundred, Steve Bielenda told me. Yet once the elation of surviving a challenge that most experienced divers forgo had evaporated, I found myself wondering if it had been worth it. The vagaries of the North Atlantic, the dangers of sharks, hypothermia, oxygen toxicity, nitrogen narcosis, equipment failure, and entangling myself in the grip of a wreck two hundred feet underwater made me think twice.

I realized that I had not wrestled myself free of her lure. The *Andrea Doria* was more than just a shipwreck. She was like Everest was to the mountaineer, something that would beckon me again, a temptation, I would come to learn, that few who knew her could resist.

Regardless of what I told my wife, I knew in my heart that I would return to that spot south of the Nantucket Shoals and make that descent into the past again.

FOUR

THE PIONEERS OF WRECK DIVING

*Man cannot discover new oceans unless he has the
courage to lose sight of land.*
—André Gide

aptain Steve Bielenda told me there was a video and to see it. It
was shot on that day back in July of 1985. Bielenda had asked
Dick Masten, one of the expedition members on that trip, to
shoot it when the body was recovered so that there would be video doc-
umentation to show to the Coast Guard that Ormsby was already dead
when they brought him up. I wanted to watch it with Billy Deans.

I knew Billy Deans pretty well. I had dived with him in Key
West, on the USS *Wilkes-Barre*. Both Steve Bielenda and Gary
Gentile have called Deans a diving "guru," quite an accolade considering the sources, and I had written about him in a now defunct
dive publication called *Underwater USA*. Although he was a diving
celebrity and I was a reporter, Billy trusted me and considered me
a friend. Still I didn't want to appear to be morbidly curious, like
some rubbernecker spoiling for a view of a roadside accident. As it

91

turned out, I never had to ask to see the video; he asked me to watch it.

It came up innocently enough as we discussed the accident and various facets of it. Questions arose about Ormsby's gear configuration, and Billy was a firm believer in learning from mistakes. I knew he had spent an inordinate amount of time breaking down what had happened in 1985. Still, I was surprised when he asked, "I got a tape that will answer that question. It's John's body recovery. You wanna see it?"

Deans's attention was focused on the screen while we watched the video. Standing to my left with his arms akimbo, he narrated the video in flat tones, prefacing it by telling me it took him years before he could view it. But now he religiously showed it to all his deep-diving, mixed-gas students. He said he wanted to make them understand that you could die "down there" and that it happened, sadly, much too often and that they had to be aware of the dangers. I could certainly understand that, but God, I thought, this was Dean's best friend and not some anonymous poor devil who had met his end on the bottom of the ocean.

In one scene, the bare-chested Rick Frehsee and Neal Watson flank the dry-suited, wet, and animated Billy after he emerges from the fatal dive. The scene ends in seconds, their excited conversation unintelligible. The lens of the camera cuts to an inflatable launch with *Wahoo* crew members Donny Schnell and Craig Stemitez aboard as it speeds over to a bobbing lift bag. As the camera zooms in, a neoprene-gloved hand lazily pokes up out of the glassy seas next to the float. Another cut, and the action is again taking place on the aft deck of the *RV Wahoo*.

This time it's Steve Bielenda and Neal Watson struggling to lift the body of John Ormsby from the diving platform below the transom. They pull the body, still fully suited in diving gear, up by the tanks' manifold and drag Ormsby over so he rests on his back parallel to the transom. In a wide shot of the body, Ormsby's arms are grotesquely spread wide open by rigor mortis as if he were about to give someone a welcoming embrace. His arms were frozen like that at a depth of 206 feet when he lost consciousness.

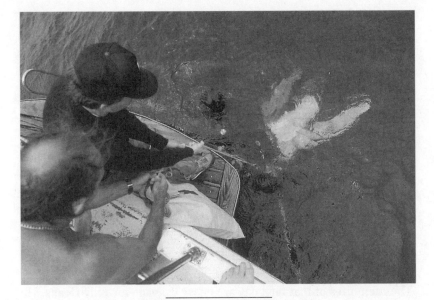

Ormsby's body near the dive platform of the *Wahoo.*
(Photo © Steve Bielenda)

Drowning is not one of the more pleasant paths to the hereafter. Because of osmosis, body fluids attracted by the salt water flooded into Ormsby's lungs, in effect making him drown in his own juices. One can only hope that either oxygen toxic shock or deep water blackout rendered him unconscious first, sparing him the terrible agony of drowning.

The camera zooms in on his upper torso. His mask is still in place. His eyes, thankfully, are hidden behind the fogged faceplate. No regulator is in his mouth. A sickening bloody bile oozes from his mouth, spilling over his right cheek and onto the deck of the *Wahoo.*

"Massive pulmonary embolism," Deans narrates dryly, his eyes still riveted to the screen. Ormsby's body cavities still contained air even though he was dead. The rapid ascent of his body, propelled to the surface by the lift bag, meant that the expanding residual air had literally exploded his lungs.

The hulking form of Janet Bieser quickly appears from the right of the screen to douse the lifeless form with a bucket of seawater, sending the rivulets of blood and body fluids cascading over the stern of the boat.

Bielenda can be heard discussing with Neal Watson how they are going to get the body into a sleeping bag, the substitute for a body bag. Watson assures Bielenda they can bend his arms and tie them in place, which they quickly do. The camera pans down the lifeless form, from head to toe, zooming in on the legs. One fin is missing and the other is pointing backward as is the foot. Ormsby's joints had twisted hideously in his death throes. Strands of black cable still bind his legs.

On the video Steve Bielenda, facing the camera, recounts the probable sequence of events that led to the fatality. When the screen goes blank, Deans turns to me and says, "As you can imagine, this tape makes an impression on my students."

The memories of that fatal day are heavy baggage for Billy Deans. He remembers that when he was in the hole with John he was on "automatic, just-do-it mode." He says he has no memory of "a higher philosophical function." He was just trying to save his friend. Deans had no concern for his own safety until Gary Gentile dropped into the hole, at which point Deans instinctually checked his gauges. He was down to 500 psi of air, barely enough to get him to the surface alive.

At his twenty-foot decompression stop, hanging from the line suspended in the vast watery void around him, he had found the time to reflect on what had happened two hundred feet beneath him. Because of the oxygen rigs at twenty feet, Deans was no longer concerned about his air supply. The reality of it all finally sank in—his friend John was dead. The subsequent sequence of events aboard the *Wahoo* have mostly been lost to Billy Deans. He remembers that Steve Bielenda was shooting lots of pictures of him, but the whirl of his camera's motor drive was about the only thing that he recalls.

The next day, during the body recovery, Deans and several others made another dive down to the wreck. He concedes that some may see it as a callous thing to do, but he reasoned John had expired and there was nothing more for him to do. He was there, there was the time, so he did his dive.

Because of his friendship with Ormsby, Deans was not tapped for the body recovery. To Deans it was of no consequence. "At that point, John was dead, however they wanted to do it—I just didn't care."

Deans was going through the classic pattern of death acceptance: denial, grief, and anger. Diving again was the denial. The anger part was intense. Deans says he was "absolutely livid that he [Ormsby] would have the audacity to do something like this, break his dive plan and go and die on us like that."

John Ormsby had unintentionally killed himself. Now his family and friends had to live with the consequences. His death changed people's lives, particularly Billy Deans's.

On landfall after the accident, at the Coast Guard station on Block Island, Billy made the call from a pay phone to John Ormsby's parents down in Florida, very late that night.

"There wasn't much I could say. I just told them that John was dead, that he died diving on the *Doria*. John's father said, 'No, no, no, it can't be true,' and burst into tears. I could hear his mother wailing and sobbing in the background. I started to cry too and then they just hung up."

John Ormsby's body was shipped from Rhode Island to his family's hometown of San Diego. Deans was never informed of funeral arrangements. He knew he was not welcome, so he never went to his best friend's interment. It was quite apparent that the Ormsbys blamed him for John's death, but in his heart he knew it was John, and John alone, who was responsible for his own demise.

Three months later, Deans got a call from Ralph Ormsby saying he wanted to get rid of his son's diving equipment. The grieving father had a face of granite when Deans arrived at his door. What Deans didn't take, Ralph, a retired naval officer, gathered up and threw in the canal behind the Ormsby home. The only piece of gear Billy kept for himself was John's speargun. John and Billy had built their guns together. They were extremely accurate and deadly, and they were a source of a lot of memories.

Whoever coined the expression *boyish good looks* must have had Billy Deans in mind. If he were younger, and if his hair were a shade or two darker, and if he had some more freckles, he could have passed for Theodore Cleaver in *Leave It to Beaver*. Deans is a compact five feet five, without a trace of fat on him. For a little guy he carries himself with the pride of a six-footer. A former competitor in the rigorous Ironman Triathlon in Hawaii, he is the epitome of a finely toned athlete. An educated and well-read man, he speaks in measured words. He is extremely friendly and seems genuinely pleased to make your acquaintance and happy to see old friends. He listens intently and with an unblinking interest, as if he can learn something from what is being said. He makes you feel at ease in his presence. He doesn't seem to have a bad bone in his body, and it is easy to see why everybody likes him.

Described in one diving publication as "the world's best diver," an accolade that makes him wince, Billy Deans came to the sport early in life. He is a third-generation Floridian, and the sun and the surf of Daytona Beach and an ocean-oriented father are the factors that formed his life. Young Billy got his first diving certification from the YMCA when he was twelve, and he and his dad started making cave dives shortly thereafter. After a divorce and a rash of cave-diving deaths in 1968, his dad decided to pull up stakes and head south for that portion of Florida that is the very embodiment of maritime living—the Keys.

The open waters of the Gulf of Mexico and the Atlantic were a safe haven to the water-addicted father-and-son team. Billy Deans took to it immediately.

After graduating from the University of Florida with a chemistry degree, Deans returned to the Keys and instead of pursuing a "real" job went to work for Reef Raiders, a dive shop located on Stock Island, the next islet east of Key West.

Because of the death of a tourist diver and the subsequent lawsuit, dive shops became leery of running trips to offshore reefs and wrecks for fear of liability suits. Deans saw this as an opportunity. He received his commercial captain's license when he was twenty-one, and he figured he had nothing to lose financially—since he had nothing. So he took over the concession of running the tourists out to sea and handheld them during their dives. In the process he learned about the ocean bottom that surrounded the Lower Keys. In the 1970s there were still a lot of virgin dive spots, which meant plenty of fish and lobster. The business of harvesting the ocean's bounty required a partner. Fellow diver John Ormsby fit the bill.

Tall and handsome, John Ormsby was the son of a navy man and a Korean war bride, the total antithesis of Billy Deans, who was short and hyperactive and the son of a devoted father and a product of a stable white, upper-class background. John's and Dean's love of diving forged a strong friendship. John had no real vices. According to Deans he liked to party, but not to extremes. "He sure liked the ladies," Deans said, but his first passion was diving. Armed with their homemade spearguns and commercial fishing licenses, they boated the underwater wealth of the fish- and lobster-attracting reefs and wrecks. The money they made fishing helped put the younger John through college and got Billy a piece of Reef Raiders in 1981.

The greatest appeal of diving to Billy Deans was exploration. In a world where there was little left in the way of frontiers, the ocean depths held out. Diving in the 1980s was still in its infancy, and its innovators were all still alive. Scuba inventor Jacques Cousteau could regularly be seen on TV leading enthralled audiences through new underwater worlds.

Diving was like space travel, but in diving you didn't have to be an elite federal employee, such as a NASA astronaut, to be part of the cutting edge. You just had to have the desire and passion, the brains, the guts, and the common sense to learn from your experience. Billy Deans had all of that. There was, however, one seemingly insurmountable hurdle to probing deeper and deeper depths: air.

• • •

Nitrogen narcosis, decompression sickness, and oxygen toxicity were the problems presented by breathing compressed air at extreme depths. All deep divers experienced narcosis—some more than others—and it was a major handicap in deep-ocean exploration. Oxygen toxicity and decompression were the more serious side effects of breathing compressed air under the pressure of several atmospheres. All three scourges of compressed air claimed their share of victims on deep dives such as the *Doria*. If sport diving was ever to make it to the next level, the problems of breathing compressed air would have to be solved. To Billy Deans the answer was "mix."

Exotic blends of mixed gases were being experimented with by the military and also by the commercial dive industry that was working the offshore oil wells in the Gulf of Mexico and the North Sea. Sport divers, however, were out of the loop, because recreational diving was just that—recreational. It was not supposed to be dangerous and envelope-stretching. The sport was always touted as a nice, safe, fun pastime. But like every other outdoor activity, diving had its extreme element. In the late 1980s, divers such as Billy Deans, Gary Gentile, Tom Mount, Neal Watson, Hal Watts, Sheck Exley and Bret Gilliam were, as they liked to call themselves, the "one percenters of sport diving," a statistical nonentity when profiles of divers were compiled for marketing purposes.

Prior to the late 1980s there were some isolated notable spikes in the development of technical diving. On an early expedition to the *Andrea Doria* in 1968, Italian filmmaker Bruno Valati experimented with surface-supplied oxygen for decompression stops, more than twenty years before it became common practice. In 1970, Hal Watts used heliox (helium displacing nitrogen in a breathing mix) on scuba for a body recovery in a Florida freshwater hole 415 feet down. Tom Mount, one of the founders of the National Association of Cave Diving, who also ran the diving program at the University of Miami, introduced a heliox training program for marine biologists.

Underwater-cave divers were the first in the sport field to see the promise of mixed gas. Sheck Exley, a world-renowned cave diver, was one of the first to employ heliox in deep-cave exploration, with great success. Still, not until 1985 did the first big innovation in mixed-gas diving open up the floodgates. That was the introduction of nitrox.

Oxygen-enriched air, commonly called nitrox today, was originally studied by the navy in the 1950s. In 1979, Dr. J. Morgan Wells, who was the diving officer of the National Oceanic and Atmospheric Administration (NOAA), collated the work done by the navy and implemented it in actual diving operations. The common nitrox mixes were 32 percent and 36 percent oxygen (as opposed to the 21 percent mix in air), the remaining percentages being nitrogen. The commercial diving industry had also been using oxygen-enriched air in operations as early as the 1960s, but due to the secrecy necessitated by competition, the decompression tables they developed were proprietary.

Nitrox was an appealing prospect to sport divers. Oxygen-enriched air has significant decompression advantages over atmospheric air since less nitrogen is inhaled and absorbed into the blood and soft tissues. It also reduces the problem of nitrogen narcosis. But nitrox imposes stringent limits on depths due to the higher concentration of oxygen in the mixture. The proportionately higher partial pressures of oxygen in breathing mixes increases the chances of oxygen toxicity hits at depths below 130 feet.

Dick Rutkowski, a colleague of Dr. Wells's at NOAA, is credited with introducing enriched air to the sport-diving community. After retiring from NOAA, Rutkowski opened a facility in Key Largo, Florida, and began to teach nitrox diving. In 1985, along with fellow deep-diving innovators Bret Gilliam, Tom Mount, and Billy Deans, Rutkowski formed the International Association of Nitrox Divers (IAND), which later became the International Association of Nitrox and *Technical* Divers (IANTD), to train those who wanted to push the envelope.

IANTD got the jump on the established dive-training organizations such as the National Association of Underwater Instructors (NAUI) and the Professional Association of Dive Instructors (PADI), who were taking a wait-and-see attitude. In 1989, IANTD got some competition from Long Island deep diver Ed Betts, who set up a rival training agency, American Nitrox Divers International (ANDI), in the hotbed of wreck diving, New York's Long Island. On a parallel line, other mixed gases for scuba were creeping into the sport world, and with the ambitious Bret Gilliam at the helm of IANTD, it was almost a given that nitrox and mixed gas would eventually gain acceptance.

Bret Gilliam was the guiding force in the push to use mixed gases, one of the few leaders in the sport-diving community with solid credentials, from his work with the navy and commercial dive operations on deep-diving systems for free-swimming divers. Gilliam himself has logged over fifteen thousand dives and as late as 1993 made a record dive on compressed air, down to the absurd depth of 475 feet.

But dives like Gilliam's are simply record-grabbing stunts. At that depth Gilliam experienced an atmospheric pressure fifteen times than that at sea level, or a 3.23 partial pressure of oxygen, putting him well into the danger zone for oxygen toxicity. The nitrogen narcosis factor, which affects each diver differently, was substantial. Dives like that are "bounce dives," where once the depth is reached, the diver quickly retraces his route back to the surface, often with little decompression penalty due to the small amount of time spent on the dive. Hence there is a relatively paltry absorption of potentially dangerous inert nitrogen gas. It is also believed that work-induced carbon dioxide buildup from heavy breathing is the triggering mechanism for oxygen toxicity hits at depths. Gilliam and other depth-record holders do no work other than to kick to the bottom on their dives.

In 1987 a watershed event for mixed-gas diving occurred. A group of cave divers, led by Parker Turner and Rob Parker, working on the Wakulla Springs Project approached Dr. Bill Hamilton. Hamilton was a well-known physiologist in the diving industry who had worked for Union Carbide, a producer of commercial gas. The commercial diving industry that serviced the offshore oil-production companies was a big customer of Union Carbide's. Hamilton's specialty was decompression, breathing gases, and the effects of pressure. The computer software and the algorithms he had devised had been proven over thousands of commercial dives, and the methodology had been tweaked and adjusted over the years.

Hamilton was reluctant to share the wealth of his voluminous research. First of all, the decompression tables for the assortment of mixed breathing gases were all written for tethered commercial divers wearing hard hats and carrying hoses. In the parlance of the commercial industry, the divers who had surface-supplied air were "dogs on a leash"—an apt description. These cave divers were on scuba, self-contained underwater breathing apparatus. Hamilton felt blackmailed: the divers told him that either he would help them or they would figure it out on their own. Just to make sure they had a safe protocol, he produced decompression tables for them for their mixed-gas dives down to 297 feet. Although Hamilton did not want to see anybody die for lack of information, he also, undoubtedly, saw a new niche market to hawk his services.

In a series of editorials *Skin Diver Magazine* publisher Bill Gleason, along with other recognized names in the diving industry, compared nitrox trainers to "purveyors of snake oil." He said the use of nitrox was "stretching individual responsibility to the limits." Gleason ruminated that nitrox would lead to other "exotic gases," and that proponents of nitrox were actually champions of "hyperdeep diving" as well. Gleason then expressed his real fear: nitrox accidents would be "another bad rap for diving and an inevitable step toward outside intervention and regulation."

Such outside intervention and regulation was the specter hanging over the diving industry. Any such governmental intrusion would cast a bad light on the pious, self-policed and safety-minded recreational activity. According to Bret Gilliam, *Skin Diver* was also under pressure from the Cayman Islands water-sports operators.

The Cayman Islands, then and now, are the most popular Caribbean destination for the enormous tourist dive market. They were also the single biggest advertiser in *Skin Diver*. On nitrox, tourist divers could make longer dives and repetitive dives, which meant Cayman operators would no longer be able to run the usual three trips a day per boat. Fewer trips, of course, meant fewer divers and less money. Tooling up for nitrox divers also involved more capital investment in equipment and training for compressor operators and dive instructors and guides.

Nitrox, as Gleason warned, was just the first step in the widening of the limits of what had now become known as technical diving. The "technical" appellation was borrowed from the jargon of mountaineering, which was concurrently undergoing radical innovations in technique and equipment. But in the dive industry that is about all they could agree on—phraseology. What exactly technical diving was, none too surprisingly given the multitude of training agencies, was beyond any agreed definition. Whatever it was, one thing was certain: it was complicated, and potentially dangerous.

The use of heliox provided a good example of the technical and physiological challenges that confronted divers who wanted to do it deeper. The benefits of using heliox had become well-known, but the expense of filling a set of doubles with the pricey blend for a multitude of dives was beyond the budget of most tech divers. Its cost was not the only problem with the helium-oxygen mix. Helium, although it produces no narcotic effect, has a smaller molecular structure than nitrogen, and more of it is absorbed into a diver's system and it took longer decompression stops to outgas it. Helium also has poorer thermal properties than regular air. Heat loss by divers breathing the cold heliox was six times faster, increasing the risk of hypothermia. Hypothermia was also a known factor in decompression sickness.

By 1992, IANTD and Billy Deans in particular were gravitating to a mix that seemed to be a godsend to the technical diving community: trimix.

Trimix is a gas in which oxygen is reduced down to 17 percent or 18 percent and helium infused to account for 50 percent of the mix, with the remainder made up of nitrogen. Not only is trimix more affordable—about half the cost of a heliox fill—it also lessens decompression times and is a "warmer" blend. The fact that the oxygen level is reduced also lessens the risk of oxygen toxicity at depths below two hundred feet.

The downside of trimix was that divers had to carry stage bottles—additional scuba cylinders containing nitrox and oxygen for decompression—with each bottle equipped with its own regulator. The auxiliary nitrox and oxygen mixes accelerated decompression stages and conversely lengthened bottom times. The stage, or "sling," bottles had to be fastened under the diver's arms to D rings on the harness. There were, of course, the problems of additional weight and awkwardness in the water. Deep diving was not only getting complicated by gas management, but it was also becoming equipment intensive.

Publications such as *Skin Diver* and *Rodale's Scuba Diving* were reluctant to report on the exploits and innovations of Gilliam, Rutkowski, Deans, Exley, and Mount. In 1990, Michael Menduno, a Californian from Silicon Valley, started up *aquaCorps,* a slim but fact-packed publication that brought out into the open the extreme things that were being done in diving. Menduno spread worldwide the word on technical diving, and there was plenty to report.

It was not unlike what was going on in the rest of the sporting world in the 1990s. Extreme sports were on the rise. A prosperous economy meant more money and leisure time. The mundane was out; bungee jumping, snowboarding, summit bagging, and deep diving was in.

One diving event of the early nineties got a particularly large amount of play in *aquaCorps* as well as in some mainstream press publications: exploration of the sunken wreck of the Civil War vessel *Monitor.*

Gary Gentile and Rod Farb won the right in court to dive on the ironclad that had spelled the end of one era and ushered in another. The famed wreck, which sank in a storm off Cape Hatteras, North Carolina, in 1863, was jealously guarded by NOAA, which routinely refused technical divers' petitions to dive the wreck. NOAA claimed the wreck—at 250 feet—was too deep to be visited safely by sport divers. The federal agency ignored that recent innovations such as trimix had greatly reduced the dangers of deep diving, and that some individuals regularly went below the outdated 130-foot limit. Gentile and Farb, on separate expeditions to the wreck, each photographed, videotaped, and chronicled the dives in documentaries and magazine articles. Deep wrecks, once beyond the realm of sport divers, had become the underwater equivalent of eight-thousand-meter peaks. Wrecks had become ripe for plucking.

No one had a better hand on the pulse of technical diving—wreck diving in particular—than Brooklyn-born Joel Silverstein. In 1991 he and his brother Jeff started up the magazine *Sub Aqua Journal*. While Menduno and his *aquaCorps* examined the big issues of technical diving, *Sub Aqua* zeroed in on wreck diving, the main interest of major New York–Long Island–New Jersey divers. In the waters off the two states, known as the New York Bight, if you wanted to dive wrecks, you had to go deep, and deep meant technical.

The circulation of *Sub Aqua* never made it much over the twenty-thousand circulation mark, but it was aggressive in promoting deep-wreck diving. *Sub Aqua* proudly proclaimed you would find "no pretty fishes" between its covers, a barb intended for the behemoth in the field, *Skin Diver*, which was prone to run covers with brilliantly colored fish shot against equally photogenic tropical reefs, usually with a buxom beauty floating nearby.

Billy Deans, Gary Gentile, and Captain Steve Bielenda were the darlings of both *aquaCorps* and *Sub Aqua*. Deans was doing mixed-gas diving and incorporating what he had learned into training programs. Divers from around the world were flocking to Key West to learn from him. Gary Gentile was blatantly ignoring any limit and making forays into wrecks along the East Coast, Great Lakes, and Europe that were well beyond "safe-diving limits." Steve Bielenda was making a reputation for taking divers to those spots.

Joel Silverstein quickly became a disciple of Deans's. Silverstein later went on to become a recognized expert in the technical-dive field, making a plethora of pioneering deep dives and authoring several instructional books as well as becoming a mainstay on the technical-

Joel Silverstein. *(Photo © Kevin McMurray)*

diving teaching circuit. According to Silverstein, it was Billy Deans who had opened up a whole new world of deep-water exploration.

"Billy Deans was doing all the deep stuff, had all the procedures down, and he ran a top-notch operation in the Keys," Silverstein said. "He always had the latest toys and the coolest of technology, and he made things happen. He had this incredibly good reputation as being the brightest, and the sharpest innovator around. He made the effort of finding a better, safer, and more efficient way of doing it."

Deans was the first to regularly use mixed gas in the open ocean. Florida cave divers had long led the way in technological advances, but underwater caving in Florida was sedate in comparison to open-ocean diving. The cavers did not have to deal with tides, unpredictable currents, bone-numbing cold water, razor-sharp steel labyrinths, or sharks. Deans incorporated cave-diving techniques and modified them so they could work in the more hostile environments.

But the 1985 accident that killed John Ormsby humbled and

stalled Billy Deans. All the resources and experiences from diving the warm waters of the Keys had not saved John Ormsby. Diving deep caves and warm-water wrecks such as the USS *Wilkes-Barre* had not prepared them for the hazards found in the cold, dark waters of the North Atlantic. Deans learned his lesson the hardest way imaginable, and he became determined to change how deep diving was to be done. It took him a few years to be able to view the video of John Ormby's body's recovery and it took him that long to reassert himself in deep diving, but when he did, it was with conviction.

Billy Deans is fond of rattling off old diving adages to his students. Three of his favorites are "Old divers, bold divers, but no old bold divers." "Plan your dive, dive your plan." "The most important artifact you can bring back is your life."

You can see in Billy Deans's eyes that they have meaning. These words of wisdom so often heard but seldom listened to come from a man who found out the hard way that the old adages are immutable truths. If I had any doubt about his convictions, Deans eliminated them when he said, "No life is worth all these fucking trinkets. Plates and all this shit, I give that stuff away. It means nothing to me. These so-called treasures that men put a value to have come to nauseate me."

These were strong words for a diver who had made his reputation in diving deep wrecks and making it back to the surface with proof of the exploits: artifacts. John Ormsby's troubling behavior and subsequent death changed all that for Billy Deans.

Deans remembered how he had pulled John Ormsby aside before the fatal dive to put some perspective on why they were there. He tried to quell his friend's "rabidity for trinkets." Deans told Ormsby he was "crazy" and tried to persuade him to "just swim around and have a good time, look at the wreck, get oriented, and relax because we're just tourists here."

Deans shook his head in dismay remembering those days. He is reluctant to place too much blame on Ormsby for his death. He said it was not so much greed and impatience but naïveté that killed him.

Now when he sees something grossly inadequate about a diver in a class, he prevents that person from diving, whether it is an attitude or equipment. "When I tell a person he's not diving, I'd rather have them upset and alive on the boat than in the water and dead and for me to have to talk to another grieving widow."

He runs his students through what he calls "dry fire drills." Fully suited up they are presented with various problems or predicaments to simulate what could possibly happen to them underwater. When they make a mistake, he tells them, "Okay, you are now dead. Think about what you did wrong and how you would correct it."

It took Deans a couple of years to muster up the will to dive deep again after his best friend's death, but he still had a business to run. Diving is, after all, his job. Deans got involved with IANTD and helped usher in the age of mixed-gas diving. In 1991, the siren of the *Doria* called again.

He buddied up with Steve Bielenda. Bielenda, through research and tentative probes, had located a china closet in the aft section of the wreck, and they would be diving on trimix. Billy went into the china closet while Steve waited on the outside in support. According to Deans, china was "everywhere." He reached in and removed one cup, one saucer, one plate, and departed. Bielenda was stunned and amused, Deans would later recall. "He told me he sent me in to bag up, only to realize," Deans said, using Bielenda's salty phrasing, "I'm fucking diving with a philosopher."

The "Mud Hole" is a wide, deep channel carved out of the Atlantic's continental shelf over countless millennia by the outgoing waters of the Hudson River. It runs southeast out from New York Harbor into the wide Atlantic like a huge drainage ditch, which in effect it is.

As the name implies, this underwater environment would never qualify for a glossy brochure touting unmatched beauty, colorful fish, teeming reefs, and limitless visibility. The Mud Hole is rife with contaminants such as PCBs, and visibility is clouded by particulates produced by the nearby megalopolis, which daily dumps unwanted waste on the passive ocean. It was and remains a bottomless dumping ground. But the Mud Hole is not a watery wasteland to everyone. It has an accessible bottom, and that bottom is a treasure trove to the hard-core group of divers who make their weekly pilgrimages there.

After five hundred years of commerce, wars, storms, and collisions at sea, the Mud Hole has claimed its share of ships. There are literally thousands of wrecks, some of them charted but most of them not.

The sea bottom off New York is relatively shallow. The gradually deepening continental shelf extends out, in some places, over two hundred miles. You could be sixty miles offshore and still be in less than two hundred feet of water. If you went the same distance out to sea off the West Coast, you would find yourself in waters several thousands of feet deep. There are wrecks there too, but you can't dive them.

In addition to the silted-up bottom there are the added hazards of monofilament fishing line and lost commercial fishing nets that envelope wrecks like spiderwebs. The Mud Hole is an underwater obstacle course sure to challenge the most daring of aquanauts. A school-teacher from New Jersey, Mike de Camp, is one who has discovered the beauty and the challenge of this wasteland beneath the sea.

De Camp got hooked on diving in 1954 when he accompanied Carleton Ray, then curator of the New York Aquarium, down to the Bahamas on a collecting trip for the aquarium. The twenty-seven-year-old de Camp used a converted old fire extinguisher as an Aqua-Lung and a weight belt made of typesetting blocks from a printing press. His only training were words of advice from Ray: "Don't hold your breath!"

Mesmerized by the underwater environment, de Camp returned north and made a visit to Richard's Army and Navy store in New York's Times Square, where he purchased some of the exotic imported diving gear. In the 1950s there were no instruction agencies, no diving classes, and precious few books on the subject of self-contained underwater breathing apparatuses, slowly becoming better known by the acronym SCUBA.

Being the determined sort, de Camp taught himself, mostly through in-the-water experience on the plethora of shallow-water wrecks within swimming distance of the beaches of the New Jersey shoreline. He recalls that back in those days there were no weight belts, no secondary regulators, and no tank pressure gauges. "You dove until it started getting hard to breathe, then you came up."

It was not long before the desire to dive the deeper, farther-off-shore wrecks began to consume him. De Camp found a friendly ear in a charter boat fisherman named Joe Galluccio. Like most New Jersey fishermen Galluccio had the "numbers" of dozens of fish-abundant outcroppings on the bottom off his home port of Brielle, New Jersey. The outcroppings were artificial reefs, made up of either discarded debris such as rocks and rubbish from construction sites or ship-wrecks, which stood out like sentinels of teeming life on the underwater Sahara. The debris and wrecks had become havens for fish seeking sustenance from the smaller organisms that attached themselves to the protuberances as well as protection from larger predators.

Galluccio was the obvious choice since he had a distinct advantage over his competitors. He had loran, an acronym for "long-range navigation." Loran was a relatively new technology developed during World War II. It utilized shore-based transmitters that determined position by triangulation. Galluccio also employed side-scan sonar or underwater radar.

In the cold months of the fishing off-season, Galluccio, and later other sport-fishing operators, took de Camp and handful of other divers to their secret spots. Like tourists everywhere, the divers naturally took home souvenirs from their underwater excursions. These souvenirs were the humble origins of the "china fever" that would consume, and often kill, those that followed de Camp.

Other diving groups began to make their presence known. A Long Islander by the name of Graham Snediker assembled a group of like-minded divers and formed the officious-sounding Oceanographic Historical Research Society, whose stated goal was shipwreck research.

Snediker and a handful of others were able to locate and dive two of the more historic wrecks in Long Island waters, the *Oregon* and the USS *San Diego*.

The British Cunard passenger liner *Oregon* sank in 1886 after a collision with a smaller vessel. In her heyday she held the then transatlantic crossing record of six days, ten hours, and ten minutes. The World War I heavy cruiser the USS *San Diego* had the distinction of being the only major U.S. warship to be sent to the bottom by a German U-boat, close to the war's end in 1918.

In 1963 de Camp and his dive buddies got the opportunity to put their passion to some practical use. A Norwegian tanker, the *Stolt Dagali*, was rammed and cut in two by an Israeli passenger liner, the *Shalom*, in the approach waters to New York. Just three days after its sinking, the de Camp crew made a dive on the stern section of the *Stolt* in 130 feet of water and reported that they had located a victim's body. At the behest of the Norwegian embassy, de Camp returned to lead a team to the wreck and successfully recovered the remains. The adoring public was impressed, especially after one of the daring divers got lost inside the *Stolt* and drowned in its underwater maze of darkened steel corridors.

De Camp's reputation as a larger-than-life diver got the attention of Peter Gimbel, who was shooting a late 1960s television series on sharks and needed an assistant. Besides filming duties, de Camp also handled the deployment of the shark cages. Their chartered boat, the *Cricket II* out of Montauk, was skippered by a legendary and abrasive shark fisherman named Frank Mundus. Gimbel was good friends with Peter Benchley, who went on to fame for authoring the underwater suspense novel *Jaws*. It was no secret that Benchley used the filming crew aboard the *Cricket II* as models for the characters in the blockbuster novel and motion picture.

One of de Camp's younger dive buddies was John Dudas, a fellow New Jerseyite who had started diving with the Passaic-Clifton YMCA as a fourteen-year-old. Dudas began diving on YMCA trips to New York's Lake George and to the Jersey shore.

• • •

Peter Gimbel and his wife, Elga.
(Photo © Michael A. de Camp)

Peter Gimbel, the heir to the Gimbel's department-store fortune and an underwater photographer of some renown, had wrangled an assignment from an editor at *Life* magazine to photograph the bottom-dwelling *Andrea Doria* just one day after she sank on July 26, 1956. With a fistful of money, Gimbel convinced a commercial fisherman, Winthrop Ellis, on Nantucket Island to take him, his wife, his twin brother—David—and James Fox sixty miles out into the ocean to the *Andrea Doria*.

With no functioning navigational gear, the wily sea captain used dead reckoning to locate the bubbling, iridescent oil slick and the orange buoy left behind by the Coast Guard amid the changeless seascape. Gimbel and Fox, wearing wet suits and double-hose regulators with no pressure gauges, pulled themselves down the buoy line left by the Coast Guard to the wreck. Gimbel managed to fire off only eight shots of the radiant white superstructure before Fox signaled

Gimbel that he was having difficulty. Gimbel pulled the nearly unconscious Fox back up to the surface. Apparently Fox had suffered carbon
dioxide buildup, no doubt brought on by the woefully inadequate regulators. The black-and-white photos shot by Gimbel appeared in the
August 6 and 13, 1956, editions of *Life*.

Life editor Kenneth MacLeish's appetite had just been whetted. Just
two months later, MacLeish organized an expedition, financed by *Life*,
consisting of himself, Gimbel, and three other experienced divers—
Bob Dill, Earl Murray, and Ramsey Parks from California—to get color
photos of what had become a major news story. MacLeish was no neophyte to the forbidding depths. In 1954, also for *Life*, he had gone down
a mile and a half in an experimental French deep-diving bathyscaphe.

After turning back twice because of poor weather, the team finally
made it to the wreck site in ideal diving conditions. The two-page color
spread was fuzzy and rather myopic in scope—a binnacle, a railing, a
porthole, and a lifeboat emblazoned with *Andrea Doria*—but the written piece was an eloquent testament to MacLeish's craft. He wrote:

"Above all, the terrible incongruity of her situation strikes the
diver's senses. Perfect (to his eyes), unscarred, seemingly impreg-
nable, still equipped with every appurtenance of her impressive calling, this vast, intricate, luxurious human habitation lies empty and
abandoned outside the realm of men. (She doesn't belong there. Your
mind can't accept the sight of her, the way she is.)"

The divers also managed to retrieve some artifacts from the wreck.
Among them was a suitcase that was returned to its rightful owner for
the human-interest photograph that closed the article, in the style *Life*
was duly famous for.

Life articles and photographs showed the public that diving the
Doria on scuba was possible. However, divers did not immediately
flock to Nantucket to charter boats. Scuba diving was still in its primi-
tive stages, and the diving ranks were thin and inexperienced. An
enterprising few, with visions of riches, slowly began to pursue the
dream.

• • •

Peter Gimbel and Ramsey Parks made another trip out to the *Doria* in 1957. They had a close encounter with a large blue shark, which made good copy in *Life*, but the pair returned from another misadventure with nothing more than a few photographs of the wreck slowly being claimed by the sea.

That same year in September, another film expedition was mounted by Frederic Dumas, for the classic series *The Silent World*, with cinematographer and future director Louis Malle. They ran into a logistical nightmare of inclement weather, equipment failure, and personnel problems. After seven weeks of work, all they got in was one dive and twenty seconds of film. Seven more years passed before the *Doria* would once again be disturbed from her slumber.

In 1964, Glenn Garvin and Robert Solomon, two businessmen from Washington, D.C., who were not divers and had no experience in marine salvage, decided that the *Andrea Doria*'s wealth had lain dormant long enough. With a refitted Coast Guard cutter rechristened the *Top Cat*, the pair hired the best-experienced salvors they could find. They set out with the nominal backing of Dow Chemical, which was interested in testing some Styrofoam byproducts for possible use in shipwreck recovery. The *Top Cat* crew again had the interest of *Life* magazine, to see if there was a story in what was worth plucking.

Life's interest evaporated when it proved too difficult to put photographers on the wreck. The underwater experiments were a bust for Dow, and they too quickly lost interest in sinking any more money into the bottom of the ocean.

Persistent, the *Top Cat* salvors enlisted some off-duty navy divers and made a third trip out to the wreck. This time they pulled off an impressive feat. Dennis Morse, Paul Heckert, and John Grich gained entry to the Foyer Deck with the help of the ship's plans and some well-placed explosives. They found the bronze statue of Andrea Doria, the fifteenth-century Genovese admiral who was the ship's namesake. Using hacksaws, the threesome freed the immortal Italian naval hero, sans his feet, from his watery grave. Despite this, no one took much notice. The bronze statue of the admiral ended up in a banquet room in a Pompano Beach, Florida, hotel, aptly named the Andrea Doria room.

So the *Top Cat* expedition was not the harbinger of things to come. It was the ragtag group of New Jersey and New York divers led by Mike de Camp, George Hoffman, John Dudas, and John Pletnik who made their way out from Montauk Point to the Nantucket Shoals two years later.

To de Camp, getting a chance to dive the *Doria* was more than a challenge; it was an obsession. The 1966 expedition was to become a momentous event in the diving community because de Camp and his companions were the first sport divers to band together and charter a

The de Camp 1966 trip, left to right: unidentified, John Pletnik, Jack Brown, Mike de Camp, Joe Hohman, George Hoffman (back), Frank Scalli (front), Dick Hilsinger, Winston Chee, John Dudas, unidentified.
(Photo © Michael A. de Camp)

boat and discover for themselves the mystery of what was to become the destiny dive for all of the divers.

Hoffman and de Camp had been dreaming of getting a dive boat out to the *Doria* ever since it went down in July 1956, yet the logistics of getting there were formidable. The technology for locating the wreck site in the open ocean was improving, mostly through the extensive use of loran. The two New Jersey divers rounded up nine other divers, pooled their money, and talked Montauk's Captain Paul Forsburg into taking them one hundred miles out into the open Atlantic. It was not a tough sell, since Forsburg had always wanted to fish the wreck, knowing full well it would be swarming with cod and pollock. If de Camp could get the loran numbers, Forsburg said, he would take them there. De Camp had got the numbers.

Forsburg's *Starlite* was a sixty-five-foot charter fisherman that made day trips out of the quaint tourist and fishing mecca of Montauk on the eastern end of Long Island. She had no bunks, so the divers had to stretch out on the deck in sleeping bags among the clanging gear for the rough ride out. As luck would have it, the *Starlite* had to lay over for shelter at Block Island from an approaching edge of Hurricane Alma in the South Atlantic, one of the earliest hurricanes of the season on record. The sea-weary group made their dash to the wreck site the following morning.

The atmosphere aboard the *Starlite*, according to de Camp was tense: "Everyone was very silent. A certain dread of the deep and gloomy water over this unknown ship filled each diver with apprehension."

De Camp, in an article in *Skin Diver* in 1967, recalled his descent down to the *Doria* as scary. He remembered telling himself, "I'll never get back from this." Still, in de Camp's words, it was "gloomy, cold, dangerous, frightening, exciting, and incredibly romantic."

The adrenaline was still pumping when he dispelled a big myth to sport divers: he touched the hallowed hull of the *Doria*, something he had always been told would be an impossible task for rank amateurs.

The *Starlite* divers had no idea where they were on the wreck. The

Doria loomed out of the darkness of the depths like some eerie apparition. De Camp swam up the black hull and reached the Promenade Deck, where he was stunned by the stark whiteness of the superstructure. With the excitement of finally achieving a dream still tingling within him, de Camp retraced his path back to the anchor line.

The myth is dispelled. A diver touches down on the *Doria*, 1966.
(Photo © Michael A. de Camp)

Diver swims along the *Doria*, 1966. *(Photo © Michael A. de Camp)*

The next day Hoffman and de Camp alighted on the Promenade Deck near the stern in 170 feet of water. They swam by the large windows still intact and acted like "a couple of tourists." The pair were surprised by large cods de Camp estimated to be in excess of fifty pounds and schools of pollock "that cascaded over the superstructure like a massive waterfall."

They peered into the portholes of the ship and swung on the empty lifeboat davits and drifted down to the lower decks of the hull. Their allotted bottom time of fifteen minutes passed much too quickly, but an image of the venerable old liner had forever been imprinted on de Camp's and Hoffman's minds.

Buoyed by their successes, de Camp, Dudas, and Hoffman planned another *Doria* trip the following season. A beginner diver who made a living making custom wet suits was determined to join them, Evelyn Bartram, who wanted to be the first woman diver to set finned foot on the *Doria*.

Bartram was not even sure the men would allow a woman aboard for an extended trip out to sea, knowing full well that mariners like Forsburg were a superstitious lot. Although she was winning the likes of Dudas and Pletnik over with her diving skills in the Mud Hole, diving the *Doria* would be a big step for her. De Camp related that Forsburg was dead set against taking a woman along, but the ever chivalrous de Camp insisted that if she was not allowed aboard, he would cancel the charter. Not willing to lose the subsidized fishing trip out to the fish-plentiful wreck, Forsburg relented.

Bartram was confident she was up to the task. Outside of John Dudas and John Pletnik, she had made more deep-wreck dives than anyone else that season. Bartram made a convincing case for her inclusion. She also had the $58 to pony up for her share of the charter.

Learning from the previous year's expedition, the divers showed up early in Montauk with hammers, nails, and plywood. They took off all the trim railing around the boat, removed the seats, and con-

The 1967 *Doria* expedition, left to right: (kneeling) Smokey Roberts, Ed Rush, Evelyn Bartram, John Dudas; (back row) Cal Preador, Jack Brewer, Dick Hilsinger, Mike de Camp, Jack Brown, boat mate (looking away), Capt. Paul Forsburg, Frank West, cook. *(Photo © Michael A. de Camp)*

structed bunks for all twelve divers. Once the bunks were built and all the diving gear was loaded on the *Starlite,* Bartram, wearing a short skirt and black stockings, and her eleven shipmates adjoined to Salavars, the local gin mill at Montauk Harbor, for an impromptu bon voyage party. Bartram barely remembers the early-morning trip out to the Nantucket Shoals thanks to "at least five martinis" and the attention of her fellow "party animals."

Captain Forsburg found the wreck quickly. The side-scan printout of the wreck profile was the "prettiest one" that de Camp had ever seen. Wearing a wet suit, double seventy-two-cubic-foot tanks, and no buoyancy control device, Evelyn Bartram made diving history when she alighted on the *Andrea Doria*.

Hoffman and de Camp had set the hook on the aft wingbridge, far away from where the expedition members had hoped to be. Bartram made her initial exploration with John Dudas. Since it had only been eleven years since her sinking, the ship was remarkably intact. Evelyn Bartram remembers they had visibility of up to one hundred feet, almost unheard of outside the warmer climes down south. The superstructure was still brilliantly white, contrasting dramatically against the black hull.

They were welcomed to the wreck by a swift current buffeting the hull. At amidships they retraced their route back, but not before Bartram pulled out of the muck an ashtray, which was quickly deposited in her goodie bag. Exhausted from their battle with the swift current, Bartram and Dudas made it back to the anchor line.

In 1967, deep decompression stops were not made. According to the authority at the time, the U.S. navy's extreme-exposure tables, decompression stops began at thirty feet. Bartram did not own a pressure gauge, so she relied on Dudas's since their consumption rate was "about the same."

The next day it was decided that the teams of divers should make their exploratory dives on the forward section of the ship near the bridge. John Dudas, being the youngest and strongest, made a solo dive and retrieved the grappling hook from a scupper hole near the stern and swam it forward against a swift current several hundred feet to secure it to the bridge area of the ship. It was difficult considering the depth, nitrogen narcosis, carbon dioxide buildup, and the unfamiliarity of the wreck layout.

Diving with Ed Rush, Bartram was unaware that the hook was now tethered to the bridge of the ship, the "holy of holies" of a shipwreck. What she saw there she will never forget: The sweeping smokestack was still in place, and in a smokestack hatchway, which was of course now horizontal, hovered the biggest codfish she had ever seen. The fish's snout almost touched the forward end, and the tail almost touched the aft end. Years later Bartram had the opportunity to board the *Doria*'s sister ship, the *Cristobal Colombo*, and stand in the twin opening of that ship's smokestack. Evelyn could comfortably fit her five-foot-eight-inch frame in the hatchway.

On her third and last dive, Bartram once again dove with Dudas. On his second dive Dudas had located one of the wingbridge's binnacles, a coveted prize to any artifact collector. Dudas managed to wrench the brass cover and compass off the pedestal, which was sent to the surface with a lift bag. The pair swam back to the anchor line. To Bartram's horror, the line had worn down to one thin strand of polypropylene due to rubbing against the wreck. That strand was all that kept them from being lost at sea almost two hundred feet down. The two made it up, but the line broke with two other divers still doing their decompression hangs. Both managed only minimal hang times before being hauled aboard the free-floating *Starlite*.

Mike de Camp and Evelyn Bartram with the *Doria*'s binnacle.
(Photo © Michael A. de Camp)

In 1968, one of the more memorable expeditions to the *Doria* was made by an Italian team of filmmakers led by producer and director Bruno Valati. Along with American still photographer Al Giddings, they gained international acclaim when they produced what would become a classic underwater film, *The Fate of the Andrea Doria*. The 16mm film captured some unforgettable moments.

The eerie black-and-white footage revealed a ship's hull that wore a threadbare shroud of fishing nets, which had become a snare for fish. Close-ups showed many of the fish in death struggles, some just skeletal remains picked clean by more fortunate and opportunistic scavenger fish. There were forays into the wheelhouse and a ghostly visit to the stern, where the name *Andrea Doria* could be still read, spelled out in brass.

In 1968, Alan Krasberg and Nick Zinkowski launched another filming and treasure-recovery expedition to the *Doria*. Krasberg, a physicist with Westinghouse, and Zinkowski, a commercial hard-hat diver, also towed along the latest in underwater habitats that could be piggybacked to the wreck. The habitat would provide divers with an underwater home that would supply breathing gases and shelter between dives. In this type of "saturation diving," the divers would remain on the bottom, so no decompression would have to be made between dives. All decompression was done after diving operations were completed in the "comfort" of the ten-by-four-foot cylinder that would be hauled up by the mother ship.

The Krasberg/Zinkowski expedition was plagued by bad weather and equipment failure. The filming end of the project, handled by underwater notables Al Giddings and Jack McKenney, had two custom-built submersible camera platforms, called Pegasus. These units were supposed to "fly" over the massive wreck and provide a photographic mosaic, but they never got out of the water after their initial runs.

The propulsion system on one Pegasus failed, and when its operator, Elgin Ciampi, tried to swim it up to the surface, he ran out of air and surfaced unconscious. The other Pegasus operator, Jacques Mayol, responded to the emergency. While rescue operations for

Ciampi were under way, Mayol tried to save the Pegasus submersibles by clipping them together, but they sank while everyone's attention was diverted to saving Ciampi.

The wreck of the *Andrea Doria* was now also the repository of the two $40,000 submarine cameras. With the loss of the units the filming of the recovery and the recovery operations were both aborted. The Krasberg/Zinkowski expedition, like so many of the dream-filled ones before it, succumbed to the *Doria*'s bewitchery. It seemed that the bigger the plans were for exploiting her riches, the bigger the failures would be. Only the modest efforts to see and explore the *Doria* seemed to have her blessing.

One would think that the film *The Fate of the Andrea Doria* would have inspired a rush by the adventurous, but it did not. *Life* magazine, Gimbel, salvors, and sport divers all seemed to lose interest—at least active interest. Mike de Camp, for one, was content that he had made three successful forays down to the mythical ship and survived. The challenge was met and conquered as far as he was concerned. John Dudas now had a dive shop in suburban Philadelphia to run. He also had a wife—Evelyn Bartram, his diving partner—and the beginnings of a family to think of. His diving was now mostly done in pools and shallow-water training dives, educating divers in what was to become the booming recreational sport of scuba.

The defection of de Camp, Hoffman, and Dudas from the ranks of divers willing to risk it all on a wreck like the *Doria* left a void. Not until a few years later would Philadelphian Gary Gentile reignite the spark for diving the *Doria*.

The *Andrea Doria*'s mystique was no accident. Her Italian builders knew exactly what they were creating. It was another masterpiece in the long line of Italian artistic achievements. Its siren call was aimed at the wealthy, art-appreciating world traveler. Little did the builder know that the *Andrea Doria* would become a magnet to an entirely different group.

FIVE

PENETRATING THE
DORIA

I n 1973 a small group from the Eastern Divers Association (EDA)
led by Philadelphian Tom Roach chartered a commercial fishing
vessel to ferry them out to the *Doria*. It had been six long years
since Mike de Camp had been to the seas off the Nantucket Shoals to
dive the ultimate deep wreck. Finding a charter captain willing to risk
his boat in the busy and treacherous sea-lanes miles from a snug harbor had been a daunting task, but Roach was confident he had found
such a vessel.

Gary Gentile was part of the EDA contingent waiting anxiously
dockside in Brielle, New Jersey, that Monday morning. Gentile had
been a certified scuba diver for only four years, but he had already
made a name for himself among the clique of deep divers exploring
wrecks on the eastern seaboard, proving his mettle on such sunken
time capsules as the *Oregon*, the USS *San Diego*, the *Coimbra*, and
the *Stolt Dagali*. The somewhat aloof Vietnam survivor had quickly
become a diving legend. For guys like Mike de Camp and John Dudas,

the recognition had come slowly over a decade, but Gary Gentile, still a diving neophyte in his early twenties, was awing this depth-tested bunch.

The group's wait was in vain. The charter boat never showed. Answering some frantic phone calls, the owner of the boat nonchalantly replied that the boat was in need of some repairs and there would be no trip. Charter fishing captains were notorious for blowing off fish charters on a whim, and scuba divers were a rung below fishermen in importance to the money-hungry characters that plied the waters of the North Atlantic. Reluctantly and chagrined by the whole affair, the erstwhile *Doria* divers piled their gear in their vehicles and made the long drive back to Philadelphia.

Tom Roach, however, did not give up. Pestering local charter operators over that diving season, he finally enlisted a ninety-foot catamaran, again out of Brielle. The *Atlantis Twin* agreed to take the foolhardy bunch out to the *Doria*.

The EDA were a group of no more than thirty hard-core deep-wreck divers who usually made their underwater forays into the New York Bight's Mud Hole. Gentile had been inspired by de Camp's tentative *Doria* probes in 1966 and 1967. He had been one of the hell-bent few, along with Roach, who had pushed for a *Doria* charter.

The *Doria* dive would push the envelope for the ambitious Gentile. He smelled adventure and intrigue and would not be denied. Their day came a year later when a collection of divers from Philadelphia, New Jersey, and Long Island boarded the *Atlantis Twin* for the 190-mile trip out into the open ocean. The barnacle-encrusted *Twin* could never best nine knots, but according to Gentile it was sheer luxury, since they had plenty of space for themselves and their gear and had a paid captain, two mates, and a cook aboard. The trip out to the *Doria* was a twenty-five-hour ordeal. Each of the twelve divers had four sets of double tanks, enough for two dives a day for the two days scheduled on the wreck.

All aboard made simple touch dives to dispel the mystique of diving the cursed lady of the deep. They also had other reasons: no one wanted to try something stupid, such as a penetration, on his first dive. But on his third dive, Gary Gentile did what had been his goal since he'd started diving: he penetrated the *Andrea Doria*.

Gentile buddied up with John Starace, the oldest diver aboard the *Twin*. Everyone hoped that the mature and safety-conscious Starace would slow down the impetuous and daring Gentile, the youngest aboard. Dubbed "the Ford and the Ferrari," the pair made their way forward along the Promenade Deck until they came upon the porthole torched out the year before by Don Rodocker and Chris DeLucchi in an attempt to pull out one of the ship's safes.

The hole was no more than two and half feet across, just enough space for one diver wearing doubles to drop in. John Starace remained outside the hole shining his light inside, giving Gentile a beacon to guide him. Slowly sinking down into the darkness, Gentile noticed the drop ceiling was beginning to separate away from the steel. Cables were draped down across it, and as Gentile went deeper, it narrowed, as if he were descending down a funnel of a spider's web. He could feel the cables brushing against him as he went deeper following the floor, which was now a vertical wall. At about 210 feet he stopped. It was dark and visibility was no more than five feet. His exhaust bubbles blocked out all illumination from above. He was very much alone in the narrow, darkened shaft of steel. "That's it!" Gentile remembered telling himself. "It's spooky. I'm scared."

Gentile inflated his dry suit with a couple of sharp blasts on the power inflator that sat just above his fast-beating heart. Above him he spied Starace's beam of light. Spreading the cables with his free hand, Gentile emerged into the green glow of ambient light that showered down from the surface.

The twelve divers from the EDA also made a startling discovery. The wheelhouse of the ocean liner, now eighteen years underwater, had disappeared. The bridge where Captain Piero Calamai had stood and watched the *Stockholm* deal the death blow to his beloved ship—which John Dudas and Evelyn Bartram had explored only seven years before—had corroded away, leaving only some twisted debris in the sand as proof of its existence. The treasured artifacts from the brain of the ship were lost forever. If divers wanted a memento of their daring adventure down into the depths of the Atlantic, they would have to search elsewhere. The 697-foot ship would provide plenty of alternatives, some of them extremely dangerous.

Gary Gentile had finally made his first penetration into the *Andrea Doria*. It was a big step for the ambitious Philadelphian. Vietcong bullets had prematurely ended any dreams of glory on the battlefield, but there was a reputation to be made diving the ultimate shipwreck and surviving. It would be years in the making and hundreds of dives would have to be logged, but it would be the infamous wreck of the *Doria* that would define his life, establish his reputation, and put him among the elite of the sport.

Six more years would pass before another charter bearing divers made the watery trek to the *Andrea Doria*. Considering the success of the de Camp and EDA charters, it was an astonishingly long dry spell. In the East Coast diving community, it was recognized that the *Andrea Doria* was a pinnacle dive that was not for everybody. It was considered sheer luck that no one had yet perished on the wreck, especially in light of the lack of deep-water experience, the ignorance of hyperbaric physics, and the inadequate gear divers used well into the 1980s.

From the 1960s to the 1980s, a tremendous aura surrounded the *Doria* and diving it, and exploring her was a huge and hazardous undertaking, equivalent to climbing Asia's Himalayas in the 1920s. Only a handful of divers were at that point willing and able to experience the mind-altering narcosis and the interminable decompression hangs in frigid water. But it was not for lack of trying, at least not on Gary Gentile's part. Gentile simply could not find a boat to take him and his pals from the EDA out there, and he tried year after year.

"Tom Roach had found fulfillment in touching the wreck," Gary Gentile later related. "I had touched the wreck too, but fulfillment for me meant continued exploration."

By 1978, without Roach at the helm, the EDA folded. Gentile was on his own and actively looking for a boat that could be the shuttle out to the wreck site. At times he had commitments from charter captains, but as the time for departure approached those commitments would evaporate. The captains usually felt they were not adequately insured to ferry divers out to such a dangerous spot. Still, Gentile persevered. One boat that Gentile had hoped to enlist was the *Sea Hunter* out of Freeport, Long Island.

One of three partners who owned the boat was Ron Burdewick, who had been on the EDA *Doria* trip in 1974. Gentile and his buddies from the old EDA would regularly charter the *Sea Hunter* for trips out to the nearby wrecks of the USS *San Diego* and the *Oregon*. Gentile thought he had an in, but Burdewick abruptly stopped diving and sold his interest out to his two partners, John Lachenmeyer and Sal Arena. At that point Gentile gave up hope, but then he learned that Lachenmeyer and Arena had decided to run a trip out to the *Doria* themselves, known as a "captain's charter" in the maritime business.

Sal Arena, John Lachenmeyer, and Ron Burdewick had teamed up to buy the *Sea Hunter* in 1973. Arena says the boat was purchased with the sole intent of diving the wrecks off Long Island. In 1973 there were no charter dive boats on Long Island, and Arena and his diving pals had to go down to New Jersey to charter them. Once the word got out about the *Sea Hunter*, the EDA kept it above water, chartering the boat virtually every weekend.

Sal Arena concocted the idea of a *Doria* trip with his good friend New Jersey diver Bill Nagle. Since Nagle had not been invited to take part in the 1974 *Doria* trip aboard the *Atlantis Twin*, he was determined to find a boat that would take him out. On a USS *San Diego* trip he asked Arena if the *Sea Hunter* would take him and his buddies, one of whom was Gary Gentile, out to the *Doria*. Arena said, "Sure, why not? What's the difference where I go? I didn't give a shit. We formulated a price and planned it for the following summer."

The *Sea Hunter II*, a small boat, only forty-two feet, replaced the first *Sea Hunter*, a three-cylinder diesel engine built in the 1930s that could never go faster than eight knots. The second *Sea Hunter* was a bit more capable of handling the offshore waters where the *Doria* rested.

According to U.S. Coast Guard regulations, since the *Sea Hunter* was not a certified vessel, she could take only six charterers plus a captain and mate. The group got around the regulations by taking seven paying divers with one of the group rotating as a mate. At the last minute, Arena had to back out of captaining the *Sea Hunter*. He told his partner, Lachenmeyer, that if he took the time off from his job as a truck driver, he would be fired.

The conditions out at sea were miserable and they arrived at the *Doria*'s watery grave late. Still, they managed to find the wreck and grapple it. Lachenmeyer shut down the engine and everybody turned in, hoping to get some much needed sleep before diving the next day. The *Sea Hunter* leaked like a sieve. When the sea-bound occupants awoke the next morning, they found themselves awash in seawater a hundred miles offshore. The boat was sinking. The water had shorted the batteries, so Lachenmeyer could not restart the engine and consequently could not activate the bilge pumps. If the boat was not bailed quickly, it would be joining the *Andrea Doria* at the bottom.

Finally Lachenmeyer remembered that they had brought along a battery in the Zodiac inflatable chase boat's outboard. Lachenmeyer, an engineer at Grumman, jump-started the engine with the small twelve-volt battery. They got the boat bailed and never shut down the engine again for the remaining two days.

The July 1980 trip, and another trip a week later, were uneventful. Gentile remembers them as "reaquaintance" dives. It had been six

Captain John Lachenmeyer with
Promenade Deck window.
(Photo © Bill Campbell)

years since he had visited the silent lady. He wanted to get comfortable
with her layout again before penetrating her.

The *Sea Hunter* charter proved once again that the *Doria* could be
dived safely and economically. Lachenmeyer and Arena were pleased
with the results. They also saw that their passion, deep-wreck diving,
could be bankrolled as well. Plans for a trip the following year were
quickly arranged. One of the divers from 1980 trip whose appetite had
just been whetted and who signed on for the repeat performance was
John Barnett.

Gentile recalled that the next year all aboard the *Sea Hunter* were
"euphoric" about returning to the *Doria*. Almost everyone to a man
had been on the successful 1980 trip. This time out Sal Arena was captaining the boat.

Gentile teamed up with his old diving buddy Bill Nagle. The pair were given the job of tying the anchor line to the wreck. They ran into trouble almost immediately. A swift current was running and visibility was poor, maybe ten to fifteen feet. The portion of the wreck where they alighted was covered with a tattered trawler net. The hook had slid across the steel plating and dropped off the side of the ship into the gloom below, coming to rest in the distant sandy bottom. Gentile and Nagle knew that retrieving the hook and tying off safely was not possible. Signaling each other in sign language, the two called off the dive after just seven minutes and returned to the surface.

Due to the *Sea Hunter*'s late arrival at the wreck site, it was decided to anchor in the sand just off the wreck and wait until the next day to try another tie-in. The next morning the current had slackened and visibility had improved to about thirty feet. This time Gentile and Nagle had no trouble tying in to the wreck on the Promenade Deck. Gentile sent up the styrofoam cups, signaling the waiting divers topside that the hook was secure and it was safe to descend down the line to the wreck.

John Barnett teamed up with Stan Smith, and they made their long swim to the bottom. Almost immediately, the two became separated. Smith did some exploring of the wreck, then returned to the anchor line. Still not seeing his buddy, he decided to go ahead with his ascent and decompression. Emerging from the water, he alerted all aboard that he had become separated from Barnett and had no idea where he was. Returning divers reported they had not seen the missing diver decompressing on the anchor line. The now anxious bunch aboard the *Sea Hunter* scanned the surface in hopes of spotting a lift bag, indicating a lost diver decompressing on an emergency upline. There was none.

By early that afternoon it was apparent Barnett had not survived his dive. Grimly, Gentile and Smith entered the ocean that afternoon with only one task on their mind—to recover John Barnett's body.

From the forward section of the Promenade Deck, Gentile and Smith worked their way aft, stopping to peer into openings on the wreck for any sign of the missing diver. In a hole burned out by the commercial *Top Cat* expedition in 1964, Stan Smith's light picked up something that did not fit. On closer examination Smith realized that his light was picking up the tips of a diver's fins some ten feet beneath him. Smith frantically flashed his light in the direction of Gary Gentile, who was busy exploring openings in the wreck with his light.

Directing his light into the blackness, Gentile immediately saw the fins protruding from a hole that was forward of the corridor that led to the lounge. Gentile dropped into the hole. The less experienced Smith stayed behind as a safety backup, his light following the descending Gentile.

Bathroom inside first-class foyer. *(Photo © Bill Campbell)*

Barnett lay facedown on what was once a wall but was now a floor to a bathroom. Gentile squeezed into the room, whose width was no bigger than the length of the door. Barnett was dead. He had been underwater for several hours, far longer than any bottled air could have sustained him, and his regulator had fallen from his mouth. The faceplate of his mask was clear and free of any blood or water, and Gentile could stare into the lifeless eyes. There seemed to be no signs of any panic. The body was not caught up in any debris or cable. Adding to the mystery, Gentile noted Barnett's gauges showed ample air. The emergency regulator connected to Barnett's spare pony bottle still hung from his neck where Barnett had secured it prior to his entry. Barnett's head was only inches from a Promenade Deck sliding window that had been wedged into the back of the little room. Perhaps he had seen it upon entering the corridor and was examining it when something inexplicable happened.

Gentile and Smith had no trouble removing the body from inside the wreck. At the surface Barnett's body was wrapped in a tarp and placed on the aft deck of the *Sea Hunter*. All diving was terminated and Captain Sal Arena headed for port to deliver the body to the authorities. All was quiet aboard the *Sea Hunter* on the sad trip back to Long Island.

John Barnett had become the first diving fatality on the *Andrea Doria*. The forty-year-old vice president of Citibank left behind a wife and four children in Pound Ridge, New York.

As with most diving fatalities, the autopsy revealed little. The official declaration from the coroner was that death was due to a massive embolism. The autopsy report had wreck divers shaking their heads. Of course Barnett had suffered embolism. Had not Gentile and Smith shot his body to the surface from the bottom two hundred feet below with lift bags once it was removed from the wreck? The remaining gases in his lungs when he was on the wreck would certainly have expanded under the reduced pressure of a rapid ascent and burst his lungs. Medical examiners had little knowledge of hyperbaric medicine and showed no inclination to learn even with the prodding of the diving community. This would continue to be a problem for divers who wanted to know what had killed their comrades while underwater.

John Barnett had probably died in one of two ways. Oxygen toxicity, unknown in 1981, might have killed him. He was at a depth where the partial pressure of oxygen was dangerous enough to have convulsed him. Little deep diving on scuba was being done at the time what with the recognized limit for recreational divers being 130 feet. As with nitrogen narcosis, oxygen toxicity could strike one diver and not his dive buddy who was shoulder to shoulder with him. There was, and still is, no way of foretelling who is apt to take a toxic hit.

Another likely suspect was what was known in diving world as "deep-water blackout." The blackout was usually a result of carbon dioxide buildup in the regulator, caused when a diver breathes rapidly in a stressful situation or overworks. The two, carbon dioxide and oxygen toxicity, may also have worked in tandem to kill Barnett.

Did Barnett have adequate skills to attempt a *Doria* dive? His first dives on the wreck the year before had gone without a hitch. But on that trip all the dives were just "touch dives," where the divers simply familiarized themselves with the layout of the wreck. No penetrations were made. On the 1981 trip, Barnett's first, and last, dive was a penetration. According to Steve Bielenda, Barnett had no business diving the wreck and certainly no business penetrating it.

Bielenda claims that John Barnett had been aboard the *Wahoo*, on a *San Diego* wreck dive, just two weeks before the fatal dive. Surfacing from a dive, Barnett had frantically signaled he was in trouble, and one of the boat's mates had jumped in and pulled him over to the boat. Barnett had had an equipment problem and had made a mad dash to the surface, luckily without a decompression mishap. The master of the *Wahoo* and Janet Bieser had taken Barnett aside and told him his skills "were way off, terrible really, just terrible." They strongly advised that he hold off on any *Doria* dives until he got his diving skills up.

Sal Arena believed that Barnett's skills were "all right" and that he simply made a stupid mistake. Arena said that for the life of him, he could not understand why a diver would want to enter the wreck. "The *Doria* is a big, beautiful wreck," Arena said, "You can do dozens of dives just swimming around it and never see the same thing twice. Why do you have to go inside? To get some old plates? What value do they have? The general population has no concept of their worth. They aren't worth shit. Most people don't know a diver risked their life getting this junk. The intrinsic value means something only to the diver who retrieved it. And is it worth risking your life for? I don't think so."

As for taking an unqualified diver to the *Doria*, Arena said that Steve Bielenda was in no position to point an accusing finger. Arena noted that Bielenda had taken Harvey Leonard out to the *Doria* after Arena had refused to take him aboard the *Sea Hunter* for a *Doria* trip. The quirky but lovable Leonard was infamous for ignoring decompression tables, something Arena says was "insane" when diving a deep wreck like the *Doria*. Bielenda, in his defense for taking Leonard aboard for a *Doria* trip, claims that, when he took Leonard, he had an agreement with him. Harvey had to follow navy dive tables or he could not dive. Leonard did and survived the trip. Leonard later died in 1998 while diving the *Oregon* from Arena's *Sea Hunter III*.

Arena says that back in 1981 nobody trained to do deep-wreck diving. It was all too new. As Bielenda found out with John Ormsby four years later, there was no way to control what a diver did once he left the vessel.

Whatever had caused Barnett's demise, one depressing thought haunted his friends and dive buddies: he had died alone under horrible circumstances deep in a watery black hole. Even veteran wreck divers shuddered at the thought. If anyone had ever thought that diving the *Doria* was overrated as a dangerous experience, Barnett's death was a wake-up call.

Nevertheless, divers lined up for the next trip.

• • •

The *RV Wahoo. (Photo © Steve Bielenda)*

Sal Arena and John Lachenmeyer were about to have company on the waters south of Nantucket. Barnett's death notwithstanding, the ease the skippers of the *Sea Hunter* had in finding the *Doria* emboldened another charter operator from Long Island to test his captain skills and the limits of his newly christened vessel—the *RV Wahoo.*

Steve Bielenda saw dollar signs. His milk runs out to the *San Diego* and the *Oregon* were profitable and easy enough, but the aura surrounding the *Doria* was hard to ignore. Running charters to the Italian shipwreck would solidify the *Wahoo's* and Steve Bielenda's reputation, and a sterling reputation attracted customers. But a dive trip to the *Andrea Doria* was daunting, and diver Julius Picatera had to talk Bielenda into it. Picatera had been a diving student of Bielenda's and had become an instructor himself.

Another incentive for making an expedition out to the *Doria* in 1981 was the twenty-fifth anniversary of her sinking. A diver from

Rhode Island by the name of Bill Campbell caught wind of the charter. Like most New England wreck divers Campbell thought of the *Doria* as his backyard wreck and was intent on diving it. Campbell had a plaque commissioned noting the twenty-fifty anniversary of the sinking and talked himself aboard the *Wahoo* for its maiden run out to the wreck.

It was a rough trip out. The *Wahoo* had to plough through six-to-eight-foot seas all the way out from Montauk. Bielenda and Janet Bieser had no trouble locating the wreck. One of the unforgettable memories of the trip for Bielenda was the laying of the plaque on the *Doria.*

Campbell had originally planned to ceremoniously deposit the plaque on the wreck and photograph the event with his dive buddy Rick Fryberg, but Fryberg was so seasick from the rough seas he was unable to make the dive. Campbell approached Bielenda about assuming Rick's duties.

Bill Campbell with a first-class china dish.
(Photo © Bill Campbell)

Before Campbell entered the water, one of his dive buddies from Rhode Island, Marty German, emerged from the water querying all assembled why they had been hanging so long on the anchor line on their ascent. Fearing German had gotten bent, Bielenda turned to John Lachenmeyer, who was crewing on the *Wahoo* for this trip, and said, "Call the Coast Guard for a helicopter evacuation."

Bielenda was tapped to carry the twelve-pound plaque to the bottom. Figuring he could save himself a laborious swim with all his gear and the plaque, he made his entry from the bow of the boat as opposed to the usual entry point amidships. Bielenda, however, had forgotten to account for the added weight of the plaque and had not adjusted his weight belt accordingly. Immediately upon entering the water he found himself plummeting to the bottom. He was forty feet down before he finally halted his rapid descent. He struggled over to the anchor line and waited for his buddy Bill Campbell.

Once they were on the wreck, Campbell took his photos of the solemn moment. That done, Bielenda signaled Campbell to ask what he should do with the plaque. Campbell signaled him to ditch it on the wreck. Bielenda laid out his goodie bag on the hull, placed the plaque in it, finished his dive, and retrieved his bag. The plaque, some twenty years later, still rests in his trophy case.

Before returning to the surface Bielenda decided to check the tie-in to the wreck. He noticed that the line had wrapped around one of the wreck's davits. Afraid that the rusting metal would wear the line, Bielenda tried to pull it off. The pitching line looped his hand, pinning him to the wreck. Bielenda waved frantically at Campbell for help. Campbell thought the *Wahoo* skipper wanted his picture taken and dutifully took one of the dismayed Bielenda. "I quickly freed my hand, but talk about miscommunication!" Bielenda could later relate.

When Bielenda climbed back aboard the *Wahoo*, Janet Bieser

Above: Marty German is evacuated by USCG helicopter. *(Photo © Bill Campbell)* Below: Marty German. *(Photo © Steve Bielenda)*

informed him that the helicopter was on its way. Marty German had indeed gotten bent. To compound the problem, with the copter on the way, the massive weight lifter adamantly refused to be taken aloft in a litter since he was deathly afraid of heights. Bielenda had to threaten the stricken diver with a crowbar before he reluctantly stretched out in the litter to be lifted up to the waiting helicopter and spirited away to a recompression chamber on the mainland for treatment.

German later died on an attempted record deep dive in the Caribbean in 1992. His body was never recovered.

The inch-and-a-half polypropylene mooring line left behind by the *Wahoo* got some more use. A few days after the *Wahoo* had left the area, Peter Gimbel and Oceaneering International arrived to start a salvage operation of the Bank of Rome's safe below the first-class gangway. They found the mooring line from the *Wahoo,* so diver and filmmaker Jack McKenney made a descent to the wreck to investigate. He found the line tied in right where they wanted to be, near the first-class loading doors. While Gimbel's project was under way, the *Wahoo* returned on a charter to locate the wreck of the *Republic,* said to be near where the *Doria* had gone down.

The *Republic* charter was the brain child of Marty Bailey, a diver who had a knack for raising money for various underwater salvage ventures. He had formed a company prophetically called the Farfetched Salvage Company and advertised in the *Wall Street Journal.* A good deal of the money raised came from actor/comedian Dan Aykroyd. The *Republic,* a White Star Line steamship, had collided with the Italian steamship *Florida* in 1909 and was said to be carrying a cargo of gold valued at the time at $3 million. Bailey hired Bielenda and the *Wahoo* to locate and put divers on her. According to Bielenda, the salvage attempt was an "abortion" since Bailey had enlisted ten divers who had little or no deep-diving experience. To add to the problems, the side-scan sonar "tow fish," used to locate underwater wrecks, had been attacked by a shark and rendered useless. While in the area Bielenda found Gimbel and his crew working the *Doria.*

After dropping off Bailey's divers at Martha's Vineyard, the *Wahoo* fueled up and headed back for home port at Captree. Bielenda and Bieser decided to take a closer look at Gimbel's operation since they were nearby. Gimbel had hired Oceaneering International, a large underwater salvage operation that had plenty of "toys" aboard their ship. The mother salvage ship, the *Sea Level 11,* called the Coast Guard and complained that the *Wahoo* was endangering their dive operation since Oceaneering had divers in the water. Bielenda said no diving operations were under way and the *Sea Level 11* was at the time just taking on supplies, so he felt within his rights to take a close look.

Back home, Bielenda decided he had better check with a maritime lawyer to see if Gimbel had any rights to the wreck and if he could prevent the *Wahoo* from revisiting the *Doria.* Bielenda had plans for a September trip. The lawyer advised him that even though Gimbel had not obtained an "arrest" of the wreck, which would give him legal ownership, he could cause Bielenda trouble with a lawsuit. Right or wrong, he was told, Gimbel's deep pockets could keep Bielenda in court with expensive legal representation for months if Bielenda returned to dive the wreck while Gimbel's salvage and filming operation was still in progress. Bielenda canceled his return trip.

Nevertheless, the success of the *Wahoo*'s first trip had his loyal following of divers clamoring for more. Ironically, it was Gimbel's salvaging of the Bank of Rome's safe that really kick-started interest in the *Doria* by wreck divers. The lure, however, was not the safes, priceless artwork, or passengers' valuables, but the china that Gimbel's cameras had spotted.

Gary Gentile saw a rough documentary of the safe salvage at the 1982 Boston Sea Rovers convention. He noticed piles of china the cameras had inadvertently captured on film. After the viewing,

First-class china inside the *Doria*.
(Photo courtesy Steve Gatto)

Gimbel pinpointed the location of those scenes for Gentile on a copy of the *Doria*'s ship plans.

The next summer Gentile was once again aboard the *Sea Hunter*. He told Captain Sal Arena exactly where he wanted to be on the wreck. Buddying up with New Jersey diver Steve Gatto, the pair secured the grapple within eight feet of Gimbel's Hole. Gentile described the hole as a cavernous "cathedral." Gimbel's divers from Oceaneering had cleaned out a wide underwater passage.

Suffering from nitrogen narcosis and a healthy dose of apprehension, Gatto and Gentile dropped deeper into the gloomy abyss.

Gentile realized they had gone too far into the wreck, and the nervous pair retreated through a cloud of stirred-up silt and dislodged rust. But while he was swimming through the foyer area, something caught Gentile's attention.

"Up ahead I saw a glimmer of white," Gentile described. "My light zeroed in on it, then waved back and forth rapidly to attract Steve's attention. It was the edge of a plate. We approached it with reverence. I touched it tentatively at first, then wiggled it out of the debris. It came free easily, but so did a swirl of thick mud. I beheld the gold-leaf trim and the crown logo; the word *Italia* stood out."

Gentile's find started a gold-rush mentality among Northeast wreck divers. Not even John Barnett's death quelled the hoopla. By 1983 Bielenda was running two, sometimes three, trips out to the *Doria* every summer. At that time the *Wahoo* and the *Sea Hunter* were the only two vessels going out to the wreck, but by 1985 Arena felt he had enough of the *Doria*. With his new *Sea Hunter III*, built in 1986, Arena found he could make more money chartering dives out to the nearby

Doria booty. (Photo courtesy Steve Gatto)

wrecks of the USS *San Diego* and the *Oregon*. Arena felt he did not need the "bullshit" of running the long, tedious trips out to the *Doria*. *Doria* divers were "whiners," said Arena. They wanted to be in a certain place on the wreck, and if the weather turned bad, they could not understand that he would have to abort and head back to safe shelter.

"They wanted their artifacts," Arena complained to me. "I wanted to get everybody home safe and sound. The difference between them and me was that they were divers first. I was a boat captain first. Besides, I was not desperate for money like Bielenda was. He started out later than me. I was always booked a year in advance. I didn't need the *Doria*. I got tired of dealing with the zealots who were always complaining that they were getting screwed by me."

Bielenda admits only to being competitive, claiming that *Doria* divers "were few and far between then and still are, and that in running a full-time charter boat money is always important."

One of the divers who was always complaining was Gary Gentile. The short-fused captain of the *Sea Hunter* and the self-righteous Gentile found it difficult to get along in the best of times. Now that the gold rush for china was on, it was important that the money-paying customers be placed near the China Hole. Gentile claimed in his book that on an 1982 *Doria* dive, Arena had sloppily hooked the wreck some three hundred feet away from the hole, forcing him to hump the hook from the pitching boat to the desired spot. Gentile claims that he grew tired of Arena's dictatorial and abusive moods and confronted the stocky truck driver. Words were spoken but no fisticuffs resulted.

Gentile claimed to be outraged when he later learned that Arena had purposely dropped the hook in the wrong place so divers would not get any of the coveted china. According to Gentile's logic, it was a way for Arena to get return customers intent on bagging some china. Arena, however, said it was just more of Gary Gentile's "self-serving bullshit," and that he always believed that it was good business to place divers wherever they wanted to be.

Steve Bielenda was happy to tap into the disgruntled Gentile's knowledge and tie-in skills. Gentile had a reputation by now, and wreck divers from all over the country called him for advice. He was in a position to recommend a boat for a *Doria* charter. With Gentile aboard, the *Wahoo*'s path to becoming the number one dive boat to the *Doria* seemed to be undisputed. But it did not come without a price. Tragedy struck the *Wahoo* in 1984.

Steve Bielenda remembers thirty-seven-year-old Frank Kennedy as a quiet, mild-mannered guy from Wrentham, Massachusetts, with a lot of diving experience, who drove down to Montauk by himself for the mid-July 1984 *Doria* dive. This would be Kennedy's first dive from the *Wahoo*.

Kennedy said all the right things during a phone conversation with Bielenda when he called to sign on for a *Doria* trip. Bielenda claims he could learn a lot about a diver over the phone. He would ask what kind of gear he used, what his configuration was, where he had dived before and with whom. Before all the advanced deep-diving certifications were available, it was the only way a boat captain could ascertain a diver's qualifications.

On his very first dive to the wreck Kennedy had a problem. He almost ran out of air. Apparently he miscalculated his time and his air consumption and could not find his reserve tank regulator. If not for his buddy Mike Moore, who found the dangling reserve regulator for him, he might have drowned on his first dive.

Bielenda says that Kennedy had his pony, or reserve air tank, configuration "all fucked up." Usual practice had wreck divers routing the regulator hose from the center-mounted tank under and through the double tank manifold and over the shoulder. Kennedy had it routed *around* the manifold, negating the bracketing the manifold afforded. The bracketing kept the regulator from falling away from the diver's grasp in case it broke free of the neck restraint. Without the bracketing, a diver would have to face downward in a prone position and hope the regulator would drop beneath him to deploy it.

Gary Gentile studied Kennedy's dive log later, and in it Kennedy confirmed the problem on his first dive with the reserve air supply. Kennedy had noted that he had to do something to correct the problem, but apparently he did not.

After Kennedy's first dive, Bielenda checked out his gear configuration and noticed the problem with the reserve air tank. He suggested the appropriate routing of the regulator. In retrospect Bielenda said he "failed" because he never checked to see if Frank Kennedy actually made the change.

After his first dive, Art Kirchner, a veteran *Doria* diver, had let it be known that he had inadvertently dropped a bag of dishes down the hole near the first-class dining room. All aboard were keen on making a quick score by finding the lost bag. On his dive down to the wreck the next morning, Kennedy dropped deep down into the hole in search of the lost bag of loot. His depth gauge indicated he had gone down 240 feet.

On his return to the surface, Kennedy's dive buddy Mike Moore claimed he was with Kennedy at the fifty-foot mark on the anchor line. Moore turned away from his buddy to survey the ocean depths around him. When he finally turned around to face Kennedy, he was nowhere to be seen.

Bielenda was standing on the starboard stern of the *Wahoo* staring forward. He remembers the water was pretty flat under an early-morning sun. Then he saw a bloated diver literally pop up out of the water. Bielenda hollered for Craig Stemitez to man the chase boat and retrieve the stricken diver. By the time they got Kennedy out of the chase boat and onto the deck of the *Wahoo*, Bielenda knew Kennedy was as good as dead.

When they got Kennedy aboard, Bielenda noticed he had not changed his gear configuration. His reserve regulator hung from his side, beyond his reach. His pressure gauges indicated he had no air left in his set of doubles. After Moore emerged from the depths, so did the story of what had happened to Frank Kennedy.

Kennedy had sprinted for the surface from the depth of fifty feet. What little air he had left in his lungs expanded rapidly under the reduced pressure of his swift ascent. Desperate to reach the surface, the doomed diver never exhaled the expanding volume of air. His lungs ruptured, releasing thousands of air bubbles into his surrounding blood system and tissues, paralyzing his body with strokes.

Gary Gentile remembers that several divers aboard the *Wahoo* were conversant with mouth-to-mouth resuscitation and cardiopulmonary resuscitation (CPR). Gentile had practiced this lifesaving technique on dummies, but never in a real situation.

Wahoo crew performs CPR on Frank Kennedy. *(Photo © Steve Bielenda)*

"We all took turns at it [mouth-to-mouth and CPR]," Gentile recounted. "This is when I learned what they didn't tell us in the course. They didn't tell us that the body in reality would be vomiting in our mouths. It was a dreadfully sickening experience for all of us."

After five minutes of administering mouth-to-mouth and CPR, Kennedy began to breathe on his own and his rescuers detected a pulse. Gentile remembers sitting back and saying to himself, "Wow, this stuff really works!"

But it worked for only a few minutes. Bielenda says it was an "artificial pulse." Besides his embolization, Kennedy was also bent. He had done little or no decompressing on his ascent, and that alone was enough to kill him. The divers and crew aboard the *Wahoo* continued to work on him for the entire hour it took for a Coast Guard helicopter to arrive, even though they knew it was in vain. Frank Kennedy was a dead man the moment he raced for the surface.

Since the Coast Guard had not ordered them off the wreck, the *Wahoo* remained tethered to the sunken ocean liner, and they continued their diving. Bielenda remembers it was a quiet trek back to Montauk.

It was the *Wahoo*'s first *Doria* fatality, but not the last. One year later, almost to the day, John Ormsby would step aboard the *Wahoo* for a reckoning with his own fate.

Bill Nagle, Gary Gentile's old friend and dive buddy from New Jersey, had purchased a thirty-five-foot Maine Coaster in 1985, which he christened the *Seeker*. Nagle had a lucrative tool sales route, and he had also inherited some family money. The money would fuel his passion in life: diving.

Looking at Bill Nagle, it would be easy to surmise that, as Steve Bielenda recalled, Nagle "had the world by the ass." With shoulder-length hair and soft features, the boyish-looking Nagle could have passed for a soap-opera idol. Bill Nagle had a well-earned reputation as an experienced, cocky, and aggressive diver. Nagle was also on the fast track to self-destruction.

One can only guess what set Bill Nagle down the road of substance abuse that killed him at the age of forty-two in 1993, but it may have had something to do with the untimely death of his diving mentor John Dudas on the wreck of the *Sommerstad* in 1982.

Legendary deep-wreck diver John Dudas was at the time an owner of a dive shop in suburban Philadelphia. He had fallen into the routine world of a scuba instructor, which meant more time spent in pools and on shallow ocean dives overseeing the training of nervous students than on the deep-water dives on wrecks that he loved so much. Gone were the days when he, along with Mike de Camp, had made their dives of discovery on the *Doria* trips of 1966 and 1967. But on July 12, 1982, John Dudas reverted back to his old form and made a pilgrimage aboard Sal Arena's *Sea Hunter* to the *Sommerstad*, the kind of a dive that had made his reputation ten years earlier.

Gary Gentile vividly recalls the dive. Gentile was returning to the anchor line, his dive complete, when he saw Dudas on his knees seemingly examining the tie-in point to the wreck at 170 feet. Frozen in inaction were divers Bill Nagle and Kathy Warehouse. It took a moment, but then Gentile realized what was wrong with the scene— no bubbles were escaping to the surface from around Dudas. Gentile saw to his horror that Dudas's regulator hung limply from his shoulder down to the sandy bottom.

Gentile sprinted forward and immediately inserted the regulator into Dudas's mouth and frantically pressed the purge button, shooting compressed air into the unresponsive diver's mouth. The air went no farther inside, spilling out into the pressing depths. Gentile reluctantly realized he could do nothing for John Dudas. He was dead.

Gentile wrote that Nagle was "traumatized and completely unresponsive" to his silent underwater pleas for help in trying to save John Dudas. All that was left for Gentile to do was to see that the body was retrieved from the ocean bottom and returned to his pregnant wife and mother of three, Evelyn.

Like most diving fatalities Dudas's death was officially listed as a drowning, but Gentile believed it was a combination of eroded deep-diving skills and equipment failure. Gentile referred to Dudas as a "dinosaur among the mammals," unwilling to progress beyond the machismo that early wreck divers had relied on. Evelyn Dudas, to this day, believes that John blacked out from carbon dioxide buildup—deep-water blackout—but she also blames Bill Nagle.

Bill Nagle, according to Evelyn, was pretty "rattled" on the day of the fatal dive. Nagle had just attended his brother's funeral the night before. His brother had committed suicide after a lifelong battle against drug abuse. Adding to Bill's woes, his mother had died that same year. Ever the loyal friend, John Dudas had driven up to the Jersey shore to spend some time with Nagle and offer him some support.

On the fatal dive, Nagle had followed John into the water. Upon reaching the bottom, Nagle had a "regulator management problem" and experienced a panic attack. After correcting the problem, he noticed Dudas kneeling near the anchor line and saw he was in trouble and did not react. Precious minutes later, Gary Gentile came on the scene.

Evelyn Dudas said that Sal Arena did not call her for six months, believing he did not want to deal with, in her words, a "hysterical pregnant widow." He need not have been so hesitant. Evelyn had rehearsed the moment she knew would eventually come. Every time she got pregnant she would stand over her kitchen sink and ponder the thought of being left a widow. She would wonder what she would do and cry her eyes out. After the phone call came from the Coast Guard, she steeled herself, to the amazement of her friends and family.

"They asked how I could be so strong," she said, "asking why I didn't just break down and dissolve. I had three kids and one on the way, and I had to survive this pregnancy."

Nagle survived too, but the booze and the drugs began to take their toll. Bill Nagle poured his energy into the *Seeker*, but the memories of the *Sommerstad* still haunted him. According to Dan Crowell, who crewed aboard Nagle's boat in later years, and who eventually bought it from his widow, Bill always refused pleas from his loyal New Jersey

Bill Nagle, 1991. *(Photo courtesy Dan Crowell)*

wreck-diving following to revisit the *Sommerstad*. It was one shipwreck he had no desire to see again.

Flush with cash and a burning desire to establish the *Seeker* as the preeminent dive boat in the Northeast, Nagle pressed ahead with his ambitious plans for his boat. He set the *Seeker* up for commercial diving, outfitting the sturdy wooden boat with an A-frame, welding rig, and heavy-duty lift bags. In 1986 Nagle made plans to dive the *Doria*—from his own boat.

Nagle enlisted a group of his old diving buddies for an expedition to retrieve the ship's bell from the *Doria*. The ship's bell was a prized artifact from any shipwreck. On a blazing hot Fourth of July the group headed out to the *Doria* from Montauk.

The job of securing the grapple to the wreck was given to Gary Gentile and Tom Packer. Conditions on the bottom were poor: a swift current was running and visibility was minimal. To make matters worse, the topside seas were heaving the small Maine Coaster to and fro, straining the anchor line. On the bottom, Gentile saw what was happening and tried to manually hold the hook to the wreck. The pitch of the boat was too much to contend with. The hook pulled free, snagging one of Gentile's pressure hoses and pulling him along the bottom like a "lassoed heifer."

Extricating himself, Gentile dropped the grapple and swam hard for the wreck. He reached the wreck where the raised letters spelled out *Andrea Doria* on the port bow. Incredibly, it was just the area where they wanted to be. Gentile deployed his sisal line, the emergency ascent line, in a hawser hole and sent the end of the line secured to a lift bag to the surface. They had their tie-in point.

After exploring the bow area, Gentile terminated his dive and made his ascent up the sisal line. When he finally broke the surface into the hot afternoon air, the *Seeker* was nowhere in sight. He hung on the jerking, arm-wrenching sisal line for an hour before he finally spotted the searching *Seeker*. He was heartily embraced by all upon emerging from the choppy seas. The complement of divers on the *Seeker* had been looking for what they thought would be Gary Gentile's lifeless body.

The next day, bottom conditions were still poor. Locating the empty davit that had held the ship's bell, Gentile and his buddy Packer theorized the bell had fallen to the bottom. The pair dropped down the hull, which was shrouded in lost trawler nets. At 235 feet the hull of the Doria ended with still no bottom in sight. Because of the curve of the bottom of the ship's hull, the brooding old hulk disappeared from view as they dropped deeper down the weighted downline. Finally alighting on the sandy bottom, Gentile glanced at his depth gauge. It read 248 feet.

With the choppy seas filtering out sunlight and with the minute particulates in the water, visibility was reduced to less than fifteen feet. Beyond their narrow beams of light there was nothing but the blackness of the deep. Caution kept them close to the downline, and they could not find the bell. Before ascending, Gentile did retrieve one memento from the wreck—a two-pound lobster.

Another full day of diving by three teams of divers did not turn up the bell. Giving up on the search, the hook was reset aft on the stern of the ship. Gentile and Packer made an arduous 175-foot swim farther aft in search of the auxiliary stern helm. At the depth of two hundred feet, the massive wooden helm appeared out of the gloom. While snapping pictures of their discovery Gentile noticed a familiar shape emerge out of the gloom: it was the aft ship's bell, totally encrusted with sea anemones.

Because of their find the group decided to extend the expedition another day to retrieve the bell. Once the 150-pound bell was raised, via some unique engineering skills, the *Seeker* lifted anchor and headed back to Montauk.

But a price would be exacted for the *Seeker*'s extended visit to the *Doria*.

The *Wahoo* was laid up in Montauk when they got a weather forecast warning of gale force winds that would be lashing the seas in the vicinity of the *Doria* wreck. Captain Janet Bieser, knowing that Nagle was diving the wreck, radioed him in the morning around 9 A.M. to warn him of the front moving in and that he "should get the hell out of there."

If Nagle had left when the warning came in, they would have got beat up for at most two hours and had the protection of Montauk Harbor before night fell. But Nagle opted for another dive and did not pull up anchor until 2 P.M. The *Seeker* took such a beating that the superstructure of the boat got cracked. Since there was no dock space at Montauk for them, the *Wahoo* let them tie up to their boat.

According to Steve Bielenda, three of the *Seeker* divers jumped off the boat to the dock and fell to their knees and kissed it. The three-some had thought they would never see land again; the waves had been so big they felt they were going down a ski slope.

Nagle bought a new boat, again christened the *Seeker*. Besides running trips out to the Jersey wrecks, Nagle took divers up to the USS *San Diego* and the *Oregon* for overnight trips.

In 1988, John Chatterton, a commercial diver and an experienced deep-wreck diver, poked around on the *Doria* and figured out a way to get into the area of the third-class dining room. No diver had ever been in the third-class dining room, "tourist class," as the Italia Line designated it. Tourist class made up the largest contingent of passengers aboard the Italian liner, and for Chatterton that meant more china, all of it up to this time untouched by divers.

In the stern of the wreck, Chatterton was able to squeeze inside a hole between two steel support beams. He quickly discovered piles and piles of plates, saucers, cups, and crystal, a veritable gold mine of china.

Back aboard the *Seeker*, Chatterton and his dive buddy Glen Plokhoy approached Nagle about running a trip with the sole intention of burning a bigger hole so there would be easy access for all to the third-class dining room. The special trip from Point Pleasant, New Jersey, was run in August.

On what Chatterton described as one of the most beautiful days he had ever seen out on the *Doria*, the massive job began. Oxygen hoses and welding cables had to be run down from the surface to the wreck for the underwater torch. Shooting video of what they were doing, Chatterton and Plokhoy burned out the hole. Chatterton related that they got "a bunch of stuff," but because of the workload not everybody could get inside. Since the ideal diving season on the *Doria* was closing, all aboard the *Seeker* decided they would run another trip the next year with the intent of exploring the new portion of the ship and loading up on artifacts. All were sworn to secrecy.

Richie Kohler. *(Photo courtesy Dan Crowell)*

Over the winter Steve Bielenda attended a meeting of the Atlantic Wreck Divers Club, and one of the members reported the *Seeker*'s success in opening up the third-class area. Chatterton claims someone in the club had seen a copy of the video, from which it was easy to determine the location of the hole.

Richie Kohler was a member of the Atlantic Wreck Divers and was at that meeting. Kohler was a frequent *Wahoo* customer, as were most of the Long Island–based members of the Atlantic Wreck Divers. Over a few beers Steve Bielenda proposed an "ultrasecret trip" out to the *Doria* to one-up Nagle and the *Seeker*.

"The bottom line," as Kohler described it, "was Bielenda wanted to fuck Bill Nagle, and it was put in those terms. But fortunately there was one member of the club who had more of a conscience than the rest of us, and he contacted Nagle and told him of Bielenda's secret trip."

Bielenda says he never set up an "ultra-secret trip," and that all his trips were advertised in advance. The *Wahoo*'s skipper claims he found out about the trip from Jon Hulbert, who helped Chatterton lay the grate over the hull just prior to the *Wahoo*'s trip out there. As for "fucking Nagle," all Bielenda says he wanted to do was to "enjoy the spoils."

According to John Chatterton, the top-secret *Wahoo* charter was tantamount to a "claim jump." Not to be preempted, the *Seeker* put together its own secret trip with the intent of beating the *Wahoo* out to the wreck site. Prior to making their run out to the *Doria*, Chatterton and his friends constructed a grate that weighed over three hundred pounds of case-hardened steel that could only be removed with a custom wrench.

The *Seeker*, indeed, got there before the *Wahoo*. All the divers aboard the *Seeker* came up with bulging bags of third-class china.

The *Seeker* and the *Wahoo* moored together at Block Island.
(Photo courtesy Dan Crowell)

When dive operations were complete, the grate was placed over the hole, and Chatterton hung a sign on it that read, *Closed for inventory. Please use alternate entrance. The crew of the Seeker.*

Chatterton says no attempt was made to block the original entrance he had squeezed into. "If they wanted to dive in there," he said, "they would have to do it the way I originally did it."

The china fever was so bad aboard the *Wahoo* prior to arriving at the *Doria* site that the divers drew straws for who would be the first to splash in. "We were going to bag up all this stuff up and leave it on the hull," Kohler recounted, "and every third team would send it up with lift bags so we wouldn't have to hang with it. We had these visions of hundreds of pounds of dishes. It was insane."

Richie Kohler remembered how shocked he was to discover the grate over the hole. He pounded on the lock with his hammer, "really freaking out," in his words, screaming in his mouthpiece, "Those motherfuckers!"

Pete Manchee, a former commercial diver from South Carolina, volunteered to dump his doubles on the hull and slip into the small space above the grate with just a single tank that he could pass in ahead of him, then drop down and bag up the china. "At two hundred ten feet," Manchee said, "a single eighty tank doesn't last very long. But you kinda get caught up looking into rooms that are just stacked up with china. I was going ballistic."

Manchee did his surveying and bagged up on some "lazy-Susan shit," as he called it, then realized he was low on air. The burly but compact weight lifter swam for the green glow of light. Still under the grate, he came face-to-face with Kohler. Manchee spit his regulator out, and Kohler gave him his primary regulator while he deployed his own reserve-tank regulator. After some anxious moments, Manchee finally squeezed through the hole, holding his breath two hundred feet beneath the surface, and got back to his doubles with the help of Kohler and Hank Garvin.

The dive team made their ascent. The threesome had overextended their stay and were low on air. While decompressing on the anchor line, they had another problem. A huge shark, the biggest one Garvin had ever seen, circled between them and the surface. "That was all we fucking needed," Garvin later said with a laugh, but the shark soon departed and the trio made it back safely to the *Wahoo*.

On Manchee's next dive, he slipped above the grate again, this time with three backup divers and a set of double tanks he could drop in between the grate bars. Coming back up from the interior of the ship was the most dangerous part of the penetration. Manchee had two bulging bags of china and no buoyancy-control vest, and the doubles he was wearing had no inflator hose to his dry suit. The bags, clipped to his harness, weighed a "ton." Standing on the edge of the corridor above the third-class dining room after emerging from the kitchen area, Manchee realized he had a serious problem. "All I could see above me was a slight green glow with a bulkhead blocking my exit, " he said. "There's no way I'm gonna swim these huge two bags of china back up to the grate with no buoyancy. Of course, I didn't want to drop the china, because that's what we came for."

What Pete Manchee then did to extricate himself from the bowels of the sunken ship with the loot certainly puts him in the pantheon of wreck divers. The dining room tables had all settled onto the bulkhead wall. Manchee figured he could jump from one table to the next and literally climb out from inside the wreck. He alighted on one tabletop, but it crumbled under his prodigious weight. The tables had laminated-plywood tops, rotted by the sea, but lucky for Manchee the pedestals were metal. "I jumped from one table pedestal to the next all the way across the dining room," he recounted, "I felt like Burt Lancaster in the *Crimson Pirate*, swinging from one to the other to get enough height to get out of there. When I got to the grate, I managed one last hard kick and jumped up and grabbed the bottom of the grate and pulled myself up."

Later that same diving season, the *Seeker* was over the wreck when the *Wahoo* arrived. Steve Bielenda was not aboard and Janet Bieser was piloting the boat. Bieser called Nagle up on the radio and asked him how long he was going to be there. Nagle replied not long, but that he still had divers doing decompression hangs on the anchor line. Bieser maneuvered the *Wahoo* in front of the *Seeker* and dropped a hook. But then the current began to take the *Wahoo* sideways toward the bow of the *Seeker*. Nagle got on the radio to find out what Bieser was doing, but there was no answer. Bieser was directing the grappling effort away from the boat's bridge. Apparently they wanted to be on the stern even though there was seven hundred feet more of wreck where they could tie off to.

Chatterton said that the *Wahoo* drifted within twenty feet of the *Seeker*'s bow before she threw her engines into reverse from neutral. Now the *Wahoo*'s grappling line was crossing the *Seeker*'s anchor line. Nagle was still trying to radio Bieser, notifying her she had crossed his line and wanting to know what she was planning to do about it, but there was still no response from the *Wahoo*'s captain.

John Chatterton.
(Photo courtesy Dan Crowell)

It was, according to Chatterton, a dangerous situation. In all his years of diving, he claims never to have seen two dive boats cross anchor lines—even on small wrecks. If the *Wahoo*'s grappling hook got pulled off the wreck, any diver on the *Seeker*'s anchor line who was decompressing would be stripped off. The crossed lines also prevented anybody aboard the *Seeker* from making any dives.

Even though he was not ready to dive, Chatterton told Nagle he would suit up and go in with Bart Malone to see what he could do. Chatterton got down to 130 feet and saw at that point that the lines crossed. Meanwhile, Gary Gentile and Gary Gilligan "splashed in" from the *Wahoo* to set their hook. Chatterton pulled his knife out and cut the *Wahoo*'s line while Gentile and Gilligan were still above him. The two teams of divers had no visual contact between them. According to Chatterton, "I solved the problem."

The *Seeker* finished up for the day, pulled her hook, and headed for home. The *Wahoo* finally set her hook on the stern, where she wanted to be. Nagle and Chatterton were irate over the incident. They claimed that Bieser had listened to her customers, who wanted to be over the third-class hole, instead of opting for a safer part of the ship to hook to. To the New Jersey divers it was a glaring blunder on Bieser's part, and they felt she was remiss in her duties as the captain of the vessel.

Bieser counters by saying the *Seeker* was deliberately making her wait, causing her group to lose dives that day. Captain Janet claims she dropped the anchor at the furthest possible place on the wreck from the *Seeker* but a strong current carried them close to her competitor. Concerned that the grapple might slip, she paid out more line to go downcurrent of the *Seeker*. Her tie-in divers were then going to take down a second line and secure it to the wreck a safe distance from the Jersey boat, but Chatterton cut their line before the tie-in divers could reach the bottom. Bieser says that where the customers preferred to dive on that particular trip had "no bearing on where the grapple snagged."

The competition between the *Wahoo* and the *Seeker* reached a crescendo over an incident on the wreck of the German U-869.

Bill Nagle had gotten a set of loran numbers for an unknown wreck from a fishing-boat captain he met at a bar. At the site sixty miles off the Jersey coast, John Chatterton and Dan Crowell were given the task of identifying the wreck. The pair went down 230 feet and immediately recognized it as a submarine from the conning tower and torpedo tubes. Two other divers followed them in: Paul Skabinski was an instructor with a lot of deep-diving experience who was a regular aboard the *Seeker*. Steve Feldman was his good friend and assistant instructor. Although Feldman did not have the experience Skabinski had, the two, according to John Chatterton, "made a pretty good team."

Skabinski and Feldman fell in love with the wreck and the romance and adventure of exploring a virgin wreck. Feldman went out and bought specialized gear and reconfigured it so he could further explore the unknown sub. According to Chatterton, Feldman came "loaded for bear" on the return trip to the sub.

Skabinski and Feldman planned a thirteen-minute dive in the deep depths to reacquaint themselves with the wreck. At the agreed-upon time for the ascent, Skabinski came off the wreck and started up. He looked down below him and saw Feldman was still on the sub, right at the tie-in point on the wreck. Skabinski waited a few minutes, then he noticed that no bubbles were being expelled by the exhaust ports of Feldman's regulator. He quickly descended to investigate. Skabinski rolled Feldman over and found a totally unresponsive diver. Feldman was not breathing, and his regulator dropped from his mouth. According to Chatterton, Skabinski at this point went "totally bonkers." Here was his good friend, his dive buddy, apparently dead.

Skabinski screamed in his regulator in hysteria. He tried to put Feldman's regulator back in his mouth, to no avail. Skabinski grabbed Feldman with one hand, the anchor line with the other, and sprinted for the surface. The current was ripping as he made his ascent. Breathing hard and unable to compensate for his increasing buoyancy from the reduction of pressure, he panicked. Kevin Brennan and

Doug Roberts were coming down the anchor line. Overbreathing his regulator, Skabinski believed he was running out of air.

Skabinski dropped Feldman and ripped the regulator out of Brennan's mouth without signaling his fear that he was out of air. Brennan deployed his emergency air regulator and stayed with Skabinski. Roberts swam down after Feldman, who had drifted away onto the sand away from the wreck. Upon reaching him, Roberts quickly realized that Feldman was dead.

Roberts assessed the situation. On the bottom he was at 230 feet and out of visual range of the wreck and the path to the surface—the anchor line. Removing his penetration-line reel, Roberts attempted to secure Feldman, but in his haste he looped his line around Feldman's head instead of his harness. Roberts then started his ascent hoping to find the anchor line, where he could decompress and secure the body for recovery later. Finding the anchor line, he fumbled to secure his penetration line to it, with Feldman on the other end.

Skabinski emerged hysterical, screaming that his buddy was dead. Skabinski reached the top of the ladder and, according to Chatterton, "did a face plant on the deck and puked. He collapsed on the deck in a fetal position, with his tanks on, and cried."

Nagle, Chatterton, and Crowell found out what had happened below from Roberts and Brennan. All that was left to do was locate Roberts's penetration line and recover Feldman's body.

Chatterton remembered thinking that the incident was "as bad as it gets." Crowell and Chatterton had already done a dive and had little of a surface interval but agreed "to fuck it and go down and get the guy."

The two crew members quickly found a thin penetration-reel line leading off the anchor line. Chatterton followed it out while Crowell stayed behind. At the end of the line was Feldman's reel with no body in sight. Chatterton was totally confused. He was ten feet off the bottom "flagging in the current" with no idea of what to do. Chatterton did a quick search using his penetration reel and line as a guide.

Finding nothing, he returned to the anchor line and Crowell. Spotting another line running out, the two reeled it in. At the end was Feldman's mask and snorkel.

Three more teams of divers entered the water and did sweeps two hundred feet out into the sand. They turned up nothing. The current had taken Feldman, and his body was adrift at the bottom of the North Atlantic.

Being a commercial diver, Chatterton knew that Feldman's body could drift for miles, but that after twenty-four hours underwater the seals on a diver's dry suit would loosen up, filling the suit with water and anchoring him to the bottom. It was too late in the day for the already nitrogen-saturated divers to mount an effective search. The Coast Guard was notified by Bill Nagle, and the *Seeker* made its quiet journey back to Brielle, New Jersey.

John Chatterton with dishes from the U-869.
(Photo courtesy Dan Crowell)

One month later, Howard Klein, owner and captain of the *Eagle's Nest*, a luxurious competitor by dive-boat standards from Point Lookout, Long Island, decided to mount a trip of his own, sanctioned by the Eastern Dive Boat Association (EDBA), to recover the body of Steve Feldman. It was something that the *Seeker* had failed to do.

Howard Klein said he simply wanted to retrieve the body of Steve Feldman, who had been a friend of his. He also knew the Feldman family. Being a Vietnam vet, Klein believed that "you don't leave your dead behind, you bring them home."

Klein also claimed it was hard to ascertain if, and how, any body-recovery operations were actually done by the *Seeker*. He did, however, call Nagle and ask for the loran numbers so that he could go out and take a look. Nagle would not give him the numbers. Klein eventually got the numbers from fellow dive-boat captain George Hoffman. According to Klein, Hoffman knew that Klein had no agenda other than to bring Feldman's body back to his family.

Klein was also trying to make amends for four fatalities on his own boat on trips to the USS *San Diego* in 1990 and 1991. Both times it took several days and crews from other boats to help retrieve the bodies. Joel Silverstein, publisher and editor of *Sub Aqua Journal* and a diver aboard during this trip, suspected that Klein was trying to inject himself and his boat into the deep technical wreck diving. Hooking up to the U-869, putting divers on the wreck, and retrieving the body would go a long way toward establishing a good reputation.

Dan Crowell and John Chatterton, two crewman and staunch friends of Bill Nagle's, believed it was simply a way for the EDBA members to make the *Seeker* look bad and get the coveted loran numbers of the U-boat. What further irked the *Seeker* crowd was that they believed Klein and Bielenda knew they would not find the body. A month had passed since Feldman had disappeared, his body had dropped down from the anchor line over a hundred feet above the wreck in a swift current, and body searches had been made two hundred feet off the wreck on the bottom right after he had disappeared.

Crowell and Chatterton believed his body was "long gone" from the site. The *Eagle's Nest* found the wreck and put divers in the water, but Steve Feldman's body was not found.

Richie Kohler believed the search was a "scam" and refused to take part. He asked some of his Atlantic Wreck Diver friends who were aboard the *Eagle's Nest* if any artifacts were taken, and he was told no. One month later, however, Kohler claims he walked into a New Jersey dive shop belonging to a friend of his and saw two dishes with the Nazi eagle and swastika displayed. The dive-shop owner, a friend of Kohler's for over ten years, had never displayed them before. When Kohler asked where he'd got them, the shop owner (Kohler would not name him for this book) admitted after some denials that Hank Garvin had given them to him. The shop owner told Kohler "not to ask questions you don't really want answered."

Kohler, a member of the Atlantic Wreck Divers and a former friend of Steve Bielenda's, said that he believes the Feldman body recovery was done simply to put "egg on the face of Bill Nagle, and all the divers aboard the *Eagle's Nest* were intent on going inside to get stuff."

On the *Eagle's Nest* trip to the U-boat, Hank Garvin and Rob Stevenson tied in to the wreck, did a brief search along the wreck, then made their ascent.

"At no time," Garvin emphatically stated, "did we ever enter the wreck, nor did we retrieve artifacts of any kind." Garvin added that the only plates from a U-boat he had were from the U-853 off Block Island, Rhode Island, which he had indeed had repaired by the New Jersey dive shop. Garvin called Richie Kohler's claim "pure, unadulterated bullshit" and stated emphatically that no one aboard the *Eagle's Nest* that day was in it for artifacts.

Joel Silverstein, who was aboard for the purpose of writing a story for his magazine, concurs with Garvin: No artifacts were taken. They were there to find a body.

Not everyone on the *Eagle's Nest* was there altruistically. John

Lachenmeyer, by this time an owner and operator of an EDBA dive boat, the *Sea Hawk*, was not aware of the body recovery effort when he signed on to dive. He thought they were simply making another wreck dive until he was told otherwise on the trip out. Lachenmeyer, nevertheless, poked around the wreck and peeked in some holes but never made a penetration nor lifted any artifacts. Of course, he added, if any had been lying around, he would have bagged them. He never made any effort to look for Feldman's body.

Steve Feldman's body was eventually recovered. He was pulled up in a trawler's net six months after his disappearance over a mile away from where he had disappeared.

Dan Crowell is an anomaly among his dive-boat-captain peers. Born and raised in San Diego, he did a reverse migration and arrived in New York as a twenty-one-year old surfer kid looking for a change from the humdrum beach life of southern California. He arrived in Staten Island, the new home of his father and stepmother, in 1984.

Separated from Manhattan and the rest of the city by the vast New York Harbor, Staten Island is a blue-collar community and a popular place for New York City cops and firemen and tradesmen to raise families. Crowell found work as a carpenter and discovered the love of his life: diving.

Certified by a local dive shop, he began making offshore dives on the wrecks that littered the bottoms of the New York and the New Jersey shores. He quickly found himself in a crowd of men who shared his passion, and one of the hard-core bunch was Captain Bill Nagle.

In 1987 Nagle had his *Seeker* exploring for new wrecks to dive, and Dan Crowell fell in with him. The group of divers who regularly dove from the *Seeker* were a hardier bunch than Crowell was used to; John Chatterton, Kevin England, Steve Gatto, and Nagle exuded an infectious enthusiasm. By Crowell's fifth trip, the twenty-eight-year-old carpenter became part of the crew. Nagle was impressed with Crowell's diving, mechanical, and people skills, and Crowell was only to happy to oblige.

Crowell knew that Bill Nagle had an "addictive personality" and would "knock one down" before arriving at the boat at the crack of dawn, but he liked Nagle and thought that he just a good guy who had a problem.

On extended dive trips, Crowell accompanyied Nagle on pub crawls at Montauk or Block Island. Crowell would keep him out of trouble and tell him when it was time to head back to the boat. Crowell and John Chatterton kept Nagle on a fairly even keel.

Nagle's descent into alcoholism drew Crowell and John Chatterton further into the operation of the *Seeker*. Chatterton employed his skills in organization—contacting dive shops, booking charters, setting up schedules. Crowell was the "maintenance guy." Most of the regulars aboard the *Seeker* thought Crowell and Chatterton had become the owners.

Crowell said it was a slow and steady transition for him and John Chatterton. The pair found themselves in charge of the day-to-day running of the boat, although there were setbacks. Nagle was in and out of rehab centers, and he duped a lot of people into thinking that he had stopped drinking. Dan Crowell knew better. Nagle called him once after emerging from one of his many fruitless attempts at detoxification, and Crowell could hear the tinkling of ice in his cocktail over the phone.

After one last shot at sobriety, Nagle succumbed to liver failure a day after emerging from another dry-out. In September 1993, alone in a rented apartment, he died, far from his wife and two children.

Nagle's widow, Ashley, tried to run the boat, but she was not a diver or a boat captain. As an absentee owner, she relied heavily on Crowell and Chatterton to do all the grunt work. Crowell bought a small dive boat on his own and started running diving trips.

Ashley Nagle approached Crowell about buying her husband's boat, but she was offended by his offer; she believed the *Seeker* was worth $360,000, what her husband had paid for it eight years before.

The boat sat idle over the winter. In the meantime the bills started to mount up. New to the world of being a boat owner, Ashley Nagle was overwhelmed by the new duties. There were slip fees, insurance, maintenance fees, and the dry-docking of the boat—all duties and costs that Bill Nagle had seen to.

In January 1995, Dan Crowell got a call from Ashley Nagle asking if his offer was still good. He said it was. The former mate now became captain of the *Seeker*, the proud owner of one of the preeminent dive boats in the Northeast.

Within two weeks of his purchasing the *Seeker* word got out to the Northeast wreck-diving community, and Crowell quickly booked eight charters out to the *Doria*.

Crowell believed the *Seeker* had the edge over his Long Island competitor, the *Wahoo*, despite the ill will generated by Nagle's drinking. As far as Crowell was concerned, Steve Bielenda, now in his late fifties, was well past his prime. The *Wahoo* was not doing anything new and rarely ran more than two trips out to the *Doria* during the season. The running of the boat was left to Janet Bieser.

The bad blood between Nagle and Bielenda was passed down to Crowell, who was not able to forget the slights and barbs tossed at his ailing boss. Several members of the EDBA, including Steve Bielenda, approached Crowell about joining, but Crowell saw the association as a do-nothing organization that could only offer inexpensive advertising. He also claimed that the EDBA had the "*Wahoo*'s fingerprints all over it." He declined to join, telling me, "I don't need the EDBA. The EDBA needs me to give them credibility."

It was inevitable that Dan Crowell and Gary Gentile would come together. I had written an article on diving the *Andrea Doria* for the Italian magazine *No Limits World*, to which I was a regular contributor. *No Limits World* touted extreme sports, and diving the *Andrea Doria* fit the bill nicely. The article appeared in their November 1993 edition. The article had a sidebar that gave readers information about how to go about doing what they had just read about. I supplied the phone and fax numbers for contacting Captain Steve Bielenda.

Over the winter of that year, Bielenda got a call from Italy. A group of divers wanted to charter the *Wahoo* for a *Doria* expedition. They had deep-diving experience, but all of it had been done in the lakes of northern Italy or in the relatively placid Mediterranean. Bielenda was reluctant to book the charter since deep-wreck diving in the open North Atlantic would be very different from what they were used to. The Italians assured Bielenda that they had no intention of penetrating the wreck in a hunt for artifacts but simply wanted to do a touch dive and see the grand old Italian liner that was a lost icon to the Italian people. Bielenda booked the trip for July 1994.

Janet Bieser was captain with Hank Garvin aboard as cocaptain, with Joel Silverstein, Billy Deans, and Gary Gentile as crew.

Captain Hank Garvin and Janet Bieser in the galley of the *Wahoo*.
(Photo © Bill Campbell)

Gentile claimed that he was alarmed that the Italians were inadequately trained for this kind of diving and were not properly equipped with safety gear and backup systems. This led to an argument between Gentile and Captain Janet Bieser that would end Gentile's long association with the *Wahoo*.

Sitting around the mess table, Gentile, John Moyer, and Deans were discussing how they could use the inflatable in case of an emergency. According to Gentile, Janet Bieser was "lurking" just outside the cabin eavesdropping on the conversation. He said she burst in screaming that she was captain of the boat and they would not deploy the chase boat under any circumstances. Bieser remembered the conversation differently. She says Gentile was upset because she would not let him fill his empty tanks off the boat's malfunctioning compressor.

The Italians did keep their promise to Bielenda and did not stray far from the tie-in point on the wreck. Diving operations from the *Wahoo* went flawlessly and the Italians flew home happy, many of them in possession of some china, courtesy of cocaptain Hank Garvin.

But back home in Philadelphia, Gary Gentile got a call from Steve Bielenda.

In a brief conversation, Bielenda informed Gentile that Captain Janet did not want him on the boat anymore because of his shortcomings as crew and his mutinous behavior. Bielenda backed her up, as always. Gentile said he was stunned by his firing and tried to reason with his friend, boatmate, and dive buddy of ten years. But Bielenda, according to Gentile, would not hear of it.

Gary Gentile was no longer welcome aboard the *Wahoo*.

Gentile received offers from both Howard Klein's *Eagle's Nest* and Dan Crowell's *Seeker*. Gentile wound up crewing on both boats for *Doria* dives, and when Klein finally stopped running expeditions out to the *Doria*, Gary Gentile became a fixture aboard Dan Crowell's *Seeker*.

Crowell was only too happy to have him aboard. Gentile may have been a "cluster fuck as a technical diver and a mess to look at," as Dan Crowell described him, but he was still one of the best wreck divers in the world. He also brought in customers who had religiously read his books on deep-wreck diving.

Because of his books and the lectures he gave, Gentile was often approached by divers for advice on how they should they go about chartering a dive boat for a *Doria* expedition.

Gentile liked that Dan Crowell did not have the guile, the sad delusions of grandeur, that Bill Nagle had had. Crowell was more laid-back and was just intent on running a nice, safe diving operation.

Gary Gentile would crew aboard the *Seeker* during what was to become the most trying time for Dan Crowell and his boat: the 1998 *Doria* diving season. It seemed that Gary Gentile was always around when it was time to recover a body from the depths surrounding the *Andrea Doria*, and many in the Northeast wreck-diving community laid some of the blame on him for the unusually high body count during that disastrous year.

SIX

THE DYING SEASON, SUMMER 1998

This chapter is dedicated to the memory of
Craig Sicola, Richard Roost, Matthew Lawrence,
and Vince Napoliello.

C raig Sicola had china fever bad.

It was apparent even to those who were not part of the hard-core wreck divers with whom the New Jersey carpenter spent his weekends diving. Two of those people were his stepmother, Susan Sicola, and his former girlfriend Karen Moscufo. They loved the hard-working thirty-two-year-old carpenter and accepted, with reservations, his dangerous penchant for deep diving. That's just the way Craig was. He never did anything half-assed. The picture-perfect homes he built on the Jersey shore were testaments to that. It was all or nothing, and *all* on a *Doria* dive meant deep penetrations into the sunken ship's hold in search of artifacts that bore the insignia of the Italia Line.

All Craig Sicola's loved ones could do when he announced he was returning to the *Doria* was shake their heads and counsel him to be careful. "No piece of china is worth your life" was a phrase Craig Sicola heard a lot before he loaded his gear into his pickup truck in

Long Beach Island, New Jersey. Nevertheless, both of the women in Sicola's life also said they would love to have a souvenir plate and that they would display it in a spot of honor in their respective homes.

During the six-hour drive to Montauk, Long Island, Craig called his father on his cell phone. Louis Sicola, like his wife and Karen Muscufo, wished Craig would turn his considerable energies to safer pursuits. His dad would often suggest that Craig explore the lush— and safer—reefs of the Caribbean. Craig's answer was always one impatient word: "Borrrring!" Diving the *Doria* was anything but boring and was the consuming passion in his young life.

Craig and his father also spoke of the previous Father's Day weekend when they had had the rare chance to spend some time together. It was special for both of them. Louis remembered telling Craig how they had to get together more often.

It was the last conversation Louis Sicola had with his son.

For Sicola, there was only one boat to take him out to the *Doria:* the New Jersey–based dive boat *Seeker*.

Craig's was a familiar face to Captain Dan Crowell, the crew, and the regulars aboard the sixty-five-foot vessel. Weekends would usually find the friendly and fun-loving Sicola diving on the wrecks that lay offshore on the sandy bottom of the continental shelf. Crowell knew that Sicola had signed on for the June 23 *Doria* expedition, and doing warm-up dives on the shallower wrecks was a good way to hone your underwater skills.

Sicola, like many of his Jersey cohorts, liked that the *Seeker* had the most experience in running trips to the *Doria*. The boat also catered to the Jersey bunch. By 1998 the Brielle-based boat was running eight to ten trips out to the wreck every season. Crowell would pilot the boat up to Montauk and take a berth at the Star Island Yacht Club, where he would stay for the entire six weeks of the *Doria* diving season. According to Dan Crowell, he had no trouble booking trips because of his liberal policy: if they got blown out by the weather and couldn't make the trip, all money was refunded. Another reason was that the *Seeker* put divers exactly where they wanted to be on the wreck.

Gene Peterson, a dive shop owner in New Jersey, had chartered the *Seeker* for this *Doria* dive. He watched as Craig Sicola hauled his gear down the dock to the waiting *Seeker*. Peterson was disturbed to see that Sicola was still using a lightweight, yellow nylon line as his emergency upline. On a dive on a wreck in Nova Scotia that both men had made, Peterson remembered that Craig had had problems with the yellow line, getting tangled up in it after he had overextended his bottom time and had had to deploy it. The light line got whipped around in the swift-running current and snagged Sicola, and he had to be cut free by another diver before the air-depleted Sicola could safely make his ascent. Peterson spoke to Craig about using the yellow line as his safety backup, but Sicola shrugged off the subject.

Dan Crowell believed Craig Sicola had all the right credentials, mainly because he dove with Gene Peterson.

"Gene Peterson is an excellent diver," Crowell said, "and an excellent trainer, and an all-around good guy that wouldn't let a guy on his trip if he felt he didn't belong there. Craig was a gung ho type of guy, but he was competent."

Gary Gentile was also crewing aboard the *Seeker*, and along with his buddy Ted Green, they were the first ones in the water on this, the first *Doria* dive of the season. Dan Crowell was on the bridge when Gentile climbed back aboard the *Seeker* some two hours later with a bag full of cups and saucers. Crowell noticed the distinctive oriental motif on the china. It was the most coveted type of china: first-class china. He asked Gentile where on the wreck he had gotten them. Grinning, the veteran *Doria* diver replied, "In secret spot number twenty-seven A."

Crowell remembers all the assembled divers got a good laugh from Gentile's response, but he also recalls a lot of "oohing and aahing" over the artifacts that Gentile removed from his mesh goodie bag, his "greedy bag,"' as some were known to call it. Craig

Sicola was one of the divers admiring the loot. Crowell, of course, knew the location of Gentile's secret spot. Upon returning to the surface, Crowell said to the surprised Gentile, "No, Gary, the spot was twenty-six B!"

Crowell said the spot was the "perfect hole," under a staircase on the Foyer Deck, down the corridor beneath Gimbel's Hole. The narrow doorway that led to the staircase had corroded away, leaving a gaping abyss. At the bottom of the staircase a little cubbyhole for storage had been exposed. In it were crated boxes of unused first-class china. Crowell had "a blast" reaching into the tight hole and removing one plate or cup at a time. The captain of the *Seeker* remembers thinking it was so perfect because no one could be a pig: the hole was so narrow a diver could pull out only one or two pieces at a time, leaving plenty more for the divers who would follow. Crowell claimed you could even see sunlight streaming down from Gimbel's Hole.

Craig Sicola got one dive in on the first day out, teamed up with buddy Paul Whittaker. They quickly found Gimbel's Hole and dropped in. The pair planned "a nice, easy penetration" just to familiarize themselves with the area into which they would do a deeper penetration later. But the two divers overshot where they had intended to go. Whittaker thought it was time to bail, and he wanted to get out. He signaled his buddy that he was exiting the wreck, and Sicola nodded in agreement. Both Whittaker and Sicola clambered aboard, burdened with their heavy gear and suffocating dry suits, empty-handed but elated. They could not wait to get back in the water the following morning.

That night, as the *Seeker* rocked in the gentle swells, the topic of conversation in the boat's salon was getting some first-class china. Craig Sicola was especially intense. This was his third trip out to the *Doria*, but he had no china to show for it. Three was going to be the lucky number for him, he told anyone who would listen. This time he would bring some *Doria* artifacts back to his Long Beach Island home.

His rabidity caused a few of the men aboard to tell him to "calm down, relax, and take a breath," and Crowell assured him that everyone would get a chance to bag up.

The plan for the following morning was set: Dan Crowell would go in first and run a line from Gimbel's Hole to the secret spot so everyone could find his way in and out. According to Crowell, it would be "no big deal."

The following morning Craig Sicola would dive alone. Experienced wreck divers commonly did so. The belief was that with redundant safety features such as backup regulators, reserve air tanks, buoyancy control in the form of dry-suit inflation and vests, knives, and gauges, a dive buddy could often be more of a hindrance than an aide. A buddy could slow down an ambitious diver, and if he had a problem, you would be obligated to see him back to the surface. Going it alone made better sense for someone who was intent on scooping up as many artifacts as his goodie bag could hold. Sicola finally made his much anticipated first dive of the second day at approximately 10:40 A.M.

Upon reaching Gimbel's Hole, Sicola came upon his buddy from the previous dive, Paul Whittaker. Whittaker was now diving with Lyn Del Corio. They were exiting the hole. The two divers flashed the thumb-to-forefinger salute to Sicola indicating that everything was okay, and they watched as Sicola entered the hole. Whittaker and Del Corio made their way back to the anchor line, and Sicola disappeared into the blackness of Gimbel's Hole.

For some unknown reason, Sicola entered the wreck and immediately swam into the kitchen of the first-class dining room on the foyer deck. Sicola had to kick down the corridor and then across the inverted dining room to get to the kitchen. According to Dan Crowell, the U-shaped dining room was a tricky area and demanded a level of experience that Sicola did not have. But the area was known for its wealth of artifacts.

The first-class dining room was now a jumble of tables and chairs heaped in indistinguishable piles of gray debris beneath the swimming diver. In the weightless world of the deep depths, it is easy to get disoriented. Unless you are intimate with the ship plans and how the sea has wreaked havoc on the once stately rooms, a simple quarter turn can turn that underwater world into an unfathomable maze to the eyes of the myopic diver.

Back on the boat, less than forty-five minutes later, Crowell and his crew spotted a yellow lift bag that had breached the surface. The letters on the bag spelled out the name SICOLA. The lift bag flopped over, and Crowell remembers thinking, "What an idiot! He probably did not have enough line on the bag, freeing it and causing it to deflate."

Crowell and Steve Gatto motored out in the inflatable chase boat to check the lift bag. No telltale bubbles were percolating to the surface of the placid seas. Determining there was no one below, they hauled the line into the boat. Inspecting the line, Cromwell noticed the end was chafed. The worried pair returned to the *Seeker*. Seven to eight minutes later, the seriously bloated Sicola popped to the surface.

Dan Crowell jumped into the water and swam out to the floating form. He rolled Craig Sicola over and saw that his face was blue and blotchy. The eyes behind the mask were bloodshot and lifeless. Captain Dan Crowell knew immediately that Craig Sicola was dead.

Back aboard the *Seeker*, CPR was administered to the unresponsive Sicola. John Moyer and Jim Schultz pulled out their knives and cut Sicola out of his tight-fitting dry suit. A bloody bile oozed from Sicola's mouth. Although they made every effort to revive their fellow diver, in their hearts they knew it was hopeless.

The Coast Guard was notified. Within an hour the helicopter, dispatched from Nantucket Airport, hovered over the *Doria*'s grave, and Craig Sicola's body was lifted from the deck of the *Seeker*. His comrades watched sadly as he was flown away, knowing full well that all that awaited him was a cold-storage niche in a hospital morgue.

Craig Sicola had become the eighth diving victim of the *Andrea*

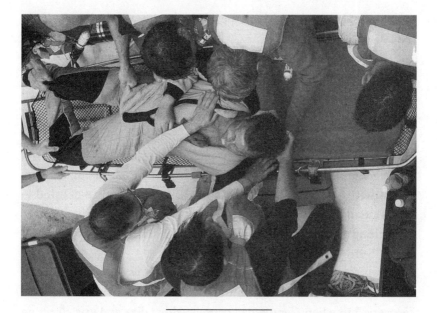

Coast Guard and *Seeker* crew ready Craig Sicola for air evacuation.
(Photo © Jennifer Samulski)

Doria, who had once again extracted her toll from those daring enough to challenge her.

The emotionally drained Crowell, trying to understand what had happened to one of his charges, checked Sicola's gear. The doubles containing his bottom mix were empty. Both of his stage tanks containing his decompression mix were full, as was his reserve, or bailout, tank. He also noticed that Craig had dishes from the first-class kitchen. To Dan Crowell, it was pretty obvious what had happened: Craig Sicola had overstayed his time inside the ship, probably from getting lost inside the kitchen or spending too much time bagging up china. Once he emerged from Gimbel's Hole, he most likely could not find the anchor line, which was about seventy-five feet forward of the hole. Lost, low on air, and probably panicking, Sicola shot his lift bag, secured it to the wreck, then made his way back to the surface. It was the same yellow nylon line that had disturbed Gene Peterson when they'd made the wreck dive in Nova Scotia.

Crowell measured Sicola's emergency ascent line. It was only 165 feet long, not enough to reach the surface from the top of the wreck. Crowell believes that either one of three things happened: Possibly the line was tied in poorly and slipped its knot. It could also have broken off in Sicola's hand, or it simply was not long enough. Whatever the scenario, Sicola was seriously low on air or, even worse, completely out. Sicola "punched out," raced for the surface, and suffered embolization. He did not have the presence of mind to grab one of his reserve-tank regulators and insert it in his mouth, something that should have been second nature to an experienced deep diver.

Gary Gentile was in the water and on the wreck at the time of Sicola's fatal dive. He never saw Sicola, nor did he witness his body recovery. But when Gentile had completed his dive and was climbing up the ladder to the deck of the *Seeker*, Jennifer Samulski, Crowell's girlfriend and boat partner, leaned over and said there had been an "incident." She did not want Gentile to be shocked to see a body stretched out on the deck. Jennifer quickly filled Gentile in on what had happened. Crowell and other crew members were giving the motionless Sicola CPR and mouth-to-mouth resuscitation. There was nothing for Gentile to do but help other divers emerging from the depths get safely aboard and alert them to the efforts to save one of their fellow divers.

Gentile remembered that Sicola had come to him for advice the night before. Sicola was so "insistent" on getting china that Gentile had tried to downplay it. "I tried to scare him," Gentile said, "to warn him of potential risks. He started to talk to me about dropping down the staircase, and I said, 'Don't do that alone.' There were cables and lines down there. He was very aggressive; still, I didn't give him any directions, just warnings."

In retrospect, Gentile feels that Sicola was not pushing his luck since he did get out of the wreck with china in his goodie bag. He had the presence of mind to pop a lift bag. The question for Gentile was why Sicola did not get back to the anchor line. Perhaps he got disoriented and swam the wrong way, something that was easy to do. Sicola could also have swum right by the anchor line without seeing it. Gentile himself had missed the lifeline to the surface on many occasions and had to deploy a lift bag and emergency decompression line.

Sicola, says Gentile, did the smart thing in popping the lift bag. But things happen fast underwater. Gentile thinks that Craig's ascent line may have gotten tangled in his sling bottles, or decompression gas tanks, preventing him from using them. He cut the line and went adrift, lost neutral buoyancy, and rocketed to the surface.

Crowell thinks another problem may have contributed to Sicola's demise. Crowell later learned from the autopsy that Craig Sicola had a heart condition known as cardiomegaly, or an enlarged heart. Cardiomegaly is hard to detect in an apparently healthy individual. There are usually no symptoms. Only a chest X ray or an echocardiogram (an ultrasound examination of the heart) could have detected the problem. Cardiomegaly could reveal itself through weakness, reduced exercise tolerance, and shortness of breath. It can also lead to heart failure.

Despite the findings of the autopsy and Crowell's suspicions, the coroner declared Craig Sicola's death was a result of "drowning and barotrauma due to a rapid ascent in salt water." According to the skipper of the *Seeker*, the coroner never even did a blood-gas analysis. "I called those guys and asked them to do these checks, but their attitude was 'What does this dopey boat captain know about physiology?' They just list it as a drowning and are done with it."

Craig Sicola had a memorial service befitting his lifestyle. After the funeral at St. Thomas of Villanova Catholic Church in Surf City, New Jersey, several of his surfing buddies had a ceremony of their own. Paddling out past the breakers on their surfboards, they laid flower petals on the tranquil sea while calling out, "We love you, Craig."

Craig Sicola was the third fatality aboard the *Seeker*, the first since Dan Crowell assumed responsibility for the boat and its divers.

That Sicola had been a regular on Crowell's boat made the trek home all the more difficult, and introspective.

That same season, Richard Roost's dream of diving the *Andrea Doria* was finally close to realization.

After twenty-five years of diving, Roost was on the threshold of making his pinnacle dive, though the Michigan native had been close before. Just the previous season he had been ready for a trip out of Montauk to the waters south of the Nantucket Shoals when poor weather had forced the hand of Captain Dan Crowell. A forecast of stormy seas by the National Weather Service had put Crowell on the phone to the charterers that he would have to abort. Disappointed, Roost had contented himself with another year of poring over the ship's plans that Crowell had sent him. Like many before him, Richard Roost was intent on retrieving the coveted china from deep within the bowels of the sunken liner.

Roost was, of course, aware of the death of Craig Sicola just two weeks before. Roost was plugged into the Internet, specifically the newsgroups and chat rooms that scuba enthusiasts tuned in to. The Internet was extremely popular with divers, who were by nature technically oriented. The relatively new medium was abuzz with the underwater faithful, who were never short of advice and opinions nor shy in sharing them.

The consensus of on-line divers was that Craig Sicola was another hapless victim of the "Everest of the Deep." His luck had just run out. If Sicola's death bothered Roost, he did not show it. His enthusiasm for exploring the mother of all shipwrecks had not waned. That he was making his second long drive from Ann Arbor, Michigan, to the eastern end of Long Island in one week was testament to that.

Just days before, yet another trip to the *Doria* had been cancelled due to poor weather. Roost, an owner of two scuba shops in his native Michigan, had businesses to attend to. Dutifully he had returned to Michigan, only to make the long, tedious trip back to New York after getting a few days of work done.

Roost was a diving celebrity in Michigan. Not only had legions of scuba neophytes passed through his stores, but many of them had trained under this diligent professional instructor. Just about everyone in the Great Lakes region of the country had either received instruction from or had dived with the forty-two-year old bachelor. Even police-department scuba rescue-and-recovery teams trained under him. Richard Roost was a "scuba god" in Michigan.

Joe King, a student and ardent admirer of Roost's skills, was supposed to make this expedition with him. According to King, Roost was the best diver he had ever seen and a man with absolutely no ego, a quietly confident diver who had the respect of everyone. King had felt honored that Roost had agreed to dive the Everest of wreck dives with him.

Unfortunately, unlike Roost, King did not work for himself. He did not have the luxury of the self-employed to take yet another week off after the cancellation to pursue his passion. Roost would have to find another buddy aboard the *Seeker*.

As Roost traveled along the two-lane blacktop that led to Montauk, he spoke with Scott Campbell, one of his shop managers back in Michigan. Roost rubbed it in that he was on leave from the mundane duties of running two successful scuba shops and about to make the deep pilgrimage to the *Andrea Doria*. Somers, jokingly, asked if his boss did not make it back, could he lay claim to one of Roost's prized possessions, his antique Mark V diving helmet. Not missing a beat, Roost had replied, "Sure!"

On July 7, the *Seeker* bobbed from its anchor line in the gentle swells of the Atlantic. The rival *Wahoo* was also tied to the wreck, but it was no big deal to Captain Dan Crowell. The seven-hundred-foot wreck could accommodate both comfortably, although Crowell was not overly friendly with the *Wahoo*. Too much ill will had accumulated over the years, starting when Bill Nagle had been behind the helm of the *Seeker*. Relations between the crews were cordial, however, and each respected their counterpart's accomplishments. Dan Crowell just liked to keep his distance, professionally and socially. They were competitors after all: the two boats vied for the loyalty of the small but devoted wreck-diving community of the Northeast.

Within minutes of the *Seeker*'s being securely shackled to the wreck, diving operations had begun. Gary Gentile had done his usual tie-in, and all "newbies" on the trip were advised by Captain Crowell to make their touch dive so that they could dispel some of the anxieties the infamous wreck imbued in first-time visitors, even experienced deep divers such as Richard Roost.

According to Joseph Gaddy and Robert Ryan, two other first-timers on the wreck, Roost played it conservatively. The Michiganer kicked along the Promenade Deck and seemed to be content just poking his light into openings on the wreck and peering inside. At the prescribed time, Roost made his ascent and safely boarded the *Seeker*. The dive had been exhilarating yet routine, just the way your first dive to the *Doria* should be.

Back on the pitching deck of the *Seeker*, others had a little more to show for their efforts, including as always Captain Dan Crowell and Gary Gentile. Richard Roost could only watch with envy as the two veteran *Doria* divers pulled piles of plates, cups, and saucers from their goodie bags. Before turning into his bunk for a much needed sleep, Roost studied the ship plans yet again. The next morning would call for a bolder dive; Roost would come back with souvenirs of his own. After all, Roost had invested over $10,000 in all the latest high-tech, not too mention most of his adult life, pursuing his passion.

Once on the wreck Roost located the same hole that had tempted the unfortunate Craig Sicola. He recovered only one artifact, but thought that he needn't be too greedy on his second dive. He was content with his meager find. Blasting air into his buoyancy-control device, he carefully negotiated the confining quarters, avoided the clinging cables, and exited safely into the green glow of filtered sunlight.

Back aboard the *Seeker,* Roost proudly showed Dan Crowell the fruit of his efforts. Crowell was impressed that the fresh-water diver from the Midwest had made a penetration into the wreck on only his second dive and retrieved a piece of china. Roost said all the right things.

"He went there, he went here on the wreck," Crowell said, "but what he explained to me was very comforting because he did things only a very experienced person would do. He was looking back to where he had been and to where he was going and other options of finding your way out. He knew what he was doing." Dan Crowell no longer worried about this newcomer to the depths of the North Atlantic.

Roost made a second dive that day. At around 2:30 P.M. he splashed into the waiting Atlantic. With twenty to thirty minutes on the bottom and his decompression hangs, Roost's estimated time of arrival back on the deck of the *Seeker* should have been no later than 4:00 P.M.

Diver Steve Berman had entered the water within minutes of Roost, but when he returned, he didn't see Roost on the anchor line doing his decompression hangs. Berman was worried and told Jennifer Samulski so. The appointed time for Roost's arrival back aboard the dive boat came and went. Samulski penciled in "overdue" next to Roost's name on the clipboard listing all the divers and their dive plans.

Samulski then notified Crowell. "Not another one!" was all Crowell could think. He radioed over to Janet Bieser on the *Wahoo.* The reply came back from the *Wahoo* that no diver from the *Seeker* was on their anchor line. A disoriented diver often made his ascent up the wrong line, as each boat's line looked indistinguishable from another. The crew of the *Seeker* formulated a search plan. The Coast Guard was also notified, and the euphoria aboard the boat evaporated amidst the grim realities of another body recovery. The Coast Guard would dispatch a helicopter, and all nearby ship traffic would be alerted to keep an eye out for the lost diver. Crowell could only hope that Roost had surfaced away from the boat unnoticed and been carried away by the current.

The chopper made sweeps of the sea surrounding the *Seeker* in a standard search grid for almost two hours, but there was no sign of Richard Roost. Breaking off its search, the Coast Guard left it to the divers aboard the *Seeker* to locate the remains of the man from Michigan. Dan Crowell reluctantly huddled with Gary Gentile and tried to figure out the likely location of Roost's body in the huge steel hull.

It would take thirty-one hours to find him.

There was and is to this day much speculation about what happened to Richard Roost. Some held that Roost, unfamiliar with the wreck, simply got lost and drowned. Gary Gentile believes it was something altogether different.

Gentile remembered Roost from a diving expedition ten years before to some wrecks in the Great Lakes. Roost, an intensely private and nonverbal man, had not spoken with Gentile during the trip out to the *Doria* nor once out over the wreck. First-timers to the *Doria* usually sought Gentile out.

Following Roost's disappearance, Gentile spoke with the divers Roost had been with on the first dive and the ones who had seen him on his second dive. From those conversations, Gentile became convinced that Roost had gone back for china in the same locale he had been scouting on his first two dives.

Gentile and John Moyer, late on the afternoon Roost was reported lost, searched that area. Other divers who were customers and not as conversant with the wreck volunteered to do exterior searches, leaving the penetration work to the more experienced. Divers from the *Wahoo* also pitched in.

On the darkened Promenade Deck, Moyer swam high at two hundred feet and searched from above with his light. Gentile swam low at two hundred ten feet scouring the bottom with his narrow beam. Since the body's buoyancy was unknown, it could be pinned against the ceiling or anchored to the floor on the wreck. Gentile then ducked into the transverse corridor beyond a stairwell while Moyer stayed behind as backup. Gentile would not consider entering this area unless he had a backup diver to monitor his movements because it was so dark and confining in there. There was no other exit from the A deck in this section of the huge ship.

Entering the A Deck, with Moyer's light as a beacon, Gentile made a cursory search. Gentile was surprised not to find Roost's body, convinced that this was the area where he had become lost. Reemerging from the A Deck, he swam over and looked around at the terminus of the staircase. He saw nothing.

The pair continued their search aft, through the dining room all the way to the next bulkhead, beyond which lay the kitchen. Gentile discovered a new opening where a revolving door had once been. Gentile figured that Roost would never have gone inside here because it would have been way beyond his experience level in an unfamiliar wreck. The two retreated, once again searching high and low for the lost diver. Then Gentile noticed something else new on the deteriorating wreck: part of the deck had collapsed, exposing the entrance to the ventilator smokestack. Perhaps Roost had discovered the new opening and decided to investigate. Gentile took a look inside, but again, there was no sign of Roost.

Moyer and Gentile continued their search forward of the china hole, swimming into the chapel area of the foyer deck. Much to their great surprise, they swam out of the wreck. The whole ceiling of the Foyer Deck and the wall of the Upper Deck were gone. Anyone kicking as far as they had would have escaped from the bowels of the ship. After twenty-five minutes, Moyer and Gentile returned to the *Seeker*.

They reported where they had been on the wreck to Dan Crowell, who made his own search of the same area and came up with the same results.

That evening there was more talk about where they should look for the body. Some of the more experienced divers thought that Roost had gone through the small opening at the bottom of the staircase into the A Deck. According to Gentile, if that was the case, that was where he was going to stay. The resident *Doria* expert would have no part in searching that area of the ship since it was way too dangerous and "spooky" for him. Gentile explained that if a diver dropped into that narrow hole, he would have to find that same small hole upon his return and squeeze himself through it. That task would be all the more difficult since the silt would be stirred up, dropping visibility to virtually nothing.

"I'll do anything to recover a body," Gentile said, "but not risk losing another life to do it. That crazy old marine mentality of charging a hill just to bring back the dead? No, I don't believe in that."

Crowell and Gentile agreed the next course of action would be to "mow the lawn," a routine exploration of the areas of the wreck where the body could be. The next morning John Moyer and Gary Gentile would kick down the length of the Promenade Deck. Gentile thought he would just be discounting areas of the ship.

Dropping into the last doorway of the Promenade Deck nearest the stern, Moyer and Gentile swam forward down the narrow deck space. Again John swam high, Gary low. The pair passed under numerous window openings in the two hundred feet of wreck they traversed. At amidships they passed the center double doors of the deck, at which point they entered the first-class bar, an area with which Gentile was familiar. The decks and bulkheads had collapsed on each other, making it difficult for the experienced *Doria* diver to know whether he was kicking through the Promenade Deck or the Upper Deck. Reaching the first-class bar at the depth of two hundred ten feet, Gentile discovered Richard Roost's body. It was approximately 1:22 P.M.

The body was not entangled in any cable. Roost was lying face-down at a slight angle with his regulator still in his mouth. If he had convulsed, his regulator would have been dangling beneath him. Both of his stage bottles containing his decompression gas were full and still clipped to his harness.

Gentile signaled to Moyer who was above him. Gentile then tied the body to his reel line, exited, and tied the loose end of the line to the outside of the wreck. The two divers reentered, following the just-deployed guideline. Lifting the slightly unbuoyant body, they carried Roost out of the wreck. Since they were over a hundred feet from the anchor line and low on air, the pair decided to leave the body for another team to recover. "It's just not worth it to stress your own safety to recover a body," Gentile said. "You just don't do that. We had to leave the job to someone else."

Gentile had sent up a slate with the body's location penciled in on it, and Crowell splashed in with Greg Mossfelt. It took the two divers just minutes to find the body. They towed Roost over to the anchor line, clipped him to the line, and sent him to the surface. Richard Roost was freed from the grip of the sunken ship.

Rick Kleinschuster, a mate aboard the nearby *Wahoo*, watched the disturbing scene unfold. Both boats had been cooperating on finding Roost's body, and *Wahoo* cocaptain Hank Garvin had even motored over to the *Seeker* to lend any assistance he could.

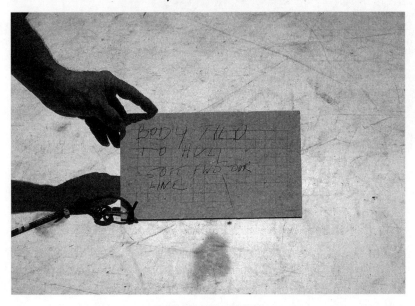

Gentile's slate indicating where Roost's body was left.
(Photo © Jennifer Samulski)

Richard Roost's body emerges from the depths.
(Photo © Jennifer Samulski)

When Roost's buoyancy-control vest was inflated and his body sent to the surface, a *Seeker* crew member had the distasteful job of waiting for the body to emerge on the anchor line. Kleinschuster could imagine what the *Seeker* crewman was feeling as the body sang up the anchor line with increasing speed as the air expanded both in the body cavities and in the buoyancy vest. Roost's body, his dry suit grotesquely bloated with air, broke the surface near the bow of the *Seeker*.

"He came up headfirst," Kleinschuster said. "His arms were rigor-mortised in a semicircle form. The body then lay back and rolled to its back. You could see that the surface recovery guy was upset. After untying him and bringing the body around to the stern, it was pulled aboard. The recovery guy followed the body up and I could see him throw his gear around in disgust."

Even though Roost's bottom air tanks were empty, Gentile believed that Roost did not run out of air and drown. He had full stage bottles. According to Gentile, a diver knows that decompression gases are potentially toxic in oxygen, but if that is all he has, he will use them and chance the toxic hit. You breathe anything you have—if you're conscious.

Roost had been in the area where his body was found the day before. Portholes with light streaming in were above him. He could

Roost's body is brought aboard the *Seeker*.
(Photo © Jennifer Samulski)

have found his way out of there. Crowell tested the gas in Roost's buoyancy control vest, which was fed by the bottom mix. It was the correct mixture and precluded oxygen toxicity as a cause of death. Like John Barnett some seventeen years before, Richard Roost had expired for reasons that deep divers such as Gentile and Crowell could only blame on deep-water blackout.

There are many examples of this potentially fatal phenomenon. Gentile remembers one instance when Jim Gatto, diving on the wreck of the *Texas Tower* at 180 feet with his brother Steve and Tom Packer, lost one of his fins. Trying to keep up with his fast-moving pair of buddies, Jim passed out and began to drift away. Luckily his brother and Packer looked back to see Jim lifeless in the water. They quickly grabbed him and brought him up, where the shallower depths revived him. If someone had not noticed his predicament, there would have been another body search on still another deep wreck in the North Atlantic.

I myself was aboard the *Wahoo* when another episode of deep-water blackout occurred. On the wreck of the *Coimbra*, lying in 190 feet of water, diver Tom Bernstein tied in the grappling hook with his buddy Pat Rooney. Engrossed in the effort, Rooney did not notice Bernstein lose consciousness and fall to the sandy bottom. Rooney grabbed him and swam for shallower depths up the anchor line. Bernstein regained consciousness and lived to dive the wreck later that day.

Yet Richard Roost was an experienced diver, famous for his ability to squeeze bottom time out of his air supply, known as "skip breathing." This uncanny knack for maximizing his dive time may have been his undoing.

Carbon dioxide is the triggering device in breathing. It makes you want to breathe. Carbon dioxide buildup by itself is not fatal, but when you are over two hundred feet below the ocean's surface, blacking out usually means one thing: death.

Richard Roost probably lost consciousness and continued to breathe from his bottom mix in the dark of the first-class bar until his

tanks ran dry and he asphyxiated. That would explain his empty double tanks and why he never deployed his decompression mix. Unlike
John Ormsby, Richard Roost most likely slipped into eternity unaware
of his predicament. It was little solace to his family and friends.
Michigan's "scuba God" was, indeed, mortal.

The *Doria* diving season of 1998 continued to be a nightmare for the
Seeker's Captain Dan Crowell. Jack Moulliet, an experienced *Doria*
diver on both the *Seeker* and *Wahoo*, was aboard with Crowell for
another visit to the Italian liner just two weeks after the Roost incident. Moulliet would be using air as opposed to trimix.

In 1992 trimix was quickly becoming thought of as the magic bul-
let for the more troublesome dangers encountered by deep divers.
Trimix was a custom blend of breathing gas that consisted of 17 to 18
percent oxygen, 50 percent helium, and the remainder nitrogen. The
theory behind the new blend was that by reducing the oxygen and
nitrogen content in deep breathing gases and supplementing them
with helium, a diver would reduce his risk of an oxygen-toxicity hit,
nitrogen narcosis, and decompression sickness. In conjunction with
the deep breathing gases, divers would have to carry stage bottles,
slung under their arms, containing oxygen-enriched air (nitrox), and
pure oxygen, which would be deployed at various depths on ascent to
accelerate decompression stops. The bottom line was that trimix was
safer than air and allowed deeper dives and shorter decompression
stops.

The sudden popularity of the new mix created a stampede down to
Billy Deans's Key West Diver, the only reputable training locale in the
country for the new gas technology. The course was highly technical,
intensive, time-consuming, and expensive.

Crowell had instituted a policy of only allowing trimix-certified
divers aboard for *Doria* expeditions, but after certification divers were
still permitted to use air. Crowell's belief was that the knowledge of
deep-diving physics and breathing-gas options was available, and any

diver intent on making a *Doria* dive should be trained to utilize it. Whether the diver employed that knowledge was his or her business. Crowell just asked that divers using air limit their depth to 190 feet to avoid an oxygen-toxicity hit.

Under a hot July sun, Crowell heard a cry for help coming from the seas just off the bow of his boat where the anchor line plunged down to the hull of the *Doria*. Jack Moulliet was screaming that he had run out of air and blown off his decompression stops. Crowell hollered for him to go back down the line to twenty feet and deploy one of the regulators that was hooked to an onboard oxygen tank used for decompression. Once Moulliet submerged, Crowell quickly rigged up a set of tanks and had Steve Gatto splash in with them.

Gatto got Moulliet to hang at a hundred feet, checked his gauges, and found how deep he had been and how long he was at that depth. Gatto emerged with the information. Crowell put together a decompression plan by doubling all the navy air tables for the length of time and the depth Moulliet was at. Crowell sent a diver down to Moulliet with underwater writing slates with the decompression plan penciled in. After five hours underwater, the exhausted Moulliet climbed back aboard the *Seeker*. The exasperated Crowell asked him what had gone wrong.

Shivering from the cold, Moulliet confessed that this had been his first dive this year. Down on the wreck he had run a penetration line inside so he could bag up some china and had got tangled up in it. In his pursuit of china, Moulliet had hastily and improperly tied off the line to the outside of the hull. It took him five precious minutes to free himself. Upon emerging from the bowels of the sunken ship, he ran out of air and had to do the "Johnny Weissmuller swim" to a safe depth to deploy his oxygen-rich decompression mix. A stream of bubbles poured out of the valve. Panicking, Moulliet punched out and shot to the surface.

According to Crowell, the "shit hit the fan about six times" for the anxiety-ridden Moulliet. He got tangled up in his own line inside the wreck; he ran out of air; he sprinted to a depth where he could jam his decompression-gas regulator in his mouth, then believed he was out of air again. He climbed over five divers who were on the line decompressing and never reached out for help, even though they could have supplied him with emergency air. In his panic, Moulliet forgot all his training.

Crowell was beside himself, although relieved that Jack Moulliet had not succeeded in killing himself. What really angered Crowell was that Moulliet had never let go of his goodie bag, which was bulging with china. The first thing he should have done when he initially got into trouble was drop the heavy bag of plates. An irate Crowell banished Moulliet from his boat for all future dives, saying he did not need the headaches from sloppy divers.

Cursing himself for his bad luck, Dan Crowell could only guess at what further problems the 1998 season would present. He would not have to wait long.

Vince Napoliello was as experienced a *Doria* diver as they come. He had begun diving the Italian liner about the same time as Captain Dan Crowell. In all, he had ten expeditions out to the *Doria* under his belt, and Dan Crowell never had to worry about Vince. He was well liked among the tight circle of wreck divers and had an attitude that Crowell found especially refreshing.

"He was one of those guys whenever anything funky happened and he didn't feel right about it, he would just blow the dive off," Crowell said. "He was careful."

The August 3 expedition, Napoliello had promised his fiancée, would be his last. Vince had been feeling the pressure to curtail his dangerous love affair with the Italian shipwreck for some time now, and his job at the Wall Street brokerage company of Legg Mason demanded more of his time. On diving trips on the *Seeker*, it was a common sight to see Vince on the stern of the boat yelling into his cell

Vince Napoliello
aboard the *Seeker*.
*(Photo © Jennifer
Samulski)*

phone over the roar of the boat's engines. Vince was always being kid-
ded about his lucrative job and yuppie lifestyle, but he took it in stride
and often gave it right back in spades.

David Murphy was a fellow stockbroker at Legg Mason and
was Vince's best friend. Murphy had always been in awe of his
thirty-four-year-old buddy who hailed from Jersey but who now
resided in New York's Brooklyn Heights. David Murphy had had
many a conversation about Vince's dangerous obsession, and
Napoliello had expressed his fears about diving the ultimate deep
wreck. Still, in Murphy's view, Vince was the most confident and

competent guy he had ever known. Vince was meticulous and safety-oriented and well aware of the dangers a diver confronted on the *Doria*. Murphy never for a moment doubted Vince's ability to survive a *Doria* dive. In a week's time he expected him back from yet another expedition with another bag full of china and more adventures to relate over lunch. Specifically, Murphy was sure he would hear all about the "secret spot" Vince had discovered on an earlier expedition.

According to Murphy, Napoliello had found what he believed to be an untouched china closet deep inside the ship. The closet was sealed shut and was sure to yield a plethora of china. Vince was anxious to find out for himself. David Murphy never doubted his friend's ability to do just that.

When the *Seeker* finally arrived over the grave of the *Doria*, another dive boat was already there. This time it was not the *Wahoo,*but the *Sea Inn* out of Manasquan, New Jersey, chartered by Nick Caruso, a scuba instructor for a shop in Hillsdale, New Jersey, Caruso and Crowell knew each other well. Caruso had been a familiar face aboard the *Seeker* from years before. In July 1992 he and thirty-three-year-old Matt Lawrence from Miami Lakes, Florida, had taken their third trip out to the *Doria* on the *Seeker*, doing their dives then for the first time on trimix.

Caruso and Lawrence, however, had one problem. According to John Chatterton, at the time neither of them was certified to use trimix. It appears the pair managed to get trimix fills. Caruso and Lawrence planned to squeeze every last minute out of the expensive mix by each using a set of doubles twice, by starting their second dive with half-empty tanks.

Once on the wreck they dropped their stage bottles at the tie-in point and deployed a penetration line to enter the number one cargo hold. After bagging up, Lawrence and Caruso began their exit with Lawrence leading the way. Caruso then had a problem.

He had fouled his reel and took a few minutes to undo it. Returning to the tie-in, Caruso saw Lawrence's stage bottles were untouched. Low on air, Caruso could not afford to commence a search for his buddy. He made his ascent and did his decompression stops. Once aboard the *Seeker* he spat out his fear about Lawrence's disappearance.

From the information Caruso supplied, John Chatterton, Dave Bright, John Yurga, and Bart Malone focused their search for Lawrence near the number one cargo hold. In the sand beneath the cargo hold, at a depth of 254 feet, Malone found the body of his friend Matt Lawrence. His gauges showed he had run out of air, probably just after exiting the cargo hold. Malone hastily rigged a lift bag to Lawrence's tank manifold, released his weight belt, and sent him to the surface—or so Malone thought. After doing an especially long decompression because of the deep depths he had reached, Malone was surprised to learn the body had not surfaced.

The next morning John Chatterton found Lawrence. He and the lift bag attached to his tanks had gotten hung up under the cargo booms. Chatterton noticed that Matt Lawrence had a goodie bag full of rosaries clipped to his harness.

The *Seeker* had left Montauk late, at about 10:30 P.M. the night of August 3, 1998. The ten-hour trip out meant that divers could expect to get one dive in early the following morning and one in the afternoon. They would have two more days before Crowell turned the bow of the *Seeker* west for the return trip to its summer home.

Shortly after hooking to the wreck, Napoliello and his dive buddy Denis Murphy, a New Jersey police officer, were one of the first teams to splash in. The pair made an uneventful first dive. Their second dive of the day was, however, entirely different. Within minutes of their entry, the pair were bagging up on china deep inside Gimbel's Hole.

The two men were ten minutes away from their agreed-upon departure time that would give them a twenty-five minute bottom stay. Without warning, Napoliello ripped Murphy's regulator from his mouth. Momentarily stunned, Murphy fumbled for his backup regulator, then quickly inserted it into his mouth. Vince grabbed Murphy by his harness and frantically pointed to Murphy's back-mounted tanks. Murphy thought Vince was telling him there was a problem with his tanks, perhaps a leak. But why had he torn Murphy's regulator from his mouth? Murphy thought Vince was out of air. Denis kept screaming into his mouthpiece over and over again, "You out of air?" Napoliello just shook his head from side to side. Then Napoliello returned Murphy's primary regulator and deployed his secondary regulator attached to the second tank of his doubles.

Perplexed and feeling his heart, thumping panic, welling in his throat, Denis Murphy's only thought was to get out of the wreck. The darkened corridors seemed to close in on the pair. What just a few minutes before had seemed like a beckoning well of wealth was now close to resembling a tomb.

Kicking out of the hole, Napoliello swam off in the wrong direction. Murphy did not know what to make of Napoliello's behavior. Napoliello knew the wreck as well as anybody, and surely, Murphy thought, he must have known what he was doing. Napoliello may have believed the distant anchor line of the *Sea Inn* was their lifeline to the surface. Despite his misgivings and fear of looking like a fool for coming up on the wrong boat, Murphy followed his more experienced buddy. He watched as Napoliello swam past the other boat's line.

Out of the blue-green void, Dan Crowell, video camera in hand, and John Moyer swam up to Murphy and Napoliello and signaled to ask if all was okay. Crowell was running video of the two. Murphy, hanging on the *Sea Inn*'s line, signaled back that he was okay. But Murphy was pushing his time limit on the bottom. After his exchange of signals with Crowell, Murphy looked beneath him for Napoliello. Visibility was good, about fifty feet, but he saw no sign of him. Even after the harrowing experience inside the wreck and Napoliello's unusual wanderings once outside the hull, Murphy was still confident that Napoliello knew what he was doing. With that thought Murphy made his slow ascent up the *Sea Inn*'s anchor line.

Minutes later, aboard the *Sea Inn*, Nick Caruso noticed a diver floating in the water face down not more than fifty feet from the boat. He watched for a few moments thinking the diver was adjusting his gear. There was no movement. Alerted by Caruso, Tom Surowiec dived into the water and sprinted out to retrieve the floating form. Aboard the *Sea Inn*, Caruso and Surowiec immediately began CPR on the unconscious Vince Napoliello. Other divers unzipped Napoliello's dry suit and cut his wrist and neck seals, stripping Napoliello of the tight-fitting suit.

All the commotion aboard the *Sea Inn* did not go unnoticed on the *Seeker*. Jennifer Samulski was standing in for Dan Crowell and found out over the radio that the stricken diver was one of their own. Tom Surowiec recognized him from his days as a crewman aboard the *Seeker*.

Knowing that Crowell was doing his hang times on the anchor line, Jennifer sent down a slate with a diver saying "Vince is on the *Sea Inn*. Helicopter is on the way."

Crowell was not overly alarmed at the abbreviated report. Napoliello was too good a diver to have punched out. Crowell figured Vince might have run too low on air and broke off some of his decompression stops. As for his being aboard the *Sea Inn*, Crowell believed that Napoliello had made an understandable mistake. The helicopter was surely just a precautionary measure.

As the messenger turned to return to the surface, Dan Crowell reached up and grabbed him. Face-to-face, Dan shouted into his regulator to ask if Vince was okay. The other diver just shook his head.

Crowell closed his eyes and bowed his head in frustration thinking, "Oh, man, not again."

Back aboard his boat, Crowell was on the radio to the *Sea Inn* and the Coast Guard. Not believing the crew of the *Sea Inn* was capable of handling an air evacuation, Crowell made plans to transfer the victim to his boat, but the helicopter was only ten minutes away. John Moyer still had ten minutes of hang time left, which meant that Crowell could not move his boat.

Vince Napoliello's helicopter evacuation from the *Sea Inn*.
(Photo © Jennifer Samulski)

Vince Napoliello never responded to the resuscitation efforts. Like many of the fatalities on the *Doria* before him, his fate was sealed before he reached the surface.

Once Napoliello's body was airlifted off the *Sea Inn*, Crowell went over in his inflatable to collect Napoliello's gear. There he was told they had opened up Vince's isolator valve on his double tanks' manifold. The valve was used to shut down the equal drawing of gas from the two tanks from one regulator. Once the valve was shut, each regulator, the primary and secondary, would work off only the tank it was attached to. By opening the valve, Nick Caruso had eliminated any chance of determining if a bad mix had killed Vince Napoliello. The segregated airs of each tank were hopelessly intermixed once the valve was opened. If the tanks had been filled separately with different blends, that could have explained the death.

A lot was made of the fact that Napoliello's stage decompression mix was too rich in oxygen, some claiming that it was 80 percent instead of the usual 36 percent. In fact, the decompression mix had been labeled 80 percent. In the *Newsday* series on the fatalities that summer, reporter Joe Haberstroh, who is not a diver, gave credence to that theory. Dan Crowell, however, does not.

First of all, Crowell said, Napoliello knew the bottle was mislabeled and that when it was pointed out to him by another diver, Vince simply ripped off the tape and below there was another tape with the correct decompression mix of 36 percent so noted. Second and most important, Crowell was the last person to see Napoliello alive. He even caught the image of him swimming off to his fate on video. Napoliello was still breathing his bottom mix. He never deployed his decompression mix. Those tanks went untouched.

That his isolator valve had been closed may indicate that Napoliello had, unwittingly, sucked one of his tanks dry. Thinking that the valve was open, Napoliello may have believed he was totally out of

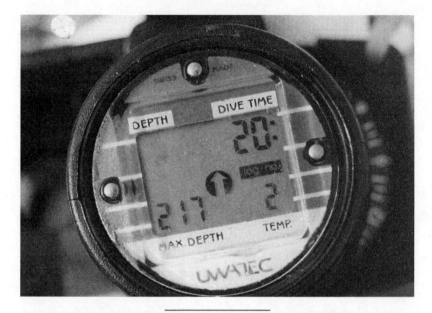

Napoliello's dive computer read-out of the fatal dive.
(Photo © Jennifer Samulski)

bottom mix when he was inside the wreck with Murphy. Panic may then have gotten the best of him. Perhaps that is why he grabbed for his buddy's regulator. Regaining his composure, he may finally have realized that his isolator valve had been shut and deployed his secondary regulator. He still had half his bottom mix plus his reserve tank and his two decompression cylinders.

Another nagging question was why Napoliello swam off in the wrong direction once he emerged from Gimbel's Hole. Maybe, as Dan Crowell theorized, he mistakenly thought the *Sea Inn*'s tie-in was the *Seeker*'s. But why did he then swim past the other boat's tie-in as well? It is unlikely that he was suffering from nitrogen narcosis since his bottom mix was trimix containing a high percentage of helium instead of nitrogen. Perhaps something caught his attention and he kicked off in that direction to investigate. No one will ever know.

The captain of the *Seeker* polled all his clients about staying. No one was in the mood to do any more diving, so Crowell terminated all dive operations. No one seemed to mind that they had shelled out $900 for three days of diving. On the cruise back, friends of Vince Napoliello's clinked bottles of beer together in his memory, but otherwise silence ruled the *Seeker* on its ten-hour trip back to Montauk. Crowell remembered it was as if his body were lying there right on the deck instead of in some morgue tray in Nantucket.

When Crowell got his hands on the coroner's report, he was shocked to learn that the robust thirty-four-year-old Wall Street trader had "occlusive coronary artery disease with severe atherosclerosis of the left anterior descending coronary artery." That revelation changed Crowell's thinking as to what had happened to Vince during that fatal dive. To the master of the *Seeker* Napoliello's heart condition was the "smoking gun." Not pretending to understand all the nuances of cardiac medicine, Crowell still believes it is a matter of gas mechanics and the diffusion of gas through the bloodstream that explains what happened to Vince Napoliello.

Basically, Napoliello became disoriented after having a problem inside the wreck and his adrenaline level was high. Because of his heart problem, Napoliello was not off-gassing or on-gassing efficiently with the restriction of blood flow. He was probably not expelling carbon dioxide effectively nor getting enough oxygen. That would explain his behavior once he was outside the wreck. Either a carbon dioxide buildup or a restricted intake of oxygen could have dazed the deeply immersed diver—or sent him into cardiac arrest.

Robert Jackson, M.D., professor of medicine in the Division of Pulmonary, Allergy and Critical Care Medicine at the University of Alabama at Birmingham and a certified trimix diver, wrote a research paper, "Diving-Related Respiratory Problems," about how a heart obstruction can explain a death attributed to panic and drowning. "Each year several divers die because of known or previously unrecognized coronary artery disease," Jackson wrote. "Some diving deaths attributed to panic or drowning are found on forensic investigation to be due to cardiovascular disease. . . . Cardiovascular disease that limits exercise tolerance or increases risk of sudden death, and metabolic or neurological conditions that could lead to unpredictable loss of consciousness, are among the accepted relative contraindications to scuba diving."

Napoliello's best friend and fellow worker at Legg Mason, David Murphy, also believed that Napoliello succumbed to heart trouble underwater. According to Murphy, Napoliello's father, a doctor himself, had been told by the coroner that his son may have been a victim of a heart attack due to the arterial blockage. That made sense to Murphy. He could not envision his good friend panicking and doing something stupid.

"Vince was absolutely neurotic about planning and executing a dive," Murphy said, "There is no way he screwed up. Vince was courageous, but I would never describe him as a daredevil. He never would take an uncalculated risk. That just wasn't Vince."

Back in Montauk, Dan Crowell tried to understand what had gone so wrong that 1998 season. He was just weeks away from taking part in an expedition to the *Britannic* off the coast of Greece in the Aegean Sea. The *Britannic,* the sister ship of the *Titanic,* was sunk by a mine during World War I, and she lay in almost four hundred feet of water. The immensity of the far-off expedition and the dangers it presented now demanded his full attention. But he could not give it its due. The deaths of Craig Sicola, Richard Roost, and Vince Napoliello were tormenting him.

"I was hammered emotionally," Crowell said. "I've tried to set in place probably the safest dive-boat operations for doing this kind of stuff by requiring of my people experience and training.

The experience level of my crew—everybody is trained in CPR and oxygen treatment—is unmatched. I've tried to make this such a professional operation then, not just a bunch of shit, guys doing things by the seat of their pants. And now I got these three fatalities."

To Captain Dan Crowell there was simply no reasoning to the three deaths, all in one season. They were all so dissimilar. What was he to do? How could he correct a problem that did not exist? Was it simply bad luck?

Adding to his misery, Crowell found himself dealing with the "idiots" in the media who had little knowledge about the intricacies of deep-diving dangers. Not only *Newsday*, but also the *New York Times*, the *Boston Globe*, and others were badgering the reticent Crowell.

According to Crowell, the media were getting an earful from his competition about what had possibly gone wrong. They had given a platform to people who, according to Crowell, were misinformed or just malicious. The public was a willing listener because people had died, and someone had to shoulder the blame.

It had seemed to Crowell that he had finally rid the *Seeker* of all the baggage the boat had acquired in the Bill Nagle years and had dispelled some of the myths of deep diving, its renegade reputation. In a few short weeks, it was all lost in a flurry of bad press and irate postings on the Internet.

The only explanation Dan Crowell could give was that the *Seeker*, outside the *Wahoo*, and occasionally a rogue boat were the only ones doing this highly technical, cutting-edge kind of diving. Seventy percent of all the diving done in 1998 from the decks of the *Seeker* was in depths below two hundred feet. In retrospect it was inevitable, just as it was inevitable that climbers would die on Mount Everest. Still, it was little consolation to the brooding boat captain.

Dan Crowell felt old before his years. He shed many a tear, not only in frustration for a lack of understanding on how so much in such a short span of time could go wrong, but also for lost friends who had spent their last days with him aboard his boat. The owner-operator of the *Seeker*, by his own admission, was devastated by the events of the 1998 season.

Maybe, Crowell thought, it was the price you paid for being an explorer.

SEVEN

BACK TO THE *DORIA*

n spring 1998 I got an assignment from *Yankee* magazine to do a feature story on diving the *Andrea Doria*. *Yankee* had recently done a piece on climbing deaths on Mount Washington in New Hampshire. The *Doria*, I believed, would have the same appeal: adventure and death on a New England icon.

In June of that year, after the story was completed and accepted, I took another assignment to do a piece on rock climbing up in New Hampshire. While relaxing around the pool at the White Mountain Hotel after a day of climbing, I noticed the headlines of the *Boston Globe* and sadly read about the death of Craig Sicola.

Diving the *Doria* had been getting more and more popular. Upscale young and middle-aged men, flush with Wall Street money and a thirst for adventure, were embracing the new advances in scuba. Snagging the brass ring—diving the *Doria*—had become akin to scaling an eight-thousand-meter peak in mountaineering.

Dan Crowell of the *Seeker* and Steve Bielenda of the *Wahoo* were fitting extra trips out to the wreck into their seasonal schedules. Sal

Arena and John Lachenmeyer, respectively of the *Sea Hunter* and *Sea Hawk,* were handling the overflow, along with a few other rogue boats.

Gone were the days when the veteran hard-core wreck-diving bunch virtually owned the infamous wreck. Now divers with less than two years of diving experience and fewer than one hundred dives under their belts were exploring her remains.

Trimix and accelerated decompression schedules were imbuing the newcomers with a false sense of security, but I knew different: gas and decompression theory aside, the *Andrea Doria* was as dangerous as ever.

As early as 1993 when the new gas technology was just getting popular, I went down to Key West to train with Billy Deans at his trail-blazing Key West Diver. That spring, with an assignment from *Underwater USA,* I found myself suited up and burdened with the latest equipment ready to dive the USS *Wilkes-Barre* with Deans.

The *Wilkes-Barre* was a U.S. navy heavy cruiser that had been used as a target in the early 1970s for new missile technology being developed for the navy. Now resting in 250 feet of water not far from the Stock Island docks where Deans moored his boat, the rediscovered ship had become another kind of training ground. This time scuba divers, not missiles, were penetrating her hull.

The wreck was ideal for such an endeavor. The warm and clear waters of the Gulf were much safer for explorations of the deep than the icy and murky waters of the North Atlantic. After we dropped over the side of Deans's dive boat, the wreck was visible almost immediately, partially obscured only by the populous schools of tropical and pelagic fish. For someone like me used to seeing an underwater wreck only when I alighted on it (and then only small portions of it), the old warship's visage was indeed impressive. In an effort to simulate actual war situations, the navy had left all her armaments intact: big guns protruded out into the swirling masses of fish, ready, it seemed, to fight one last sea battle.

What amazed me even more was the narcosis-free mind-set I

experienced on trimix. Gone was the mind-numbing throb of the rapture of the deep. The gas I was breathing seemed colder and drier, but the clarity of thought was an entirely new experience. It was if I had been roused from a deep slumber with caffeine coursing through my veins. It was exciting and revealing. I learned firsthand what all the buzz was about in the deep-diving community. Trimix, indeed, was all it was cracked up to be.

The deaths of Richard Roost and Vince Napoliello followed in rapid order, and newspapers far and wide jumped on the story. Jon Krakauer's runaway best-seller *Into Thin Air* inspired reporters to draw parallels between the disaster on Mount Everest when six perished and to what had happened in the depths off the Nantucket Shoals in 1998.

My editors at *Yankee* and I were not immune. I quickly updated my piece on the *Doria* with the 1998 deaths so as to accommodate a July 1999 publication. *Outside, National Geographic Adventurer,* and *Esquire* all had major stories in the works on diving the *Doria* and news programs such as ABC's *20/20* also did segments on the ultimate dive. A media frenzy was on.

And so it was time for me to go back. Things had changed dramatically since I'd visited the wreck eight years before. The technological advances in scuba made *Andrea Doria* expeditions more like a NASA space shot than a seat-of-your-pants adventure. I wanted to take a writing assignment on the advances in diving the *Doria,* and I wanted to take a formal trimix training course.

Billy Deans was again my first choice for an instructor, but Deans was hard to nail down for a week's worth of training in the new mixed-gas technology, involved as he was in offshore U.S. wrecks and on the West Pacific island of Guam. Deans recommended Joel Silverstein, a diver and writer who had covered the new trends in his magazine, *Sub Aqua Journal. Sub Aqua* was an altogether different diving publication from the likes of the "big two" of diving, *Skin Diver Magazine* and

Rodale's Scuba Diving, which were written for the entry-level scuba diver. These glossy magazines were full of articles on resort locations, basic gear, technique improvement, and always, photo essays on marine life; but extreme-diving stories were verboten. The cutting-edge stuff was, however, the meat and potatoes for Joel Silverstein and *Sub Aqua*.

Silverstein was a scuba instructor on New York City's maritime province of City Island, where he also operated a recompression chamber. The recompression chamber was hooked into the Divers' Alert Network (DAN) and treated divers (as well as burn victims in need of hyperbaric treatment) who suffered from symptoms of decompression sickness, which was becoming an increasing problem in sport diving.

Silverstein became a disciple of Billy Deans's, and before long the hulking and ambitious Brooklyn-born Silverstein himself became one of the few trainers offering technical trimix certifications. In May 1999, I loaded up my gear for my trimix course at Morehead City on North Carolina's Outer Banks, an ideal locale for trimix training. The Outer Banks was known as the Graveyard of the Atlantic, and its often-violent seas had claimed many vessels.

Because of the treacherous shoals that extended eastward off Cape Lookout into the Atlantic, ship traffic is forced to swing wide into deep water. During World War I and World War II, this put ships directly into the sights of prowling German U-boats. The two world wars had added to the list of thousands of unfortunate ships that rested under these waters—along with a few of the hunters.

Silverstein told me the course would be, in effect, a five-day boot camp in absorbing lessons on the new breathing gases. I had to obtain numerous manuals, dive tables, and gear.

The National Association of Underwater Instructors (NAUI) was the certifying agency for the course.

Silverstein and Dr. Bill Hamilton had been given the job of writing the training manuals for the course of instruction. Officials at the

National Oceanic and Atmospheric Administration (NOAA) had been impressed with their efforts for NAUI and had enlisted the pair to produce the materials that became the standards for training mixed-gas scuba divers for federal government agencies. Silverstein and Hamilton had become the authorities on mixed-gas diving.

Home base for the trimix instruction was the Olympus Dive Center in Morehead City. The dive shop and training facility was consistently rated by diving publications as one of the top dive resorts in North America. The shop sat just off the docks where their three dive boats were moored. Across the street was a dormitory-style barracks for divers.

Silverstein promised an intensive crash course in the highly technical understanding of gas physiology. It had been a few years since I had taken any courses in physics, and the various laws of Boyle and Dalton regarding the interaction of inert gases and oxygen under pressure were pretty tough going.

Equally challenging were the new gear configurations popularized by Billy Deans and championed by Silverstein. Back on the *Doria* in 1990 I had jerry-rigged an old BC (buoyancy control) vest to accept two eighty-cubic-foot tanks with a center-mounted pony bottle as my bailout gas. Each tank had its own regulator, and I had to monitor my air supply for each tank. When the first tank was half-empty, I switched to the second. When that tank was depleted to half, I reverted back to my first tank and began my ascent, leaving half of all my air supply for my decompression. This was no small task, considering I was heavily intoxicated by the pressurized nitrogen.

My pressure gauges and inflator hoses swung free. I monitored my decompression stops by penciled scribblings on a slate secured on my forearm, and my newfangled dive computer that was my timepiece spat out my backup decompression plan, which I did not quite trust. The new thinking on gear configuration in Morehead City replaced all my old gear for a new streamlined look that eliminated the "danglies" that had killed Ormsby. Everything had to be snuggly secured to the diver.

One of the bigger innovations in deep diving was the introduction of "wings" to the confusing array of gear. Deep divers no longer wore buoyancy-control vests. The inflatable wings were now mounted to the backplate on the double tanks, freeing the diver's front for securing gauges and other paraphernalia needed to probe the depths. In the old days of *Doria* diving, inflating one's dry suit was often the only way to maintain buoyancy, since wreck divers considered BCs too uncomfortable. BCs also eliminated the use of a harness for tool deployment. With wings instead of BCs a diver had buoyancy redundancy that also allowed for the use of a harness.

My bottom mix was now contained in a twin set of 120-cubic-foot tanks, which were joined by a manifold. The manifold had an isolator valve that was kept open, allowing for the equal drawing of gas from both cylinders. If one tank or regulator malfunctioned, the tanks could be isolated by shutting the valve. A diver could then rely on his functioning regulator and tank to make his ascent.

The bottom mix contained a lower content of oxygen, generally 17 to 18 percent, negating the possibility of an oxygen-toxicity hit. Helium made up approximately 50 percent of the bottom mix, thereby reducing the nitrogen content to around 30 percent. By reducing the nitrogen, narcosis was virtually eliminated. But because helium is a lighter, a less dense gas than nitrogen, a small bottle of argon (a highly dense gas) has to be included in the diver's gear configuration, usually slung from the backplate and resting on the hip, connected to the dry suit by a low-pressure hose.

The argon was needed because of the poor thermal properties of helium. Argon gave the diver the luxury of more comfortable decompression hangs, by warding off the numbing cold of the open sea. It also reduced your chances of a decompression-sickness (DCS) hit, since hypothermia was a factor in the debilitating and potentially fatal affliction.

For an old-timer like me, the biggest adjustment was getting used to the stage bottles under each of my arms. They were clipped into my harness, which was fitted to me like a straitjacket. One bottle contained nitrox (enriched air with 36 percent oxygen) and the other pure oxygen. On my ascent I had to switch to the nitrox at about one hundred feet and breathe it during decompression, which accelerated the outgassing of the inert gases that caused DCS. At the twenty-foot stop I deployed the pure oxygen, further ensuring the purging of potentially harmful gases.

I learned that deep diving had become extremely gear-intensive. Monitoring the positions of the gear and the gas supplies was an intimidating task for the beginner. It was also a job that would have been impossible to perform on the narcosis-inducing nitrogen-rich blends of the past.

Nevertheless, many of the old guard continue to dive deep on air. They welcomed the narcotic effect of the air that made them more paranoid—it also made them careful. Diving on simple compressed air also meant less gear to purchase, cheaper tank fills, and fewer hardware malfunctions to worry about.

For a wreck diver, few places rival Carolina's Outer Banks. The offshore wrecks are immersed in waters with clarity sometimes equal to the Caribbean's. The nearby Gulf Stream brings pelagic and tropical fish of every description around the old wrecks, including the photogenic and snaggletoothed sand tiger shark.

Being loaded down with so much ungainly gear made waddling around on a pitching boat difficult. After several hours of being cocooned in a stiffling dry suit under an unrelenting sun, I had happily entered the chill Atlantic—but not until a lot of checking and rechecking of gear was done. A diver from New York had drowned just months before diving these same waters.

Tony Smith, who had a reputation for being a competent but sloppy diver, had come down to North Carolina to tune up for a *Doria* dive. Diving with his buddies from New York City's Sea Gypsies Dive Club, Smith did a back roll off the gunwale of the *Atlantis V*. There had been a competition among the group as to who would be the first in the water, as the Sea Gypsies liked to have a good time. In his haste to splash in, Smith had neglected to open his tank valves or connect his BC inflator hose, although he remembered to wear his weight belt. Dragged down by twelve pounds of lead, Tony Smith both won and lost at the same time.

Smith, a big man, sank like a stone to the bottom, 145 feet below. In his uncontrolled descent, he may have ruptured his eardrums, resulting in vertigo and hopefully quick unconsciousness. He probably never had a chance to drop his weights or attempt to turn on his air.

No one aboard the *Atlantis V* knew about the quick demise of Tony Smith until one of the crew members went down to untie from the wreck. Smith was directly beneath the boat, dead of course.

Our first dive was to the USS *Schurtz*. At 130 feet, the sixteen-hundred-ton warship was a step back into the beginning of the early twentieth century. The *Schurtz* was an Imperial German Navy vessel that had made the mistake of seeking shelter in Honolulu, Hawaii, away from the Japanese warships seeking her destruction in the early years of the First World War. Since the German ship had violated America's neutrality laws, the ship was promptly confiscated and refitted as an American vessel. Her tenure as an American warship was short. On June 21, 1918, she was inadvertently rammed in a fog by the steamship *Florida* while obeying a wartime directive to run without her lights to avoid detection, ironically by German submarines.

In the following days we made dives to the *Naeco* and the *Papoose*, both victims of Nazi U-boats. Deeper wrecks such as the *Yancey* followed in rapid order, and our last dive was to the U-352.

The German submarine had been looking for her first kill in April

1942 when she mistook a U.S. Coast Guard cutter for a freighter and launched a torpedo attack. The torpedo missed its mark and exploded harmlessly, and the sub's position was quickly deciphered by the cutter. In short order the U-352 was sent to the bottom, entombing fourteen of her crew.

The wreck of the U-352 heels slightly to her port side, the conning tower thrusting up from her rusting hull into the aquamarine void clouded with schools of fish. The conning tower is the repository for most of the German sailors' remains. They fled the flooding pressure hull in hopes of escape through the conning-tower hatch, which is where the war ended for them. One can only imagine the horror they must have experienced as the rising water snuffed out each life one by one.

Back home I looked into the prospect of signing on for another expedition out to the *Doria,* eager to put some of my new training and gear to the ultimate test. But taking the time and shouldering the expense made me hesitant. My wife was not overly enthusiastic either. I had survived one visit to the wreck, she said, why challenge fate again? But during the early days of June, I received a phone call from a New York literary agent who had read the article in *Yankee* and saw book potential. Within days I had a publisher, and in rapid order I was on the phone to Steve Bielenda, begging for a spot on the *Wahoo* on the next charter out to the *Doria.*

My trip to the *Doria* in the first week in July 1999 coincided with a heat wave. The temperature climbed to 105 degrees Fahrenheit. On the usually blustery Montauk Point there was not even a hint of a breeze.

Getting suited up on a stable platform, I believed, when nothing was on the horizon but blue sky, would have a calming influence. Besides, having the added experience from my extensive training dives on trimix in North Carolina just weeks before, I felt ready and confident about another deep descent to the *Doria.* It was just another dive, and not the intimidating one it had been nine years before. I had survived it then, and I would survive this one too. I had no great ambitions. I just wanted to revisit an old friend.

Belowdecks, the *Wahoo* was a sweltering sauna mixed with the odor of perspiration from a dozen men and the ever-present diesel fumes. Few if any of us got any sleep. Tony Maffatone, for one, wrapping himself in a blanket, opted to sleep outside against the boat's transom beside his underwater scooter.

Maffatone had a storied past. A former navy SEAL, he was now an owner of a security outfit that saw to the well-being of celebrities like Dolly Parton and Elton John. Maffatone was reportedly also the model for Sylvester Stallone's Rambo character. Stallone had befriended Maffatone when he doubled for Stallone in one of his early movies. Maffatone's credentials were impressive. He was a veteran of seven

Tony Maffatone being assisted by Rick Kleinschuster aboard the *Wahoo*.
(Photo © Kevin McMurray)

tours of Vietnam and only one of eleven from a thirty-man SEAL team to survive the war in Southeast Asia.

Retrieving the two missing Pegasus diver-propulsion vehicles from the failed Giddings-McKenney expedition in 1968 had become Maffatone's quest. Both vehicles, equipped with cameras for montage images of the wreck, were lost when operator Elgin Ciampi had mechanical difficulties with his unit and ran out of air, surfacing unconscious. In an effort to rescue Ciampi, fellow operator Jacques Mayol was forced to abandon the vehicles, and they quickly joined the *Doria* on the bottom. Maffatone had designed and built his own eight-foot-long diver-propulsion vehicle complete with a deck-mounted davit to launch it and a custom scuba system. With six hundred cubic feet of breathing gas in seven tanks, Maffatone could stay underwater more than four times longer than most systems allow. The former SEAL was rumored to have spent over $100,000 on the design and construction of his self-contained system.

With the vehicle, Maffatone could survey vast stretches of the bottom alongside the *Doria* for the Pegasus units. There was only one problem: the motor noise, which attracted curious sharks who dogged him and snapped at his fins. His military background served him well as, despite the aroused seas and a continual wash of seawater on the aft deck, Maffatone slept soundly the night before our dive. I did not. I arrived at the *Doria* wreck site exhausted from the marathon trip and was lucky to have gotten just a few hours of sleep.

This time, because I was diving on trimix and carrying the extra stage bottles, I had more difficulty entering the water. In the past we were somewhat dependent on the crew for assistance in gearing up, but now divers are absolutely reliant on them. Gone are the days when exploring the *Doria* and diving machismo demanded self-reliance.

It's a tedious process: donning tanks, clipping into a harness, routing regulators, attaching inflator hoses, snapping the proper stage bottle under the correct arm. None of it could be done without

Above: Entry into the ocean over the *Doria.*
Below: Exit from the ocean over the *Doria. (Photos © Kevin McMurray)*

the help of another set of hands, but all of it has to be monitored by the diver. The diver's preferences on placement of gear must be respected. In an emergency, at two hundred feet beneath the surface, if you go to grab a needed piece of gear and it's not where it's supposed to be, a "situation" could deteriorate quickly to a full-blown panic attack. Underwater panic attacks have a way of killing you.

One of my biggest fears is that a tank valve would mistakenly be shut down. Sucking hard on a regulator mouthpiece deep underwater and getting nothing surely rates as a diver's number one nightmare. Consequently I am forever checking to see that all five valves are open, and I recite in mantralike tones, "Righty-tighty, lefty-loosey." The childlike chant always makes me feel like a fool, but I have never entered the water yet with a valve shut down.

These are anxious moments, these times when entry is imminent. I am uncomfortable, sweating profusely in my dry suit. Burdened with all the gear, I am convinced that, once I step wide into the ocean, I will rocket down to the bottom like the unfortunate Tony Smith. Trying to remember everything about my dive plan and how I plan to manage the deployment of gear only adds to my stress. It's early in the morning and I'm still fatigued from lack of sleep. The last thing a crewman asks: Am I set to go? Already sucking on my regulator, I indicate my readiness with the thumb-to-forefinger salute. Actually I'm scared shitless, but I splash in anyway.

The ocean restores some semblance of normalcy. The weight of my gear evaporates and the cold waters cool me. Purging air from my wings, I slowly submerge. The noise of men and gear cease, the blistering sun beating down on me disappears. This is the time when most of my anxieties dissipate. In this moment, the *Doria* is just another dive. I am comfortable, I am confident, and I am alone as I sink deeper into the open ocean. The *Andrea Doria,* my underwater Everest, awaits.

Diving alone is a heresy that is perpetrated endlessly on *Doria* expeditions. Every entry-level diver walks away from his or her certification course with the hammered-in belief that you should never dive alone. On this dive, everyone aboard the *Wahoo*, except for a pair of first-timers, dives alone. *Doria* machismo has a lot to do with it, but there is also an unstated belief common among *Doria* veterans: a dive buddy will only get you into trouble. With all the redundancy of gear and the multitude of breathing gases, a diver has plenty of options in bailing out of a dive. There is also the emergency upline that everyone carries. If a diver cannot rectify a problem underwater, there is little a buddy can do to help. Chances are if you punch out, you might take your buddy with you. Panic can be extremely contagious.

The *Doria* has changed dramatically in the nine years since my last visit. The hull, which stretches far beyond my line of sight, now appears dull gray, its blackness forever masked by a fine silt and a carpet of sea anemones. The *Wahoo*'s anchor line is shackled at a point not far from Gimbel's Hole amidships. The once-rigid steel hull seems to have yielded to the weight of the ocean and appears to have sagged, precipitously in some spots. Checking the position of my stage bottles and making sure their regulators were secured, I drop over the side of the hull and slowly sink down into the black depths. I cast a quick, furtive glance back to the anchor line, trying to ingrain in my memory its location. I don't want to waste my precious air supply on my return searching for my lifeline to the surface. Resorting to the emergency ascent line would be an act of desperation.

The Promenade Deck is almost entirely open now. I slip into the former main street of the ship and kick along the corridor that now is populated only by curious fish, who eye me suspiciously. The beam of my light illuminates rusted-out portholes and jagged gashes that pock the hull. Still, it's easy to imagine how passengers once strolled these very decks some forty-three years ago. It reminds me why I am here: to experience an era of history that few have the nerve to explore.

I count the number of windows I pass under. Retracing my route and successfully reuniting with the anchor line is an obsession of mine while swimming through the old wreck. It's simply a matter of turning around and counting back the window holes.

My bottom mix of gas lives up to its hype. My mind is clear; the old drunken feeling brought on by compressed nitrogen that I had experienced in the past on the *Doria* no longer exists. Trimix gives me a clarity of thought: no tunnel vision, no confusion, no paranoia. The mix seems colder in my lungs, but maybe it's just because I am more aware of it. I am, however, comfortably warm in my dry suit, which is fed by the dense argon gas specially rigged to my backpack. Streamlined, with all hoses and straps secured tight to my body, I present a svelte profile resistant to the ensnaring clutches of the wreck. I realize, even down this deep, that I am overconfident and blithely oblivious to the dangers of the recumbent ship. I remind myself I am on the *Doria*, a ship who has claimed better divers than I.

Back at the anchor line, I rehearse my decompression plan, noting my tables for the dive and checking my wrist computer. I begin to pull myself up the line. The air in my dry suit and wings expands, giving

The *Seeker* from the deck of the *Wahoo* over the *Doria*.
(Photo © Kevin McMurray)

me a gentle, reassuring lift up from the bottom. At the hundred-foot depth, I remove the bungeed regulator from my nitrox bottle, and in a flash I spit out my bottom-mix regulator and insert the one that delivers the oxygen-enriched air. I do not miss a breath.

For spending twenty-five minutes at 210 feet I must spend seventy-three minutes decompressing. The early stops at ten-foot increments starting at one hundred feet are thankfully brief. At twenty feet the tediousness of long hangs kicks in. Having switched to my pure-oxygen stage bottle, I hang for a torturous sixteen minutes. At ten feet, the wait goes on for another twenty-eight minutes. I bide the time watching divers' bubbles percolate up from the bottom.

Other divers are waiting below me. Like me, each has deployed a jonline—a line that the diver ties into the anchor line that permits him to suspend himself away from the up and down tug of the anchor line and the traffic of other divers. It is a bizarre scene to watch. Still minutes from emerging, I stare at my computer readout, willing the elapsed time forward.

The hot sun that had me wishing just over an hour and a half ago for the comfort of the deep is now a welcome relief. As the warm, moisture-laden surface air fills my lungs, I whisper a word of thanks to the scuba gods for another successful return to the surface.

All aboard the *Wahoo* have the option of a second dive that first day. Most of us take a four-to-five-hour surface interval to allow for the remaining inert gases to be expelled. On a second dive, I would have to add five minutes to my actual bottom time and decompress accordingly. Another twenty-five minute dive at 210 feet would have to be calculated as a thirty-minute dive, which would add up to ninety-four minutes of decompression, or twenty-one more minutes hanging than on my first dive. That's the penalty for not extending my surface time adequately to expel residual nitrogen.

Toward the end of my last dive, I noticed that the current had picked up and the particulate matter in the water had increased, reducing visibility. Reports from returning divers confirmed that conditions have deteriorated. I am not about to make a second plunge to the bottom in less than ideal conditions, not while I am nearing exhaustion, so I sit out the second dive.

The next day, the early divers report that visibility is still poor on the *Doria*, just fifteen to twenty feet. The minute organisms, or particulate matter, in the water are still heavy, so I plan on a midday dive to take advantage of the better light of a high sun.

I splash in right behind Joel Silverstein, who is crewing aboard the *Wahoo*. Prior to the dive Joel and I had formulated a dive plan that would have us, as a team, exploring the Boat Deck of the ship. We had calculated our decompression stops and times and agreed there would be no penetrations into the wreck. Joel and I meet on the bottom and begin our exploration together.

The Boat Deck is the level of the ship from where the lifeboats were launched. Because the *Stockholm* knifed into the *Andrea Doria* on its starboard side, the *Doria* listed dramatically to that side shortly after impact. None of the lifeboats on the port side could be launched since the boats could not dropped into the water because of the listing hull. Only the boats on the starboard side could be launched. If not for the prompt arrival of the gallant rescue ships and the *Doria*'s seeming reluctance to sink, the death count would have been significantly higher. The starboard-side Boat Deck is now buried in the sand under the massive hull, and only the port side-Boat Deck remains for exploration.

The empty davits that still jut out from the hull make for an eerie sight. One after another they poke out into the underwater void, speaking volumes without words about what happened that night. When history is this tangible, a diving experience can be overpoweringly rewarding. I momentarily forget the worries of another deep dive and just marvel at the sights before me. In that moment, all the dangers of the dive seem more than worthwhile. Few ever see such a dramatic face of history. I am one of the lucky ones.

• • •

Dan Crowell and the *Seeker* appeared to have weathered the storm of bad publicity in the wake of the disastrous 1998 *Doria* diving season. The monikers *Death Boat* and *Morgue Boat* were thrown around on the Internet, but Crowell's eight-week Doria dive schedule was once again full.

On the July 20 slot, Crowell had the Cincinnati Dive Shop penciled in. Most of the *Seeker's Doria* charters are private, and filling the boat on private charters is the duty of the charterer, who takes the whole boat for an agreed-upon sum. It's also the charterer's responsibility to vouch for the qualifications and physical fitness of all aboard.

When it was a captain's charter, Dan Crowell was a stickler when it came to the qualifications of divers. He required all divers to be trimix certified, the highest and most technical of scuba certifications. However, when the boat was privately chartered, that was not the case. Crowell would make an allowance for instructors whose students were making training dives on the *Doria*. The student diver was then the sole responsibility of the instructor. As Dan Crowell would say, he was then just a "bus driver."

Student diver is a misleading term. Once a diver is training to use trimix, he must have become, in all aspects, an expert diver. Trimix training is the last rung in the scuba-training ladder. The final checkout dives are usually just a formality.

The *Doria*, according to Crowell, was an ideal wreck for trimix training. A diver could get his checkout dives done with the kind of depths needed for trimix usage. Yes, it was far out to sea, but the visibility was better than at the closer in-shore wrecks of the New York/New Jersey Mud Hole, where a lot of trimix training was done. In Crowell's mind, if you had the time and the money, diving the *Doria* for the certification was the best way to go.

Many veteran *Doria* divers disagreed and held that the *Doria* was too dangerous a place to run training exercises. Crowell ignored them, believing that the members of the old guard were taking umbrage because having student divers on the "Everest of wreck diving" demeaned their achievements.

Christopher Murley was one of the Cincinnati group led by Joe Jackson, owner, operator, and instructor for the shop. At forty-four, Murley was one of Jackson's most gung ho students. Even though he had been diving only two years, Murley had progressed in scuba expertise, racking up specialty certifications in less than eighty dives, a not uncommon occurrence. Scuba often became an obsession with new divers. Once bitten by the bug, newcomers to the underwater world became the most ardent practitioners of the sport. It was like falling in love. New divers often lived and slept the sport, and Christopher Murley was one of the smitten.

Murley was a bear of a man. At six feet seven inches tall, he weighed over 350 pounds. Crowell was alarmed by Murley's size when he arrived at dockside at the Star Island Yacht Club in Montauk. But Murley had signed the waiver that required any participant in a deep dive to acknowledge that he was in good health and had no physical affliction that he was aware of.

Joe Jackson also assured Crowell that Murley was one of his best students, a fast learner, and that he would not be a problem. Crowell set aside his reservations about the hulking diver again, even later when Gary Gentile witnessed Murley "run out of breath" just getting his gear on.

On July 17 due to bad weather conditions out over the *Doria* Dan Crowell piloted the *Seeker* to an alternative wreck site off of nearby Block Island. The wreck of the U-853 rested in only 119 feet of water, a good warm-up dive for the deeper *Doria*. Chris Murley completed one dive on the wreck.

Returning to Montauk at noon on the following day. Murley retired to his bunk and slept the rest of the day and well into the next. His fiancée Mary Beth Byrne rousted Murley from his bunk on Monday the nineteenth for a day spent sightseeing around the town of

Montauk. The couple returned to the *Seeker* at 6:00 P.M., and the boat departed for the *Doria* five hours later.

Murley's girlfriend and Joe Jackson were concerned about Chris's lethargic behavior and his lack of appetite. During the rambling conversation, the subject of Murley's recent diagnosis of diabetes and how it would effect his diving came up. Jackson related how the disease was not a reason not to dive but that he would have to be more careful.

Of the eleven people aboard, Murley was only one of two divers who were paying customers. Besides the six-man crew, Cincinnati Dive Center's Joe Jackson and Rick Vanover received a free ride because they had arranged the trip. Mary Beth Byrne would not be diving. She was just along for the ride.

The first dive on the *Doria* on the morning of July 20 was a harbinger of trouble ahead. Buddying up with Jackson, Murley aborted the dive on the surface, complaining of having trouble getting his bottom mix from his demand regulator. Jackson continued with his planned dive. Murley was observed to be having trouble returning to the boat and had to strip his gear in the water since he was unable, so encumbered, to climb up the ladder to the deck on the *Seeker*.

Murley returned to his bunk and dutifully wrote in his dive log that his tanks "must have been anal [analyzed] wrong—difficulty breathing blue haze in sight." He later told Mary Beth the vision problem—the blue haze—disappeared after he got some rest and food in him.

The next morning Murley again buddied up with Joe Jackson. This time they made it to the bottom as a pair. It was an uneventful dive. The two Midwesterners kicked along the Promenade Deck to Gimbel's Hole and made a shallow penetration before returning back to the anchor line. The dive lasted a total of sixty-one minutes. The deepest depth they reached was 189 feet. Murley was all smiles aboard the *Seeker*. He had finally touched and explored diving's holy of holies, the *Andrea Doria*.

After lunch and a nap, Murley teamed up again with Jackson for an afternoon dive. Rick Vanover and Rick Lay joined them. The plan was for the foursome to proceed once again down to the wreck and over to Gimbel's Hole, where Jackson and Vanover would make a penetration. Murley and Lay were to wait outside the hole. Murley had previously confided to Mary Beth that he was not happy about the plan but acquiesced to his instructor's wishes.

Murley entered the water wearing all the gear needed for the technical trimix certification. Jackson followed him in but then swam ahead and began to make his descent. Swimming along the drift line over to the anchor line, Murley once again began to have trouble and cried out for help. Steve Nagiewicz, a New Jersey dive-boat operator, was crewing for his good friend Dan Crowell. Nagiewicz quickly spotted the flailing diver and saw that Murley's regulator was not in his mouth, and his buoyancy compensator and dry suit were not sufficiently inflated. Nagiewicz jumped in and swam over to the struggling diver. By the time Nagiewicz reached Murley, Jackson had resurfaced and asked the pair what the problem was. Murley was incoherent. Nagiewicz pushed the panicking Murley back to the boat while Jackson pulled. Reaching the stern of the boat and the ladder up to the deck, the two rescuers began to strip Murley of his gear. Some aboard shouted out that Murley was not breathing. With the help of another diver who had jumped in, the threesome immediately began resuscitation procedures in the water.

Despite the efforts of five men, Murley could not be lifted out of the water and onto the deck of the *Seeker*. A boat davit had to be used to hoist the now-lifeless body up. CPR efforts were continued on the *Seeker*, along with the administration of oxygen until a coast guard helicopter arrived about an hour later. Chris Murley was airlifted to Cape Cod Hospital in Hyannis, Massachusetts, where he was promptly pronounced dead at 7:30 P.M.

In a matter of hours the news of another death aboard the *Seeker* started circulating around the Internet. Rumor had it that the overweight man from Cincinnati had died because he was hypoxic. The low blend of oxygen in his bottom gas, said the buzz, had triggered a heart attack.

Divers from the Midwest commonly dived on a low-oxygen, high-helium trimix, characteristically 10 percent oxygen, 50 percent helium, 40 percent nitrogen. The mix was called heliair. It was popular in the Midwest in part because, fairly easy to mix, it did not require an elaborate gas-mixing station, which were practically nonexistent in that part of the country. Tanks were half-filled with helium and then topped off with compressed air, giving them the heliair blend. Heliair was an acceptable bottom mix on a three-hundred-foot dive but it could cause problems at lesser depths and on the surface. Conceivably a diver could become hypoxic on the surface if he was physically exerting himself and under stress. To some in the diving community, using heliair on the surface and at shallow depths was insane.

That the Midwesterners did not increase the oxygen content of their heliair mixes had always "pissed off" Dan Crowell. But other than advising on richer oxygen mixtures, he felt he was in no position to dictate gas blends. "Besides," Crowell later told me, "Murley was not breathing from his bottom mix when he ran into trouble. So, blaming his death on hypoxic mix was bullshit."

Crowell related he had noticed that Murley, upon entering the water, was going to use his heliair bottom mix on a tune-up dive on the U-853 off Block Island. Crowell asked him what he was doing using the 10 percent oxygen mix on the surface. Murley replied that it was "okay" since he would make an immediate descent. Crowell had to point out to him that he would have to first kick along the drift lines to the mooring point before descending down the anchor line. That would be a long swim on the light mix. Murley understood his predicament and switched to his 36 percent oxygen nitrox mix, or his decompression gas. Crowell said on Murley's fatal dive attempt on the Doria the next day, he had checked to see if Murley had deployed his nitrox mix when he splashed in: he had.

The *Seeker's* captain later conceded that had he known that Christopher Murley had only two years of dive experience and only eighty-plus dives, he would never have allowed him on the charter. But Murley, says Crowell, was Joe Jackson's student and his responsibility. Jackson had vouched for Murley, and Crowell could not investigate everyone's credentials. It was not practical. There had to be a certain amount of trust when it came to something as serious as diving the *Doria* or else no one would be diving the wreck. The deep-wreck-diving community was, after all, small and tightly knit, and trust was the binding glue.

To many in the diving community, that Joe Jackson was the charterer did not absolve Dan Crowell, and many of those who weighed in against him were his competition. They suggested that he should have been more vigilant about whom he allowed on his boat for deep dives such as the *Andrea Doria*. Rumors also started to spread that the Jersey-based boat was cursed.

Joel Silverstein had met Murley and seen him dive. Silverstein believed that Christopher Murley should not have been allowed on the charter. Silverstein had been invited to a talk on "Technical Diving and Enriched-Air Diving for the 21st Century" at the Ohio Council of Scuba Divers Conference in Columbus, in February 1999. He described Murley as "a big tall guy, bigger than me," who looked older than his forty-four years and who did not look to be in the best of shape.

Murley introduced himself and told Silverstein he was planning on diving the *Doria* as part of his trimix training class that summer. Silverstein recalled that Murley said he was a little hesitant about it but thought "he would be okay." After hearing that he had not gotten all his training dives in yet, Silverstein advised him to wait another year until he had some "better experience" before he attempted such a dangerous dive. Murley said he would take it under advisement.

Joel Silverstein bumped into him again in March at the Beneath the Sea Conference in New Jersey. Silverstein was concerned that

Murley still had not gotten in any more training dives and that he was still planning to do the *Doria* from the *Seeker*.

In June 1999, just one month before Murley's death, Silverstein ran into him yet again at the Gilboa Quarry in Findlay, Ohio, during one of the enriched-air diving courses that Silverstein gave around the country. The Gilboa Quarry was a popular spot for divers in the Midwest to do deep-training dives. In Silverstein's opinion, the "brain-numbing" cold water of the quarry was adequate for preliminary technical training but not for advanced training.

Silverstein noted that Murley's stage bottles were not marked with the mix they contained. Being a self-described "inquisitive prick," Silverstein asked him what was in them and how Murley could tell one tank from the other. He replied that one of them had a yellow regulator and the other had a green one. Silverstein informed him that all colors were filtered out below thirty feet. Murley said he "would think about" correcting the potential problem.

Silverstein asked Murley if he was still planning to do the *Doria* dive in one month's time. Murley confessed that he was still uncomfortable about the looming dive, citing his lack of experience. Silverstein again suggested that it be put off for another year, but Murley said that the reservation was set and already paid for. That was the last time Silverstein saw Christopher Murley. In the back of his mind, he later related, he knew Murley "was not going to have a successful dive on the *Doria*." He was, in Silverstein's words, "an accident waiting to happen."

That same month, Murley made a trip down to Pompano, Florida, to make some more training dives with Joe Jackson. According to his finacée, when Chris Murley was not diving he was sleeping, and he did not go out to eat with the rest of his dive buddies in the evening. Mary Beth also related that Jackson informed Murley that because of Murley's poor performance in the water, Jackson was withholding permission for Murley to take part in the *Doria* expedition one month later. Only later, at the beginning of July, did Jackson inform the anxious Murley that he could take part in the *Doria* expedition. Between the time of the Pompano dives and the *Doria* trip, Chris Murley made only six training dives, three of them in water less that sixty three feet deep.

After Murley's death Dan Crowell had several weeks still left in his *Doria* diving season. All he could do was try to ignore the storm of controversy and do what he did best—pilot his craft out to where divers wanted to be. However, the *Doria* had yet to claim one more life before the 1999 season would end.

Charlie McGurr was a fifty-two-year-old auto mechanic who had been crewing aboard the *Seeker* for just a year. The former Vietnam Green Beret's most prized possession was a china plate bearing the Italia

Charlie McGurr.
(Photo © Jennifer Samulski)

Line inscription he had bagged on the *Doria* in 1998. Dan Crowell remembered that Charlie lived for diving—and diving the *Andrea Doria* in particular. Crowell also recalled McGurr as the hardest-working crewman aboard the *Seeker*. "Charlie was a workaholic," Crowell said. "You would have to tie him up and staple his feet to the deck and say, 'Hey, relax, Charlie, you don't have to do this. You're one of the better crew anyway.' "

Somehow, Charlie McGurr never found enough time to secure a trimix certification, probably because he worked so much, says Crowell. But the *Seeker* now required a diver to have that highest level of scuba training for a *Doria* expedition, so McGurr had no choice but to get the coveted trimix card.

McGurr made several dives with Crowell and Gary Gentile on the advanced gas mix. Gentile was duly impressed and told Crowell that McGurr was "one smooth operator underwater." Gentile's good opinion of the crewman meant a lot, and McGurr was deemed ready.

Before leaving for Montauk, McGurr and Dan Crowell stopped by a restaurant in South Belmar, New Jersey, managed by McGurr's wife, Kathleen. Kathleen always worried about her husband on these deep dives, and they had discussed the risks involved. McGurr promised her that if something did not feel right, he would always abort.

His taking time off from work to take part in the expedition, Kathleen recalled, was a birthday present to himself. Kathleen saw her husband for the last time for just a brief moment when he came to the restaurant to say good-bye.

On July 28, one week after Christopher Murley died, Charlie McGurr crewed on the *Seeker* and made his first trimix dives on the *Doria*. His first dive went without a hitch.

On the second day of diving, McGurr, fellow crewman Peter Wohlleben, and customer Darryl Johnson splashed in at approximately 9 A.M. They followed a team of three divers from North Carolina into the water. The two *Seeker* crewmen were to escort Johnson over to Gimbel's Hole and explore that area of the ship.

Dropping down the anchor line, the threesome experienced a swift-moving current.

Strong currents are one of the hazards that divers encounter on the wreck. Currents can appear out of nowhere without notice, making it extremely difficult to navigate the sunken ship.

Down on the line, McGurr signaled to Wohlleben that he was going to abort his dive. Wohlleben gave him the okay signal and proceeded with his dive plan, not concerned that McGurr was returning to the surface so soon. McGurr was a safe diver, known to terminate a dive if he felt uncomfortable in adverse conditions. The strong current may have been too much for the fifty-two-year-old McGurr, unaccustomed as he was to all the new gear he was carrying.

On the way up the anchor line McGurr encountered three more divers on their way down at the 150-foot depth. It was the last time Charlie was seen alive.

After a twenty-five minute dive at 230 feet and a lengthy decompression, Michael Kane, one of the three who had seen McGurr, emerged from the cold water and was informed by Dan Crowell that Charlie McGurr had not yet surfaced. Crowell wanted to know where Kane had been on the wreck and if he had seen McGurr anywhere. He had not.

Everybody aboard scanned the seas around the *Seeker* in hopes of spotting a lift bag belonging to McGurr bobbing on the surface. A lift bag would indicate that McGurr was alive and was doing his decompression. No bag was spotted. Once again, a Coast Guard helicopter was called in to conduct a search for a missing diver.

Kane had a pretty good idea of what had happened to McGurr. On his ascent from the wreck Kane had experienced a "ripping current" and had tethered himself to the anchor line during decompression with his jonline and "held on for dear life." If the older McGurr had drifted away from the anchor line, he might not have been able to get back to it. That would have had dire consequences.

An hour into the Coast Guard grid search of the ocean around the

Seeker, Crowell and J. T. Barker decided it was time for them to go down to the wreck and look for Charlie.

Nineteen minutes into their search they found him.

Charlie McGurr was resting on the Promenade Deck at a depth of 202 feet. His regulator was not in his mouth. His wings were inflated and his emergency upline and lift bags were undisturbed. It was as if McGurr had just lain down on the wreck and died. Crowell secured the body to the anchor line and released McGurr's weight belt. His body gently ascended from the depths.

Kane and two other divers swam over to McGurr's body when it breached the surface and towed it back to the boat. Since McGurr had been underwater for several hours and showed no signs of life, the threesome saw no point in performing CPR. Charlie McGurr was obviously dead.

McGurr's pressure gauges showed that his bottom tanks were nearly full and his stage bottles were untouched. The general consensus among those aboard the *Seeker* was that McGurr had somehow gotten separated from the anchor line at 150 feet, where he was last seen alive, and had struggled against the swift current. That effort could have resulted in a carbon dioxide buildup, precipitating a deepwater blackout, or in the case of the middle-aged diver, a heart attack.

U.S. Coast Guard lieutenant Tim Dickerson was the investigator assigned to look into McGurr's death, as he has been with all the fatalities over the last few years on the *Doria.* From the coroner's report, Dickerson believes that McGurr succumbed to a heart attack while underwater. Despite what some divers believe, including Michael Kane, McGurr was not the victim of a lack of experience, equipment malfunction, or adverse conditions on the wreck. Dickerson's findings seemed to absolve the *Seeker* of any blame.

Nevertheless veteran *Doria* diver John Chatterton believes that McGurr was unprepared mentally for the unexpected, explaining that the unexpected leaves you desperately reaching at the worst possible moment for an urgently needed answer, and in deep water it too often leaves you dead. His "unexpected" situation may have precipitated his heart failure.

John Chatterton, Dan Crowell's best friend and sometime crewmate, knew that the 1999 season was tough on the *Seeker*'s captain, coming on the heels of the disastrous 1998 year. Losing Charlie McGurr was especially hard on Dan Crowell.

According to Chatterton, "It was just entirely too close to home, much like the death of a family member. Charlie was a good guy, a very good guy. He just got in too deep on the wrong day."

The 1998 and 1999 seasons would not go away for Dan Crowell. Lieutenant Tim Dickerson called for a meeting at the Coast Guard Field Office in Coram, Long Island, to discuss the rash of fatalities on the *Andrea Doria*. Dickerson is the assistant senior investigating officer for the Group/Marine Safety Office for the Long Island Sound, headquartered in New Haven, Connecticut. Normally the Providence, Rhode Island, field office of the coast guard would handle any matter regarding the waters off the Nantucket Shoals, but no investigating officer there had diving experience. Dickerson was a certified, but inactive, scuba diver. Also attending was Coast Guard civilian employee Bob Higgins, fishing-vessel safety coordinator, who reviewed all diving casualty cases in the Boston First District. Higgins, as the Coast Guard liaison, was also working with Duke University and the Divers' Alert Network (DAN) to set up a Memorandum of Understanding (MOU), a pilot program so that more investigative work could be done on diving fatalities.

Crowell thought the whole meeting idea was "bullshit." Everyone knew that the Doria lay in international waters so the Coast Guard had no jurisdiction. Crowell believed that Dickerson had been pressured by some politicians, particularly Congressman William Delahunt of Massachusetts, leader of the thirty-member Congressional Coast Guard Caucus, to do something, in Delahunt's words, "to stop all the carnage" out on the wreck. Crowell said the meeting was just the result of some elected officials "trying to attach themselves to anything just to get some publicity."

Dickerson denied he was under any pressure from anyone to conduct the "informal workshop" on what had happened out on the *Doria* in 1998 and 1999. He says he called the meeting on his own initiative after conferring with Bob Higgins. Dickerson also claimed that the Coast Guard *does* indeed have the jurisdiction to conduct investigations and assign blame for diving deaths on the *Andrea Doria*. "The Coast Guard has jurisdiction over any U.S. vessel anywhere in the world," Dickerson said, "or any vessel in U.S. waters. In these cases they were diving off a U.S. vessel. We can't prevent diving out there, but if an accident happens and we deem it due to negligence, we would then contact the U.S. attorney or the FBI to take further action."

What made Crowell particularly suspicious about the nature of the meeting was that his old rival Steve Bielenda's name was brought up in Crowell's phone conversations with Dickerson. Dan Crowell made it clear that he wanted no part in anything that the master of the *Wahoo* was involved in. Crowell believed that Bielenda was behind a lot of the "blame game" being played out in the media and on the Internet. But Dickerson persisted and cajoled the skeptical *Seeker* skipper, and Dan Crowell reluctantly attended the meeting.

The informal meeting was attended up by a who's who in the Northeast dive community: Michael Emmerman, a forensic investigator and honorary member of the NYPD Scuba Team; Captain Bill Reddan, president of the EDBA; Hank Keats, noted underwater historian, researcher, and deep diver; Bob Yeagle, member of the Massachusetts State Police and *Doria* diver; Joel Silverstein, technical-dive instructor, author, and *Doria* diver; Captains Steve Bielenda and Janet Bieser of the *Wahoo;* John Moyer, noted *Doria* diver and salvor; Dennis Burlage, *Doria* diver and amateur accident-investigator; Steve Nagiewicz, captain of the Jersey boat *Diversion.* Howard Klein, captain of the *Eagle's Nest,* and John Chatterton declined to attend.

According to Captain Steve Bielenda, Dan Crowell and fellow

Jersey dive-boat skipper Steve Nagiewicz showed up at the meeting with an "attitude."

"They actually were bucking the whole system," Bielenda said. "They made statements indicating their resentment that the meeting was on Long Island and not in New Jersey since they were the guys 'doing it' [running the *Doria* trips]. I think they were afraid what was going to come out of this meeting."

Crowell claims he did have an attitude—a good one. He believed the meeting went surprisingly well except for Bielenda's "inconsequential rhetoric." The *Seeker*'s captain added that Bielenda is "best at pointing the finger at others to draw attention away from himself."

Dickerson wanted to find out exactly what diving operations on the *Doria* entailed. According to Crowell, and Bielenda, the Coast Guard did not have a clue as to what a *Doria* expedition involved. Dickerson admitted to me that the meeting was an "education" for him because of his rudimentary understanding of dive operations.

Dickerson wanted the meeting to be an open discussion, to find out what the procedures and operations were on charter boats that took divers out to the *Andrea Doria*. He explained that the Coast Guard was concerned that there had been five deaths in thirteen months aboard the *Seeker*, and he and the Coast Guard wanted to find out why accidents had dramatically increased.

Crowell and Bielenda spoke on their respective boat's policies, specifically on required scuba certifications. Crowell explained the *Seeker*'s policy of allowing trimix students with their instructors aboard for *Doria* dives. He elaborated that because of the generally good conditions out on the wreck, it was an ideal place for that kind of training. John Moyer, a good friend of Crowell's, disagreed with the Jersey boat captain. His opinion was that the *Doria* was a wreck "you trained up to, not one you trained down on." Bielenda's opinion was that the wreck was too "remote" to have training sessions on, that they should be done on wrecks closer to shore.

The remoteness added to the stress on a diver, especially if he did not have a lot of boat experience, or his "sea legs" as Bielenda called it. The *Doria*, Bielenda later related, is a good three hours from medical treatment under the best of conditions, an often fatal distance for the kind of accidents that happened on it.

Then the issue of certification and the use of trimix gas came up, and Bielenda pressed Crowell to explain his policy. According to Bielenda, Crowell was forced to "bend" his rules because regular *Doria* divers aboard his boat such as Gary Gentile, Steve Gatto, John Moyer, and Tom Packer all dove the wreck on air, as they had for the last fifteen to twenty years. To accommodate them, the *Seeker's* rule then evolved to the requirement that a trimix certification was necessary just to understand your responsibility and exposure. A duly certified diver aboard the *Seeker* was then free to use air on deep dives if he so chose.

Crowell admitted that he dove the *Doria* about half the time on air himself. The reason he required trimix certification was that he wanted divers on his boat to know the inherent physiological risks involved with diving these extremes, something the certification would alert them to. What kind of mix they used was then their choice.

They also discussed the kind of equipment that was used on these deep dives. Dickerson learned that in a perfect world everyone would use the same gear, but that standardization was impossible to implement. Crowell and Silverstein also weighed in on extreme exposures, gas blends, and decompression schedules.

Christopher Murley's death was one of the sticking points of the meeting. When Crowell was asked if a diver with only eighty dives was qualified to be out on the *Doria*, he replied that coming up with an arbitrary number as a minimum requirement did not make much sense. At the *Doria* level of diving, a diver had to be honest with himself about whether he belonged there or not. Murley, he pointed out, was with his instructor, who was also the charterer of the boat and therefore responsible for Murley.

Christopher Murley, Crowell also said, died of a heart attack, which could have happened anywhere. Crowell believed that Murley either hid that he had a heart problem or was unaware of it. Either way, Crowell claimed, he could not be blamed for the death of someone who signed a waiver stating he was in good health when he apparently was not.

Of the five deaths on the *Doria*, the Murley accident troubled Dickerson the most. According to Dickerson, a heart attack was *not* listed as the cause of death in the coroner's report. It was a drowning, although Murley did have signs of heart disease that may have precipitated the accident.

Crowell was absolved of any blame, but Dickerson later related to me that Murley's death brought up other issues that "rang bells" in his mind: Murley's inexperience and poor physical shape prompted Dickerson to recommend to his superiors that a copy of the Murley investigation report be sent to the proper scuba certification agency for their review of the actions of his instructor, Joe Jackson of the Cincinnati Dive Shop. Dickerson suggested to his superiors that the Coast Guard should encourage the vessels to adopt their own system to check the physical fitness of people who made dives from their boats.

Dickerson admits checking a diver's fitness is a "gray area," but he has come up with standards produced by various international health organizations using body-mass indexing. To undertake the rigors of deep diving, if you have a high-risk index number, you should have had a recent physical attesting to your good health and physical ability.

As far as Dan Crowell was concerned, the meeting was a "waste." He says he spoke with other Coast Guard officials who confirmed his suspicions that Dickerson was just "kissing ass." Crowell says that he was told by his sources in the Coast Guard that nothing would come of it, and according to Crowell, nothing did.

"The Coast Guard may have actually learned something," Crowell said, "but I doubt it. One afternoon is not going to teach them about all this stuff. The Coast Guard is part of the Department of Transportation.

They have no business nor the knowledge to dictate policy to us out on the *Doria.*"

Joel Silverstein had a different take on the meeting. It was clear to him that a Coast Guard inspection at the dock of a dive boat could now find a minor infraction and prevent it from sailing. If they found one thing wrong, they might be able to find some more with a further detailed inspection. The sea cops could then "haul" the boat, effectively terminating any diving activity. According to Silverstein, that "veiled threat" is exactly what Dickerson implied.

"Dickerson was satisfied that we were professionals in what we were doing," Silverstein said, "and that the accidents were just that—accidents. It was an important public-relations issue to deal with. We showed the Coast Guard that we were more than willing to work with them, talk with them, teach them, and learn from them. I believe that meeting allowed our *Doria* charters to sail this year [2000]."

The charters did indeed sail, and I was on one of them.

It took a while to connect with Dan Crowell. The captain of the *Seeker* had been beaten up in the press. He was leery of talking to yet another uninformed writer. People had died and someone had to shoulder the blame, according to the ethos of the mass media people. He was the most likely candidate, and I was just another snooping reporter. Even though I was a diver with *Doria* dives under my belt, Crowell did not like my references.

At the time I was unaware of the intense rivalry between dive-boat captains, especially between Steve Bielenda and Crowell. I thought the names Steve Bielenda and Joel Silverstein would be an entrée into Dan Crowell's confidence. They were not, and he told me so. Nevertheless I assured Crowell I was not looking to do a hatchet job on anyone and was just interested in presenting the facts as best as I could report them. That I was a diver with over thirty years experience and had been out to the *Doria* twice allayed some of his suspicions about my qualifications and intentions. He agreed to see me.

In April of 2000 I drove down to Crowell's residence in Brick,

New Jersey, about an hour and a half south of New York City on the Jersey shore. Crowell lives on a typically suburban block a couple of miles from the Garden State Parkway. I had no problem locating his home; his garage door was wide open and it was crammed with diving gear. No mistaking his place.

Like most people, I always try to imagine an appearance to match a voice on the phone. I am usually way off, and I was with Crowell.

From articles in *Newsday* and from my phone conversations with him, I had conjured up a vision of some sun-leathered, arrogant boat captain with a bad disposition and low on patience. The man who greeted me at the door was a surprise.

Dan Crowell looks young for his forty-two years. His brown hair is shorn in the style of a California kid, casually parted in the middle and of modest length. A well-maintained mustache rides his upper lip; otherwise he is clean-shaven. He has a face that speaks of long hours on the open sea, but none the worse for it. The burnishing from the sun suits him well. He does not look like a candidate for skin cancer.

I guess him to be about six feet two. He dresses casually in jeans, T-shirt, and running shoes. A firm handshake and a genuine smile put me at ease. I had been expecting a wary welcome tinged with hostility.

Crowell's living room would be the envy of any wreck diver. Artifacts from long-lost ships take up all available shelf space. The room is a veritable showcase of shiny brass, elegant china, and fragile crystal. Looking around me, I remember that I am in the presence of a diver who has logged more dives on the "Everest of wreck diving" than anyone else.

I followed him downstairs and we entered his office. The side-by-side computer workstations remind me that he shares his domicile with his companion and business partner, Jennifer Samulski. Crowell explains her absence and adds that perhaps we can all share a meal together later at a local restaurant. The image popularized in the press of the arrogant, unapologetic boat captain goes out the window.

Over the winter when not running diving trips on the weekends, Crowell had been keeping himself busy with commercial dive work. Most of that was the distinctly unglamorous work of inspecting underwater pipes for a New Jersey utility company. Utility pipelines run through waters no sport diver would ever care to enter.

I spent over three hours in taped conversation with the captain of the *Seeker*. He was articulate, thoughtful, and patient in his explanations. That I am a diver with deep-wreck experience probably helped some. My pointed questions seemed to engage his intellect, and he appeared to enjoy my well-intentioned verbal sparring with him. I did, however, detect a touch of paranoia when it came to the subject of Captain Steve Bielenda of the *Wahoo*.

Dan Crowell inherited his distaste for Bielenda from his old mentor, friend, and former boss Bill Nagle, the now deceased *Seeker* owner who had had a long and legendary running battle with Bielenda.

Several times during the interview Crowell professed to be unaffected by the "noise" that Bielenda creates in the press and on the Internet regarding Crowell's stewardship of the *Seeker* and the boat's rash of fatalities. Later in a July 2000 feature article in *Esquire* on diving the *Doria*, Bielenda inveighed that "if it takes five fatalities to be the number one *Doria* dive boat, I'm happy being number two."

Crowell said he just wanted to be left alone and could not care less what other boat captains say about him. But he came back to the subject constantly, belying his stated indifference. I came away with the impression that Dan Crowell cares more about his perceived ethics, morals, and reputation than he would care to admit. A proud guy, he has been wounded.

Interview finished, we agree that I should dive from his boat. That way I can see firsthand how it is run, and the ride out and back will be another opportunity to continue our conversations on deep-wreck diving, and specifically going down to the *Doria*. An upcoming dive on the *Pinta* a month hence is judged ideal.

It is another long haul down to the Jersey shore and the *Seeker* from my New York home. Getting to the dock by 6:30 A.M. meant a 3:30 A.M. departure for me. I had made dives from Jersey-based boats before. This trip was another example of why I preferred the Long Island boats—they are much closer to home.

Brielle, where the *Seeker* is berthed, is in the heart of the Jersey shore abutting the ever-popular beach resort of Point Pleasant. Some say it is also the hub of Northeast wreck diving. Some of the most popular wrecks along the East Coast are within a few hours sailing time from Brielle. A visit to the *Pinta*, a shallow-lying wreck, is always an early-season dive. It is a tune-up for deeper, more challenging dives.

The 194-foot Dutch freighter *Pinta* sank in 1963 after running afoul of the British freighter SS *City of Perth*. It was never determined why the radar-equipped ships collided on a clear, calm day. The *Pinta* lies in eighty-eight feet of water on her port side. In her holds she still carries her cargo of Central American lumber.

The weather on this May 6 was more like the weather you would expect in mid-August. The temperatures were in the high eighties and the seas were glassy. The balmy weather, evidently, was a temptation to every boater in the region. The channel out of Brielle looked like a California freeway.

Gary Gentile was aboard. Sleeping in his usual spot, the bunk next to the boat's galley, Gentile was there so he could update his book *The Shipwrecks of New Jersey*. As usual, he was enduring good-natured ribbing from the rest of the crew of the boat, including Dan Crowell.

Crowell would explain, with a smile on his face, that Gary Gentile was not the most useful member of the boat's crew. Just as during his days aboard the *Sea Hunter* and the *Wahoo*, Gary could usually be found in his bunk, either asleep, reading, or writing in his journal. But on the *Seeker* there was no resentment. Gentile had become something akin to a diving eccentric, and a legend. He was also a diving celebrity, which did not hurt the *Seeker*'s reputation. Gentile was also a good friend of Dan Crowell's.

An hour and half after we departed from the dock, the motors were thrown into neutral above the underwater gravesite. Gary suited up in his inimitable way, that is, slowly and chattering away to whoever was around, then splashed in and shackled the anchor line into the wreck.

I had asked Dan Crowell if I could team up with him on the dive. I had never been on the *Pinta,* and Crowell had a multitude of dives on her. Diving with him also afforded me the opportunity of observing him in action.

Unfortunately conditions underwater did not mirror those on the surface. Particulate matter in the cold water was dense and inhibited visibility to about ten feet. I was glad I was diving with the veteran *Pinta* diver.

Since this was my first dive of the season and because of the poor visibility, I decided against making a second dive. Hanging around the decks of the *Seeker* was also an education in how things were run on the sixty-five-foot charter boat.

Dan Crowell blew off doing a second dive as well. He had been videotaping the wreck on the first dive and saw no point in doing more since the visibility was so poor. With a coffee mug clenched in his fist, Crowell made the rounds of his boat chatting and joking with customers and crew. A lot of his one-liners were aimed at Gentile. Gentile seemed to enjoy the barbed attention, often replying with a zinger of his own or feigning bewilderment at their meanings.

Gentile and I also discussed my book at length, especially the personalities of certain boat captains. As far as Captain Sal Arena of the *Sea Hunter* was concerned, Gary warned me not to bring up his name until my upcoming interview with Arena was almost concluded. "He doesn't like me," Gary explained.

All things considered, I was impressed with the *Seeker,* her captain, and her crew. Other than for the lack of cutouts on the gunwales (the *Seeker* has a wood hull) for easier entries and exits like the *Wahoo* (she is fiberglass), I could have closed my eyes and imagined myself aboard the Long Island boat. There was the same lively camaraderie, conversations, joking, and ribald comments on just about everything.

In conversations with Captain Dan Crowell, the subject invariably drifted back to his string of unusually bad luck in 1998 and 1999. The deaths that had occurred from the decks of his boat continued to haunt him. For Dan Crowell there was no making sense of them.

The thing that was hard to ignore when trying to understand why the *Seeker* was snakebit—what separated the *Seeker* from the rest of the boats—was the number of deep dives she was the platform for. Other than for the *Pinta* and a few other shallow-dwelling shipwrecks, the boat's schedule laid bare Crowell's passion for diving deep wrecks. Maybe the numbers had just caught up with the Jersey-based skipper.

In late June in a follow-up call I made to Dan Crowell for a clarification, he asked me if I would be interested in taking part in a *Doria* expedition in the third week of July. A spot had opened up, and he thought it might be a good idea, since his boat was a principal in my book, that I be aboard it at least once when it was out over the *Doria*. I could not argue with him.

I frantically tried to rearrange my schedule to take the time off needed for the expedition. In the meantime I had gotten a call from Joel Silverstein. Silverstein had chartered the *Wahoo* for a *Doria* expedition during the first week of July. He had a group of Europeans who had wanted to film a documentary on a dive to the Italian liner. The Swiss, French, and Italian divers had become a major "nightmare" for him. After five months of lining up mixed gas, accommodations, transportation, and provisions for the boat for the fussy European divers, he was having problems lining up one more crew member for the expedition. He asked if I could come along and help out.

Crewing on the *Wahoo*, unfortunately, was out of the question. I thought it was important for my book that I go out on the *Seeker*, and two back-to-back trips a hundred miles out to sea on different boats was a logistical nightmare for me. I did, however, agree to help out on a warm-up dive for the Europeans on the USS *San Diego*.

The *San Diego* was just a short two-hour trip out from the *Wahoo*'s home port of Captree Boat Basin. Arriving at the boat early Friday morning, I got a firsthand look at how much of a "nightmare" the boatload of Europeans were.

Not only were their arriving flights late, but their carrier had misplaced a lot of their luggage. They were not in a good mood when they arrived at Captree in the wee hours of Friday morning. They took one look at the *Wahoo* and complained to Silverstein how they had gotten "fucked."

Apparently they had expected more luxurious accommodations, not the stacked-up bunks belowdecks in the non–air-conditioned fifty-five-foot boat. Silverstein had reams of e-mails where he had pointedly told them the accommodations were spartan. They casually dismissed the correspondence and made demand after demand. A topside cameraman from French TV then began making demands of his own. All I could do was pity the exasperated Silverstein.

On the *San Diego* dive Silverstein at least had his fears allayed as to their diving skills. I wished I could have helped more and gone along on the *Doria* trip but was relieved, nonetheless, that I would not have to put up with the troublesome group.

The *Seeker*'s *Doria* expedition was originally scheduled to depart from Montauk on Monday night, July 17. Crowell delayed it a day because of thunderstorm activity out at sea predicted by the National Weather Service. On Tuesday night the *Seeker* was at the lift bay at the Star Island Yacht Club. The gear for the ten divers and five crew was loaded efficiently, and the boat shoved off at 10 P.M. sharp.

Conditions were ideal for the trip out. The seas were driven by a gentle swell, and the warm July night didn't prevent me from getting a full night's sleep. When we arrived at the wreck, for the first time I was well rested and ready to dive deep. As Captains Bielenda and Crowell had always said, getting out there and back comfortably was always the biggest concern. It put a diver a leg up on diving operations.

All the divers aboard had impressive credentials. When polled, not a person aboard had not made a dive to at least three hundred feet. Most of the divers hailed from the Washington, D.C., area.

None of them were under the age of forty. That was a testament to the level to which deep-wreck diving had come. An individual had to have the wherewithal to afford not only the $900 charter fee, but also the $400 to $500 in gas-mix fees and the estimated $10,000 worth of high-tech scuba gear. Deep diving was seeing an influx of highly paid white-collar professionals who were entranced with the new equipment and the mixed-gas technology that afforded them deep-adventure thrills.

Some of the Johnny-come-latelies had an arrogance that they knew it all. Diving the *Doria* had become polarized into an academic camp versus a cowboy camp. Veterans such as Crowell and John Chatterton, who called themselves "in-betweeners," sometimes had difficulty imparting their experience to the know-it-all newcomers aboard the *Seeker*. Undoubtedly the attitudes of this new wave of divers were in part responsible for the recent deaths on the *Doria*. Two of the divers who had perished in 1998 and 1999 were relatively new to deep-wreck diving.

Conditions out on the wreck were the kind you dream about—sunny skies, warm temperatures, and calm seas. But surface conditions, as always, were deceptive.

Even though not a cloud was in the sky and the sun was high, visibility underwater was poor. Sea conditions were always best in late June and early July, but visibility, often, was not. Particulate matter in the cold water would be heavy, creating almost gelatinous conditions obscuring sunlight and reducing visibility. There was a lot to be said for diving the wreck later in August and into September. During those months a diver could count on the warmer waters brought in by the Gulf Stream to clear things up, improving visibility to the neighborhood of one hundred feet. But August was also hurricane season. Storms brewing thousands of miles away had adverse effects in the

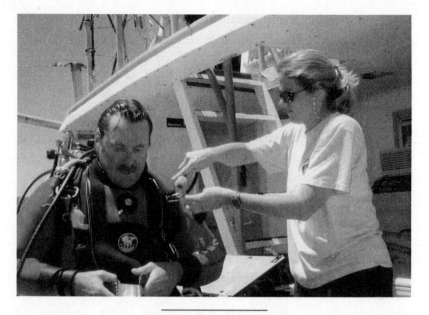

Dan Crowell gets help from Jennifer Samulski before a *Doria* dive.
(Photo © Kevin McMurray)

North Atlantic, making for unstable dive platforms that most boat captains ardently avoided.

Dropping down to the wreck, I was stunned how much it had deteriorated in just one year. We were tied into the Promenade Deck some
fifty to sixty feet forward of Gimbel's Hole near where the former
Main Street of the ship gave way to the open deck of the bow. Two
mooring bollards sprouted from the Forward Deck, indicating we
were near the working area of the ship.

Exploring the area just aft of the tie-in, I made a rather amusing
discovery. The plaque laid by the visiting Europeans just a week
before on the *Wahoo* was lying just below our tie-in on a sagging section of the Promenade Deck. Kicking over the ceramic artwork, I
smiled widely behind my mask. I recognized it immediately.
Commissioned by the Europeans, the glazed ceramic literally glowed
on the silted-over wreck. I marveled at the likelihood of tying into vir-

tually the same spot on the seven-hundred-foot wreck as the *Wahoo* a week before and finding the plaque within minutes of my dive in such poor visibility.

Kicking aft, I stumbled onto Gimbel's Hole. It was almost unrecognizable. The Promenade Deck had succumbed to the sea to such a degree that the garage-sized hole was no longer a viable entry-way into the interior of the ship. Peering into the once cavernous hole, I was shocked to see bulkheads and decks collapsed upon each other, almost as if they were melting away. Had it been like this fifteen years before, John Ormsby would never have been able to make his fatal penetration. The sea was changing the wreck from a labyrinth of decks and bulkheads into a heap of corroded steel—an underwater junkyard—almost as I watched.

I began to have problems. I had suffered through a bout of bronchitis the week before, which I thought I was over. The cold, dry mix I was breathing brought on a coughing fit at 190 feet of water. It was a frightening experience, convulsively coughing far below the surface of the sea. I could look up and see only blue-green water. When I felt the need to cough, I had to pull my regulator out of my mouth, replacing when it was time to gasp for air. My lungs felt seared by the breathing mix. I willed myself to calm down, sensing a panic attack beginning to grip me. I did a quick 360-degree turn to get my bearings, since the coughing fits had disoriented me. The shackled chain of the anchor line got picked up by my light beam. I kicked hard in its direction. It was time to abort the dive.

I had some hellish decompression hangs in my incremental climb to the top. Thankfully the current did not pick up as struggling against it would most surely have aggravated my gasping for air. A glass of water would have been nice. My throat was parched from my spasmodic heaving.

When I arrived at the surface, Crowell was there with his video camera. Crowell had told me that he would not be running dive charters forever. He had slowly been getting into the documentary-business end of diving. Crowell had already completed two based on the *Seeker's* discovery of the U-869 and his *Britannic* expedition in Greece in 1998. Both had been well received. His work on the U-869 had got the attention of *Nova,* the highly acclaimed documentary series and they had chartered his vessel and used some of underwater footage of the German submarine in the production.

Crowell had gotten the bug. A *Doria* production was in the works, hence his camera on the ready when I emerged. I related my problems on the bottom. "I hate that when it happens," was his commentary behind his eyepiece.

There were no significant retrievals of artifacts by anyone aboard. Poor visibility and the dramatic decomposition of the wreck had everyone just exploring the hull noting the changes. However, Jack Cheasty, an aviation-medicine specialist working for the U.S. army in Fort Campbell, Kentucky, did bring something up: the plaque laid by the Europeans from the *Wahoo* the week before.

Cheasty did not know what it was. He thought someone on the *Seeker* had dropped it or inadvertently left it behind. Since Cheasty was the last diver out of the water, he brought it up. Crowell bestowed on the embarrassed diver the Knucklehead of the Week Award. Showing an uncommon degree of ethical behavior for a wreck diver when it comes to underwater trophies, Cheasty decided to return the plaque to the wreck, but not until everyone had had pictures of themselves taken with it.

Calm seas and sunny, warm weather continued. Schools of tuna and an occasional whale breaching the surface made the days at sea unusually pleasant. It was my first trip out to the *Doria* where surface conditions did not conspire to make something as simple as eating a meal or maintaining your position in your bunk an ordeal. The *Seeker* floated contentedly on the ocean pretending to be a lake.

The next day, the running joke aboard the *Seeker* was the symphony of flatulence belowdecks the night before, which had been pro-

The author with the Italian commemorative plaque. *(Photo courtesy Dan Crowell)*

duced by our previous evening meal of ham and baked beans. Quickly dubbed "Blazing Drysuits," the day of diving was short. Captain Crowell notified all that the boat would pull the hook at 1 P.M. Everybody would have one more chance to dive the wreck before the *Seeker* motored back to Montauk.

Given my problems of the previous day, I had no desire to push it on the second. I planned a fifteen-minute dive to further survey the Promenade Deck at the 190-foot range. Because of my bronchial problems, the degree of collapse of the wreck, and the continuing poor visibility, discretion seemed advised. I would make no penetrations nor delve the deeper depths that are always a temptation. There would be no souvenir for me from this year's trip.

There was an attitude aboard the *Seeker*, that had obviously filtered down from its captain. Perhaps it reflected the deep-water experience of the clientele aboard for this expedition. Dan Crowell, before departing the dock, had given the standard lecture that every charter dive captain gives before a dive, including notes on the considerable curves the *Doria* throws at you. Advice was freely given, but by and large we were all expected to see to our own needs, prepare our gear, make sure of our gas mixes, and suit ourselves. We were also expected to file a dive plan, complete with gas mixes employed. Straying from your dive plan was frowned upon.

The crew of the boat was there to help, mostly in getting you into your tank harness, clipping on your stage bottles, and assisting in entries and exits. They do not check or touch your valves. I had understood that, so I had done it myself several times over. Personally, I think having the crew do a last-minute check of valves, inflator hoses, and regulators is a good idea. Had it been done for Tony Smith in North Carolina, perhaps he would still be alive today.

Every experienced diver has splashed in missing some gear, or with a valve inadvertently shut. Most of the times it is not a fatal mistake. Deep wrecks like the *Andrea Doria*, however, leave little room for mistakes.

Still the *Seeker* attitude is "Hey, you're on the *Doria* so we assume you know what you are doing." It is a flattering assessment of one's diving skills, but at the same time it is also dangerously presumptive. Would Vince Napoliello be alive today had his isolator valve been checked on the deck of the *Seeker* before he made his last dive? The stress of a near-panic situation inside the shipwreck when he thought he was out of air may have caused the problems that occurred outside the wreck that killed him. No one knows for sure, and never will, but it makes you wonder.

•　　•　　•

On the leg back to Montauk, Dan Crowell confessed that he does not spend much time thinking about the fatalities of the 1998 and 1999 seasons. "Shit happens" is how he characterized the deaths during those disastrous seasons. Life, operating the *Seeker*, and diving goes on. Death had apparently hardened him to the dangers of deep diving. "No one," Crowell said, "has to have a gun put to their head to do this kind of stuff."

It is a familiar argument analogous to that made for dozens of other dangerous activities. Yet he, like the other masters of dive boats who have experienced deadly accidents, is expected to be called to task and offer some explanation for what happened. There are no easy answers.

All the deadly accidents in 1998 and 1999 were examined from top to bottom in the hope that something could be changed to prevent future ones. Dan Crowell feels the most stringent safety requirements have been implemented aboard the *Seeker*. Still, the captain of the *Seeker* has seen twelve divers perish. He knows that there will be more, and that he can really do nothing to prevent it.

Shit happens.

EPILOGUE:

WHERE ARE THEY NOW?

GARY GILLIGAN

Gary Gilligan still does wreck dives, but it has been years since he last visited the *Andrea Doria*. He has found a new site to focus his considerable talents on: the wreck of the steamship *Lexington,* which sank in 1840 with a loss of 154 lives. The coal-burning side-wheeler, built by Commodore Vanderbilt in 1838, was en route to Stonington, Connecticut, from New York when it caught fire and sank just a few miles out in the Long Island Sound off Port Jefferson, New York. Gilligan found the wreck after gathering the most likely loran numbers from some Long Island divers who had come across an unidentified wreck in exploratory dives. From archival searches, Gilligan thought the wreck might be the elusive grave of the *Lexington,* whose story had always fascinated him.

The ship had died a painful death, and its conflagration was visible up and down the Long Island and Connecticut coastlines for miles. Little could be done for the vessel, and men, women, and children huddled on their funeral pyre, their only option to throw themselves into the freezing waters on a bitterly cold January evening.

Two divers and I joined Gilligan aboard his boat, the *Minnow*, to see what was left of the ship. This part of the sound is within sight of the skyline of New York, and the waters are dark and murky. Large cities are not always conducive to optimum dive conditions.

All ambient light disappears at seventy feet, swallowed up by particulates in the water. Even with powerful underwater lights, visibility is a scant three feet. Since the *Lexington* burnt to the waterline, little is left of her. Two attempts were made to raise her shortly after she sank with the intent of claiming the gold and silver she carried as salvage. The failed salvage attempts further reduced the wreck to what she appears to be now: a junk pile on the bottom of the sound.

Even in the poor visibility it was obvious that we were on a historic and tragic wreck. The burnt timbers, partially buried anchor chain, rusting paddle-wheel, and boilers that my light illuminated were a constant reminder that the loss of the *Lexington* was one of this country's worst maritime disasters.

Gary Gilligan was excited to locate and explore the ship remains. The experience reinvigorated the sea-loving carpenter with the same excitement he had felt when he was on the *Doria* in years past. The *Lexington* also lies a lot closer to home—only eight miles away from the East End Yacht Club in Bridgeport, where Gilligan lives on the *Minnow* with Midnight, his black Labrador.

Gilligan no longer crews on the *Wahoo*. When I talked to him about the old days out on the *Doria*, a twinkle came to his eye. I told him that I remember watching while he and Gary Gentile pulled up bags full of china and crystal on my first expedition out to the wreck in 1990. Gilligan and Gentile were stars then.

Those were heady and exciting times, those initial explorations of the *Doria*. Gilligan is proud that he was one of the early "cowboys" who blazed the path that now has become so popular, and so fatal.

Gilligan has seen other diving deaths and has taken part in more than one body recovery, but John Ormsby's death in July 1985 still haunts him. He still has vivid images of the events aboard the *Wahoo*. It was, he feels, a death that should never have happened: Ormsby was young, skilled, fearless, and he lived for diving.

Gilligan believes it's possible that the *Doria* is a cursed wreck. Although he's made hundreds of dives on her and has survived, he sees no point in pressing his luck. He is content now making short runs out to the *Lexington* and the U-835, a World War II German sub that was sunk by the U.S. navy off Block Island in 1945. I ask him if he is ever tempted to go back to the *Doria*. "Yeah, sometimes," he says, "but it passes."

SALLY WAHRMANN

Sally Wahrmann no longer dives the *Doria* either, but it is age and her weight that have conspired to keep her away. She jokes about the limitations brought on by aging, but one can detect a nostalgia for the *Doria* that is hard for her to conceal even over the phone. Now a tenured professor at Long Island University's C. W. Post Campus, time has become a commodity.

Sally, however, still dives. During the winter she vacations in the Virgin Islands and makes some dives, "the easy stuff," she says. But the easy stuff is an impetus to get back into the cold water of the North Atlantic. Sally recently bought a new dry suit and made some dives from the deck of the *Wahoo* on the *San Diego* and the *Oregon*.

She is contemplating a return to the *Doria* in 2001, to dive again on the wreck where she has logged over sixty dives over the years. Few women have made more dives than this garrulous accounting professor. Wahrmann says that if she does the dive again, she will do it on air, not trimix.

Wahrmann does not like what she sees happening in the world of deep-wreck diving. Distance and time have given her a unique perspective on what deep diving has become. Using trimix, she believes, is "overkill," a cowboy point of view that holds the gas is not necessary and is potentially dangerous.

Sally told me a story that illustrated her point: She met another woman diver at a WNBA game who had been on the *Seeker* for a *Doria* expedition. They had a pleasant conversation, the kind that two strangers have when they discover they have something in common. But Wahrmann said the woman "copped an attitude" when Wahrmann matter-of-factly said she dove the *Doria* on air.

"Snidely," Wahrmann said, "she asked me if I had remembered any of my dives, knew where I had been, and did I remember my name. It bothered me, because I think when we dove the *Doria* on air, we were safer. I think technical [trimix] divers have a false sense of security and consequently they overextend their time on the wreck. Because they're clearheaded, they think they can go places and do things that they couldn't do on air instead of using it as a safety factor."

Sally likes diving the "basics." She believes a lot of the fun has gone out of diving because everybody has become "tech crazy." She will not let that happen to her. Sally will see how she feels about diving next spring. If she is comfortable, she will be back on the *Wahoo* for another *Doria* trip. The lure of the wreck is still strong.

PETER GIMBEL

The man who started it all, Peter Gimbel, the consummate wealthy sportsman, explorer/adventurer passed away in 1987 at age fifty-nine, a victim of cancer. But Gimbel's association with the *Andrea Doria* did not end there. In a rather bizarre twist, Peter made one last descent to the *Doria*.

In 1995, Dan Crowell got a phone call from underwater photographer Brian Skeery, who related that he had been contacted by the Gimbel family. They told him that Peter Gimbel's last wish was to have his ashes buried in the hold of the *Andrea Doria*. The family wanted to know if it was possible for those wishes to be honored. Besides Peter's ashes, they also had the urns of Peter's twin brother David, and his recently deceased wife, Elga. The Gimbel survivors wanted all three urns deposited on the wreck together. Although the request was unusual, Crowell thought the *Doria* would be an appropriate final resting place for the man who had first dove the wreck. Crowell agreed to place the remains on the wreck.

The logistics of placing the ashes were a bit problematic. Two of the urns were wooden boxes, and the third was a ceramic box. Aboard the *Seeker* out over the *Doria*, Crowell did not have a lot of throwaway weights. The crew gathered up some old chains and shackles and put them and the urns all together in a catch bag. In a brief ceremony on the bow, a few words were said, a wreath was laid on the calm ocean, and then divers splashed in with the remains.

The first attempt to insert them in the wreck failed because they could not find a hole big enough. On a second dive, one of the divers found a porthole on the A Deck and slipped the package in. He watched as the weighted bag carrying the remains of the trailblazing Gimbels dropped out of sight into the darkened chambers of the sunken ship. The *Andrea Doria*, which had been so much a part of the Gimbels' lives, had now become their tomb.

STEVE BIELENDA

Steve Bielenda is now sixty-four years old, and like Sally Wahrmann he rarely dives. When he does, it is usually on spots that are close to his home port at Captree Boat Basin: the USS *San Diego* and the *Oregon*.

Some might say that Bielenda's legendary status as the skipper of the *Wahoo* is in his own mind, but that is due to his brashness and his inability to stroke other egos. Extremely outspoken Steve Bielenda, "the king of the deep," is now the old lion of wreck diving, and his opinions and experience still cannot be ignored. He may have slowed down a bit, but he is not ready to give up his crown, and he's as feisty as ever.

Bielenda is also always good for audacious quotes, and he's never diplomatic when it comes to stepping on others' toes. "Scumbags" and "fucks" are still his favorite sobriquets for those who have pissed him off—and there are many.

Bielenda was anxious to have his input on diving the *Doria* included in my book. His detractors might see it as just another example of Bielenda's hunger for publicity, but I knew better. Steve Bielenda was always an ardent promoter of wreck diving. He was a pioneer of *Doria* expeditions, and he was intent on seeing the record set straight.

We were blessed with near perfect weather conditions on an Indian-summer day in mid-October. I had experienced enough of the "snotty" conditions out on the fickle Atlantic to know that the scuba gods were smiling on us that day. Glassy seas, no wind, and clear skies greeted us when we arrived two hours after departing Captree at the spot where the 505-foot USS *San Diego* sank eighty-two years before.

For a man in his sixth decade Bielenda is impressively fit. His thinning gray hair is cropped close to the scalp with a wisp of it tied tightly in ponytail at the base of his skull, a bow to fashion one would expect from a sea captain wanting to maintain an image. He is powerfully built, a man men half his age would be reluctant to cross. Short and stout, he stills moves about the decks of his beloved *Wahoo* nimbly, as he sees to the hooking of the boat to the wreck. Captain Janet is at the helm, and Bielenda defers to her directives. She is in charge.

Bielenda wants to wait until after all the other divers are in the water, including Janet Bieser. Captain Janet wants to bag up on lobsters. We stay behind, basking in the shining sun, helping all the divers into their gear and ushering them into the placid seas off the portside deck of the *Wahoo*. In a moment of retrospection Bielenda confesses to me that time has caught up with him, that his once fabled dive skills have eroded. He now picks and chooses his dives carefully. If it does not feel right, he will not dive. He has seen one too many dive accidents. He has no intention of "dying doing what I love." He wants to expire in his bed while sleeping.

Bielenda's charges begin to emerge from the water onto the dive platform on the stern the *Wahoo*. He suits up quickly and goes over his gear rigging and examines mine. We formulate a dive plan, and he insists there will be no digression. Snapping a goodie bag to his harness, he says he wants to see if Captain Janet left any pickings for us. It's the old Captain Steve.

We expell air from our bloated wings and dry suits and drop unceremoniously down to the inverted keel of the dormant ship. Bielenda leads the way. I follow sheepishly, like some eager tourist following his guide. After following a bilge keel aft, the two of us drop over the port side of the wreck. The six-inch guns on its flank point harmlessly into the blue-green void. Other than for the hovering blackfish, we appear to be the only living things on the rusted-out hulk. The huge propeller shafts appear out of the watery gloom, timberlike silhouettes against the faint glow of the sun 110 feet above us.

Besides a guideline run by Captain Janet, there is little to see on the featureless sandy bottom as we make our way to the barge one hundred yards out from the wreck. The barge once belonged to a salvor who attempted to raise the bronze propellers off the warship in the late 1960s. The massive screw had been too much for the wooden float to lift, and it had joined the *San Diego* on the bottom.

As with most disasters at sea, the wreckage proved to be a boon to marine life and divers alike. The decomposing wood of the barge became a lair to lobsters intent on refuge. Captain Janet appeared to have bagged all the lobsters foolish enough to reveal themselves, and Bielenda shrugged his shoulders underwater with his palms facing upward. The message was clear.

We followed the line back to the iron hulk, kicking along the starboard side. Bielenda stopped on more than one occasion to cut away monofilament and errant penetration lines left behind, respectively, by frustrated fishermen and divers. I got the distinct impression watching him that he was a man cleaning up the litter on his well-maintained property. If he had spied a beer can, I am sure, he would have bagged it. I began to follow his example.

We clutched some ice-cold beers in our hands on the aft deck of the *Wahoo* on our way back to port, the midafternoon sun still warm on our backs. The beer and the misty spray of seawater rent by the bow of the boat was delightfully refreshing. Watching seagulls gliding over our wake put us in a reflective mood.

Steve Bielenda wavers from waxing nostalgic to waxing combative. The past and the future form an unbroken line for the master of the *Wahoo*. He knows he cannot rest on his laurels, and he is a proud man and worries about the future of his boat and the future of wreck diving.

Bielenda is irked that the press has crowned Crowell's *Seeker* as the number one boat when it comes to running *Doria* expeditions. Bielenda is not comfortable with being second banana. He feels he ran trips to the *Doria* long before Bill Nagle and Dan Crowell and so he deserves respect. It all comes down to mathematics, according to Bielenda: The *Seeker* runs more trips out there. More trips mean more divers. More divers mean more visibility. Gary Gentile, Bielenda's former friend and crew member, is now aboard the *Seeker*, as are other dive luminaries who have shunned the *Wahoo* in favor of what has become a veritable taxi ride out to the *Doria*.

The number of expeditions run by the *Seeker* out to the *Doria* bothers Bielenda. He does not believe there are enough qualified divers to justify so many trips. He says that Dan Crowell is too willing to take anybody out to a wreck and that the *Doria* deserves more respect. According to the Bielenda, Crowell's unbridled ambition to be the number one boat led to the deaths during the 1998 and 1999 seasons.

"I don't think he [Crowell] is responsible for all the fatalities," Bielenda said. "I never said he was. There have been certain situations that happened underwater that he had no control over. But when a guy dies on the surface [Christopher Murley], then I think you do have some responsibility, but I have never said that publicly."

With all the ill will between the two primary charter boats out to the *Doria*, Bielenda tried to smooth things over. His solution was for Crowell and the *Seeker* to join the Eastern Dive Boat Association (EDBA), but Crowell would have none of it. Crowell always disparaged the EDBA as Bielenda's "club," and he was content to wing it on his own. All he wanted, Crowell has said, was to be left alone.

The 2000 season out on the *Doria* was, thankfully, uneventful. One of the mitigating factors was bad weather. Dan Crowell was forced to cancel all but three of his expeditions out to the wreck, one of which I was on. The *Wahoo*, however, managed its usual two. There was a communal sigh of relief once the season was over. None was louder than the one emanating from the Coast Guard field office in New Haven.

Lieutenant Tim Dickerson was relieved that he did not have to mount another investigation on a fatality on the *Andrea Doria*. His work, however, is not done. All but one of the fatal-accident reports have been completed and submitted to Coast Guard officials. What if anything will be done is questionable even to him. The only thing that he can be sure of is that there will be more deaths on the *Doria*. It is only a matter of when, and there is little he or the Coast Guard can do about it.

TONY MAFFATONE

Unfortunately the wreck-diving season in the Northeast was not devoid of tragedy. Tony Maffatone died while experimenting with some new gear on the USS *San Diego* on August 2, 2000.

Maffatone was perhaps the least likely of all to perish exploring the wrecks on the continental shelf. His untimely demise proved once again the dangers of pushing the envelope of diving.

Tony Maffatone.
*(Courtesy of Joel
Silverstein
Photography)*

The fifty-six-year-old Maffatone was testing a new gear configuration. I had tried unsuccessfully to contact him about it. Steve Bielenda
and Joel Silverstein said Maffatone had decided against a *Doria* dive
until he had tested his new gear and felt comfortable with it.

Bielenda was aboard the *Wahoo* on that hot, sunny afternoon.
Bielenda remembers he was talking to Charlie Firmback and facing in
the opposite direction when Maffatone breached the surface. Firmback
alerted him that Maffatone was up. Bielenda thought that that was odd,
since Maffatone had splashed in just minutes before. Turning in the
direction that Firmback was looking, Bielenda saw Maffatone roll
from his back onto his stomach and vomit a bloody froth. Bielenda
immediately realized Maffatone was in serious trouble and threw
a line to the stricken diver. He hollered for Kevin Gannon and Art

Paltz to jump in and pull the unconscious Maffatone to the stern of the boat.

Maffatone was wearing only a dry suit, a hood, one glove, and one fin. Somehow, somewhere on the bottom he had ditched all his gear, bolting from the depth of 110 feet to the surface without any air supply.

Rife with adrenaline, all Bielenda could feel was his own pulse when he pressed his forefinger to Maffatone's wrist. Cutting off his neck seal, Bielenda stared in horror at Maffatone's carotid artery, which bulged a good quarter inch out of his neck, bloated hard with air, a sure sign of a massive embolism. Maffatone's lungs had ruptured on his frantic ascent to the surface, sending a flood of air into his blood system, causing cataclysmic blockages in all his vital organs. Staring hard into Maffatone's eyes, Bielenda saw that the pupils were fixed and dilated. No lifesaving techniques were necessary. Tony Maffatone was dead.

Maffatone was well-known in the deep-diving circles, and his innovative equipment was far beyond the realm of even the most experienced deep diver. He was considered a pioneer among pioneers. Now he was gone, a victim of his own experiments. To the diving world his loss was like losing an astronaut in space or a world-class mountaineer on a Himalayan peak.

As best reconstructed by those there, Maffatone most likely flipped under his heavy experimental gear shortly after entry due to a buoyancy problem. Plummeting to the sandy bottom with a possible air-supply malfunction, he realized his only hope was to strip himself of his gear and kick to the surface. As with many of the *Doria* deaths, the warm air of the surface is not always the answer. Just like Craig Sicola, Vince Napoliello, and Frank Kennedy, Maffatone was as good as dead the moment he realized he had a problem.

Bielenda says Maffatone probably experienced a series of problems with his experimental gear. The most critical was a likely freeze-up in his primary regulator. That he surfaced with only one fin tells Bielenda that he was struggling on the bottom to right himself.

Joel Silverstein, a longtime friend of the ex-SEAL, believes Maffatone knew he had little chance of surviving when he ran into trouble. Silverstein believes that Maffatone stripped his gear and headed to the surface because he did not want to put his friends through the distasteful effort of locating his body in the ocean depths. According to Silverstein, Maffatone's military mind-frame made him think of such things. The medical examiner's report listed his death as a "drowning/embolism."

Sally Wahrmann remembers talking to Tony Maffatone ten years ago on the aft deck of the *Wahoo*, over a beer on the trek back to Captree Boat Basin from the wreck of the USS *San Diego*. She was proudly displaying an artifact she had recovered from the World War I relic, but Maffatone was unimpressed. He told her artifacts did not interest him. He told Wahrmann he was an inventor.

"I told Tony what he was doing was dangerous, that it was overkill," Wahrmann recalled. "So he said, looking at his gear, 'Yeah, probably one day my toys will kill me, but I just have to do it.' And he continued to do it, and it killed him."

I spoke to Steve Bielenda the day after the accident. Devastated, he was uncharacteristically at a loss for words. Speaking in quiet, somber tones he finally told me that he could not understand how it could have happened.

Tony Maffatone was an experienced and fearless diver. He was Bielenda's best friend and had died diving from his boat. What made it even harder on the aging dive-boat skipper was that Maffatone's death was the first one from the decks of the *Wahoo* since July 31, 1985, when John Ormsby had died on the *Doria*.

GARY GENTILE

Dan Crowell surpassed Gary Gentile for the most dives on the *Doria* during the 1999 season, but Gentile is still considered by most in the wreck-diving crowd as "the guy," mostly because Gentile was there long before Crowell. Gentile is comfortable in the knowledge that he pioneered diving the *Doria*. All his subsequent dives on the *Doria* are gravy to him. He knows his reputation among the diving community is safely established.

Gentile still makes several dives on the *Doria* every year, but there is no competition between him and Dan Crowell. Both speak highly of each other, and Gentile crews on the *Seeker* frequently. When

Captain Dan Crowell.
(Photo © Kevin McMurray)

269

together, they kid each other good-naturedly. They dive together, and together they have recovered some of the unfortunate few who never made it back to the surface from wrecks like the *Doria*. They are such good friends that Crowell turned a blind eye toward Gentile's treatment of Bill Nagle, Crowell's former boss and late mentor, in his book *The Lusitania Controversies: Book 2*. Gentile discusses Nagle's ego, his failings, and his substance-abuse problems. It was the kind of stuff one would not want to see written about a friend. Another friend of Nagle's, Sal Arena, captain of the *Sea Hunter*, and a controversial character himself, found Gentile's descriptions of Nagle (and himself) "lower than low."

But Crowell holds no grudges. "Gary is just Gary" is how Crowell explains Gentile's writing. Life, friends, and diving go on.

A bachelor for many years, Gary Gentile lives and breathes shipwrecks, but he lives not in some ocean-fronting property but in a nondescript row house in North Philadelphia.

Gary greeted me at the door still engrossed in a conversation with a prospective client. Long ago eschewing traditional employment, he runs out of his home his modest business of self-publishing, speaking engagements, and expert testimony on diving-related incidents. He is wearing a remote phone-headset, a godsend, he says, for the hyperactive self-employed few who have to juggle the many hats when not blessed with employees. The clock is on and he is charging me for his time. As he says, this is his living. As a journalist I am not used to paying my interviewees a fee, but I was writing about the *Andrea Doria*, and I can not ignore Gary Gentile. He is, after all, "the guy."

His home is adorned with goodies from past conquests. *Doria* artifacts are everywhere—plates, crystal, and other paraphernalia fill display cases and bookshelves. From past experiences I know that Gary is not shy about displaying his successes. Why should his home be different?

Gary Gentile is opinionated and not reluctant to voice his thoughts, the kind of person a journalist loves to interview. He is fifty-

feels that trimix is bringing a lot of people into technical diving who are not skilled enough to meet the challenges, people who think they can dive as deep as they want. Gentile says that is a fallacy. It pulls divers into dangerous situations they are not capable of handling.

To Gentile, people with less than three years of diving experience going down to three-hundred-feet depths are "going from badge to badge." They do not have the experience level he had when he learned to dive on mixed gas after twenty years of doing it on air. He believes that experience is why he has survived.

Gentile echoes Dan Crowell's credo of personal freedom. "There are people who are diving deep," Gentile says, "who don't have the automatic responses, the instinctive control, to respond in a certain way in a certain situation the way I have after thirty years of experience. When something goes wrong for me, I instantly know what to do. Someone who has been diving for only three years does not have that instinct. But I'm not going to be my brother's keeper. I won't say who is qualified and who is not. A diver has to be honest with himself and make that decision himself."

Many people in extreme sports do not recognize their limitations, Gentile believes, and when they do, they are about to die.

BILLY DEANS

Billy Deans has quit diving. That fact is hard to reconcile for many in the diving community. Deans was the embodiment of the sport. Steve Bielenda, Dan Crowell, Gary Gentile, and Joel Silverstein can agree on little—and they like each other even less—but they share one belief: Billy Deans was the guru of deep diving. It makes Deans's exit from the sport all the more difficult to accept. Yet he has.

Deans lives on Big Pine Key, approximately a twenty-minute drive east of Key West. Although divers used to tease him that he "never had time for a girlfriend," he has slipped comfortably into a relationship with a woman twenty years his junior. Billy and Kendra share the same roof in a typical Florida Keys home—airy, extensively tiled, brightly painted, and constructed in the favored Moorish style. It abuts a canal that leads out to deep water.

Key West Diver on nearby Stock Island was sold after Hurricane Georges in September 1998. The shop was damaged in the storm, so Deans took the insurance money and sold what was left and embarked on a new career. He is studying to be a geriatric nurse, a profession he says he always felt attracted to. For Deans it was an easy decision.

Deans could not see himself getting ahead of the "power curve" in the dive industry. Even though his income from his business was "okay," he never put anything away for retirement, and he always knew that diving was a young man's sport. Diving, according to Deans, is a recreational industry, not an industry in which professional people make vast sums of money.

He also watched as other dive operators lowered their standards to make money, something he could not do himself. Ever since John Ormsby's death, Deans could not live with the justification that he was just a "bus driver," taking anybody out on the ocean, watching them splash in, then leaving them to their own devices.

It was human nature, Deans ruefully concludes. He was tired of people calling him who wanted to dive the *Doria* in "zero to two years." Deans said he could not go to bed at night knowing that he had not done everything to make it safe. Although charging a premium dollar for a premium service cut him out of a lucrative market, compromising his integrity and principles was not an option. After twenty-five years in the business, his energy for diving had ebbed. Expending it was just not worth the return.

There was also the ominous cloud of legal action against dive operations. Deans believes the recreational industry of diving is ripe for lawsuits. Another reason Deans quit diving was the physiological consequences. Deans believes that in deep diving you are "insulting the brain," loading the vital organ with high doses of nitrogen and high partial pressures of oxygen. The brain is sensitive to that, given that it does not regenerate cells.

Deans finds that he often loses a word or phrase, short-term memory—neurological damage that he attributes to his deep diving. There is not a lot of medical information on the effects of diving, according to Deans, because it is a relatively new phenomenon. Until the death of Jacques Cousteau, most of the pioneers of scuba were all still alive. But the "neurological deficit" has to have some permanent effect, and the continuing damage to your body can age you prematurely.

Deans explained, "The powerful oxidizers produced by the high partial pressure of oxygen grab electrons. One of the first places it happens is in the DNA code. These mutants damage the DNA, which cannot replicate themselves, and cause aging. They can also produce cancer cells." He posed an important question: "How can a 25-year diving career *not* cause damage, and how much damage do you want to chance?"

Deans also credits Kendra for his change of lifestyle. He is grateful to have a reason to spend more time at home. "Boring," as he related, is good: getting up on a Sunday morning, having a quiet and leisurely cup of coffee and reading the newspaper, is new to him—and he likes it.

Billy Deans always wanted to go back to school. He is thrilled to have the chance in his nursing program to help treat disease and people from a holistic standpoint. He left diving because of a fundamental spiritual change. Was his legacy going to be *Doria* dishes or helping people?

"It's a good feeling," he said. "You walk out after a day's work at the convalescent center and you have done something positive for the energy flow of the human race. There's a critical nursing shortage and I want to help. But primarily it is something that I can devote my time to and it is worthy. It will bring me some financial gain, but also it will give me a personal wealth."

For all his talk of leaving the underwater world for good, he admits he still feels its tug. He has kept his rebreather, a closed-circuit scuba system, and from time to time he uses in the canal behind his house. "Just keeping in shape," he says.

Billy Deans slips easily into reminiscing about his former life, the adventure diving around the world and the exploring of virgin wrecks, but getting up at "zero dark thirty," captaining a boat, and getting ten guys in the water, however intense and exciting it was, just wore him out. The possibility of getting killed diving was always with him after John Ormsby died. The horrible memories are still fresh.

Billy Deans will never forget being deep inside Gimbel's Hole while his best friend and dive buddy was hopelessly entangled in the sagging cables. Deans could only watch in helpless frustration as the

Billy Deans after Ormsby's fatal dive. (Photo © Steve Bielenda)

life ebbed out of John's eyes and the bubble trails ceased. No amount of pulling, tugging, cutting, and pleading with his God could free his friend from a cold, suffocating death in a watery black hole. It is the stuff of nightmares, and it will always be Billy Deans's nightmare.

Rich Hickey has been diving for twelve years now. It has been a slow, incremental inching up the ladder of scuba expertise for the thirty-one-year-old resident of Telford, Pennsylvania. "This is the year," Hickey told me, "that one way or the other I'll be out on the *Doria*."

Diving the *Doria* was not always paramount to Rich Hickey. He first diving experiences were in the Caribbean. Hickey quickly tired of it. He echoes a familiar refrain among wreck divers when describing the easy, safe recreational kind of diving that is done in the warm, gin-clear waters: "boring." "You see one pretty fish, you've seen them all," Hickey says, "In wreck diving it's always challenging, and different, and there's always the chance you may find some interesting artifact. I also get a chance to use my planning and analytical skills. I love it that wreck diving combines science and adventure."

Hickey, who works for a pharmaceutical company that calibrates instruments, is emblematic of what deep-wreck diving is all about: acquiring skills, experience, patience, attention to detail, and a healthy respect for the ocean in plumbing the unknown depths.

I had met Rich Hickey aboard the *Seeker* on the *Pinta* dive early in the 2000 dive season. He was diving with his new closed-circuit scuba rebreather, the lastest technological innovation in the sport. Later in the season he would travel down to North Carolina to dive the deeper wrecks but these dives were all just warm-ups for the ultimate: the *Doria*.

Hickey told me he had one more training dive on trimix before he would have the hard-won certification. He hoped the gas would give him a clearer head, help him with the long decompression hangs, and reduce the possibility of an oxygen-toxicity hit on the *Doria*.

I could detect a tinge of impatience in his voice when I spoke with him over the phone about the *Doria* expedition in the upcoming season. Hickey was tuned in to the world of deep-wreck diving and knew the sunken ship was deteriorating fast. He had heard that Gimbel's Hole was no longer a viable entry point into the holds of the wreck and that the *Doria* was quickly becoming a "rubble pile," as he called it.

Hickey had journeyed out to Montauk five years ago to board the *Seeker* for an expedition out to the *Doria,* but the trip had gotten blown out by the weather. He was glad it did, because he now knows how little he knew back then. It's different now. He says he now has the experience, the skills, and the knowledge. "I am a lot more prepared now than I was then," Hickey related to me. "Now when something comes up, I can handle it. I know exactly what to do. I'm ready now."

The *Doria* awaits.

BIBLIOGRAPHY

Gary Gentile. *Andrea Doria: Dive to an Era*. Philadelphia: Gary Gentile Productions, 1989.

Gary Gentile. *The Lusitania Controversies, Book 1: Atrocity of War and a Wreck Diving History*. Philadelphia: Gary Gentile Productions, 1998.

Gary Gentile. *The Lusitania Controversies, Book 2: Dangerous Descents into Shipwrecks and Law*. Philadelphia: Gary Gentile Productions, 1999.

William Hoffer. *Saved! The Story of the Andrea Doria—the Greatest Sea Rescue in History*. New York: Summit Books, 1979.

Alvin Moscow. *Collision Course: The Andrea Doria and the Stockholm*. New York: G. P. Putnam's Sons, 1959.

BIBLIOGRAPHY

NOTES

39 "As for the rest of the ship": Alvin Moscow, *Collision Course* (New York: G. P. Putnam Sons, 1959).

42 "Dignified but distant": Hoffer, *Saved!*

49 "The *Stockholm* was turning": Ibid.

49 "I was thrown": "Survivors of Another Night to Remember," *New York Times*, 8/1/99.

52 "All of a sudden": Ibid.

52 "Eventually, my mom": Ibid.

53 "tremendous thud": Moscow, *Collision Course.*

54 "we heard a big explosion": Ruth Roman obituary, *New York Times*, 9/11/99.

56 "The *Stockholm* was, in effect": Hoffer, *Saved!*

57 "The majority of the blame": Interview with Captain Robert Meurn (USMM), 1/21/00.

58 "In those days": Ibid.

CHAPTER THREE:
MY FIRST DESCENT

69 "Bag of tricks": Interview with Captain Steve Bielenda, 7/28/99.

72 See Appendix A for the *Doria* expedition waiver.

CHAPTER FOUR:
THE PIONEERS OF WRECK DIVING

95 "At that point": Interview with Billy Deans, 11/5/99.

95 "absolutely livid": Ibid.

95 "There wasn't much I could say": Ibid.

101 "purveyors of snake oil": "SDM Editorial," *Skin Diver*, November 1992.

105 "Billy Deans was doing all the deep stuff": Interview with Joel Silverstein, 12/6/99.

106 "No life is worth": Interview with Deans.

106 "Just swim around": Ibid.

107 "When I tell a person he's not diving": Ibid.

107 "Okay, you are now dead": Ibid.

Notes

107 "He told me he sent me": Ibid.

109 "You dove until it started": Sean J. Holland III. "Father of Northeast Wreck Diving—Michael A. de Camp," *Immersed* 3, no. 2 (Summer 1998).

112 "Above all, the terrible incongruity": Kenneth MacLeish, *Life,* 9/17/56.

115 "Everyone was very silent": Michael A. de Camp, "Unreal Trip to the *Andrea Doria,*" 1/67.

115 "I'll never get back from this": Ibid.

118 "that cascaded over the superstructure": Ibid.

119 "At least five martinis": Interview with Evelyn Bartram Dudas 12/22/99.

CHAPTER FIVE:

PENETRATING THE *DORIA*

127 "That's it!": Interview with Gary Gentile, 10/26/99.

130 "Sure, why not?": Interview with Captain Sal Arena, interview, 5/8/00.

135 "were way off, terrible": Interview with Captain Steve Bielenda, 9/29/99.

136 "The *Doria* is a big, beautiful wreck": Interview with Arena.

144 "Up ahead I saw a glimmer": Gary Gentile, *Andrea Doria: Dive to an Era* (Philadelphia: Gary Gentile Productions, 1989).

145 "They wanted their artifacts": Interview with Arena.

149 "We all took turns": Interview with Gentile.

150 "traumatized and completely unresponsive": Gary Gentile, *The Lusitania Controversies, Book 2: Dangerous Descents into Shipwrecks and Law* (Philadelphia: Gary Gentile Productions, 1999).

151 "They asked how I could be so strong": Interview with Evelyn Dudas, 12/22/99.

153 "lassoed heifer": Gary Gentile, *Andrea Doria* (Philadelphia: Gary Gentile Productions, 1989).

156 "The bottom line": Interview with Richard Kohler, 5/26/00.

158 "If they wanted to dive": Interview with John Chatterton, 5/24/00.

158 "We were going to bag up": Interview with Kohler.

158 "At two hundred ten feet": Interview with Pete Manchee, 6/9/00.

159 "All I could see above me": Ibid.

159 "I jumped from one table pedestal": Ibid.

163 "did a face plant": Interview with Chatterton.

283

Notes

165 "you don't leave your dead behind": Interview with Captain Howard Klein, 6/2/00.

166 "egg on the face": Interview with Kohler.

166 "pure, unadulterated bullshit": Interview with Captain Hank Garvin, 5/31/00.

169 "I don't need the EDBA": Interview with Captain Dan Crowell, 4/19/00.

172 "cluster fuck as a technical diver": Ibid.

CHAPTER SIX:
THE DYING SEASON, SUMMER 1998

175 "Gene Peterson is an excellent diver": Interview with Captain Dan Crowell, 4/19/00.

180 "I tried to scare him": Interview with Gary Gentile, 10/26/99.

181 "I called those guys": Interview with Crowell.

183 "Sure!": *Newsday*, 6/21/99.

185 "He went there": Interview with Crowell.

188 "I'll do anything to recover a body": Interview with Gentile.

189 "It's just not worth it to stress": Ibid.

191 "He came up headfirst": Interview with Rick Kleinschuster, 7/1/00.

195 "He was one of those guys": Interview with Crowell.

204 "Diving-Related Respiratory Problems": Robert M. Jackson, University of Alabama at Birmingham.

205 "Vince was absolutely neurotic": Interview with David Murphy, 7/24/00.

205 "I was hammered emotionally": Interview with Crowell.

CHAPTER SEVEN:
BACK TO THE *DORIA*

232 "an accident waiting to happen": Interview with Joel Silverstein, 8/9/00.

234 "You would have to tie him up": Interview with Captain Dan Crowell, 4/19/00.

237 "It was just entirely too close to home": John Chatterton e-mail, 8/1/00.

238 "Trying to attach themselves": Interview with Captain Dan Crowell, 5/6/00.

238 "The Coast Guard has jurisdiction": Interview with Lieutenant Tim Dickerson, USCG, 8/18/00.

239 "They actually were bucking": Interview with Captain Steve Bielenda, 8/19/00.

241 "The Coast Guard may have": Interview with Crowell, 4/19/00.

242 "Dickerson was satisfied": Interview with Silverstein.

EPILOGUE:
WHERE ARE THEY NOW?

260 "Snidely," Wahrmann said: Interview with Sally Wahrmann, 8/22/00.

268 "I told Tony": Ibid.

268 when John Ormsby had died: See Appendix C, "*Andrea Doria* Fatalities."

272 "It's like blaming Edmund Hillary": Interview with Gary Gentile, 10/26/99.

273 "There are people who are diving deep": Ibid.

275 "The powerful oxidizers": Interview with Billy Deans, 11/7/99.

277 "This is the year": Interview with Richard Hickey, 11/19/00.

APPENDIX A

WAHOO CONTRACT

ANDREA DORIA ALL EXPEDITION'S 2000
DEEP EXTENDED RANGE DIVING
ANDREA DORIA'S EXPEDITIONS CONTRACT, RELEASE,
WAIVER, INDEMNIFICATION AGREEMENT AND ASSUMPTION
OF RISK AND ACKNOWLEDGMENT TO MY EXPERIENCE TO
MAKE THESE DIVES.

For and in consideration of permitting the Undersigned to participate in The Andrea Doria Expedition to the wreck site of the Andrea Doria, in any and all activities associated with the expedition (including, without limitation, meetings, social gatherings, instruction, dives and equipment loans) and for other good and valuable consideration, the Undersigned hereby voluntarily releases, discharges, waives and relinquishes Captain Steve Bielenda and/or his officers, agents, and employees from any and all actions or causes of action for personal injury, property damage and/or wrongful death, or otherwise, occurring to him/her self arising as a result of engaging in the aforesaid activities incidental thereto, whenever, wherever and however the same may occur.

The Undersigned agrees that Captain Steve Bielenda, Under Sea Adventures Inc., the Wahoo, any officers, agents, servants and employees are only responsible for transport via boat to and from the site of the Andrea Doria and are in no way responsible for any diving related activities, including, but not limited to, breathing gas or gases, dive planning, back-up or emergency plans, diving gear, safety equipment, and diving tables.

The Undersigned further agrees that under no circumstances whatsoever will he or his heirs, executors, administrators or assigns prosecute any claim for personal injury, property damage and/or wrongful death, or otherwise, against Captain Steve Bielenda, Under Sea Adventures Inc., the Wahoo, and/or his officers, agents, servants and employees for any of said causes of action.

The Undersigned hereby assumes all risks arising out of or pertaining to his/her participation in the aforesaid activities, and enters into this Agreement with the express intention of exempting Captain Steve Bielenda and/or his officers, agents, servants and employees from any and all liability for personal injury, personal damage and/or wrongful death, or otherwise, caused by negligence or otherwise.

The Undersigned, for him/her self, his/her heirs, executors, administrators and assigns, agrees that in the event any claim for personal injury, property damage and/or wrongful death or otherwise has been brought, he/she shall indemnify and save harmless Captain Steve Bielenda, Under Sea Adventures Inc., the Wahoo, and/or its officers, agents, servants, and employees from any and all claims or causes of action wherever, whenever, and by whoever made, for personal injury, property damage and/or wrongful death, or otherwise.

Date:_____signed:_____end page one

Andrea Doria Expedition's 2000 (continued) Page 2

The Undersigned has made the above representations to Captain Steve Bielenda, his crew or agents in order to induce said person to allow him/her to participate in the aforesaid activities. The Undersigned acknowledges and understands that diving to the site of the Andrea Doria is potentially hazardous, with inherent dangers, and is considered beyond the limits of recreational diving. Furthermore, the Undersigned acknowledges and understands that the minimum depth of this wreck site is approximately 170 feet of sea water (FSW), approximately 52 meters of sea water (MSW), which is beyond the diving depth established by all United States' recreational SCUBA diving training agencies. Dives to this wreck may entail decompression, which carries with it a higher risk of decompression sickness than recreational diving. Also, the Undersigned agrees to accept full responsibility and liability for the use of any breathing gas including, but not limited to, air, oxygen, NITROX (oxygen enriched air), Trimix (oxygen/helium/nitrogen) or Heliox (oxygen/helium). The Undersigned agrees to accept full responsibility and liability for the use of any and all diving tables, decompression or otherwise, used on this trip or in training for this trip. Under no circumstances will the Undersigned, or any person associated with the Undersigned, hold any person, persons, or organization liable for injury or death resulting from the use of any diving tables associated with the expedition. Use of mixtures other than air is not recommended by United States recreational SCUBA training agencies, and is by my own choice._____. Initials

I_____, hereby affirm that I have been well-advised and thoroughly informed of the hazards of making Deep dives like the "Andrea Doria" by my own extensive deep diving experience. I also affirm that Captain Steve Bielenda of Under Sea Adventures Inc. has informed me that deep scuba diving has its risks and I informed Steve Bielenda I have the experience to scuba dive the "Andrea Doria." I understand this is a very deep dive (up to 250' FSW), and potentially very hazardous dive, and the hazards include, but not limited to, the following: decompression sickness, nitrogen narcosis, rapid depletion of air supply, strong current, poor visibility, oxygen poisoning, entanglement, "silt out," entrapment, air embolism, and drowning. By signing this release, I certify that I am fully aware of all these risks.

I understand that neither Captains Steve Bielenda, or Janet Bieser, Under Sea Adventures Inc., and the Wahoo and crew may be held liable in any way for any occurrence on this dive expedition which may result in personal injury, property damage or wrongful death; and the Undersigned does for him/herself, heirs, executors, administrators and assigned hereby release, waive, and discharge, and relinquish any action or cause of action, aforesaid which may arise for his/her heirs, executors, administrators and for his/her estate, and agrees that under no circumstance will he/she or his/her heirs, executors, administrators and assigns prosecute or present any claim for personal injury, property damage or wrongful death against same the crew of the vessel "Wahoo" for any said cause of action, whether the same shall arise by negligence of any of said persons, or otherwise.

IT IS THE INTENTION OF _____BY THIS INSTRUMENT, TO EXEMPT AND RELEASE CAPTAINS STEVE BIELENDA, JANET BIESER, UNDER SEA ADVENTURES INC., THE VESSEL WAHOO, AND THE CREW OF THE VESSEL WAHOO, FROM LIABILITY FOR PERSONAL INJURY, PROPERTY DAMAGE OR WRONGFUL DEATH CAUSED BY NEGLIGENCE.

Date:_____Signed:_____end page 2

Andrea Doria Expedition's 2000 (continued) Page 3 of 3

The Undersigned for him/herself, his/her heirs, executors, administrators, or assigns agrees that in the event any claim for personal injury, property damage or wrongful death shall be prosecuted by or on the undersigned against Captains Steve Bielenda, Janet Bieser, Under Sea Adventures Inc., the crew of the "Wahoo," he/she shall indemnify and save harmless the same from any and all claims or cause of action by whomever or wherever made or presented from personal injury, property damage or wrongful death.

I have read all three pages and accept all the risks involved in diving the Andrea Doria by signing below. This agreement also includes photo and image release with no compensation for any and all use of photos/images & video before, during, and after the expedition.

Being part of the expedition does not mean you must dive. Diving is only part of the experience, if for any reason you do not feel like diving, DO NOT DIVE.

Review this document with your family and loved ones, diving the Andrea Doria is EXTREME DIVING AND HAS ITS RISKS. Ins._____.

This contract covers any change in dive locations.

Date of your expedition_____.

FILL IN DATES

DATE SIGNED:_____

Participant: _____ Date_____

(Print Name)

Social Security #:

Divers Insurance #:

Notary—Print Name:

Or witness: _____ end page 3

Next of Kin/ Spouse: _____

(Print Name)

_____ Date: _____

(Sign Name)

Doria 2000. After signing and notary, please make a copy of this contract for your file.

APPENDIX B

SEEKER CONTRACT

Deep Explorers, Inc.
Liability Release

Initial each numbered section to which you agree. Print the word "VOID" in the space provided for initials if you do not agree, or if the statement is inaccurate, untrue, or you do not understand the intent of the statement.

_____ 1. It is my intention by this instrument **to give up my right to**
initial   **sue** Deep Explorer, Inc. IANTD, TDI/SDI, and their officers, agents, servants, and/or employees, whether specifically named or not, and it is also my intention to exempt and relieve Deep Explorers, Inc., IANTD, TDI/SDI and their officers, agents, servants, and/or employees and to hold these entities harmless from any liability for personal injury, property damage, or wrongful death caused by negligence or gross negligence and **I agree to assume all risk** in connection with my scuba diving activities.

_____ 2. I am a certified diver and have been taught and understand
initial   that scuba diving has inherent risks and dangers associated therewith including, but not limited to, decompression sickness, embolism, equipment failure or malfunction, acts of fellow divers, depletion of the diver's breathing gas supply, becoming lost or disoriented at depth, becoming entangled or entrapped by objects on the sea floor or wreck, onset of sud-

293

den illness at depth, or other perils of the sea which could cause injury or drowning, and **I SPECIFICALLY ASSUME SUCH RISKS.**

<u>   </u> 3. I understand that breathing gases other than air, diving
initial deeper than 130 feet, and conducting dives requiring mandatory decompression, only increase these inherent risks, and I have received training specifically to aid me in managing these increased risks.

<u>   </u> 4. I fully understand and am fully aware that there are no US
initial Navy repetitive dive tables for dives deeper than 190', although computer driven software exists to create any dive schedule desired. I understand it is not recommended to conduct repetitive dives beyond 190' and in doing so **I SPECIFICALLY ASSUME ALL RISKS** involved with my activities.

<u>   </u> 5. Within the last year, I have conducted wreck dives well in
initial excess of 130 feet and I am familiar with the extensive preparation necessary to conduct such dives and understand that **I am solely responsible** for such preparation, **OR** I am currently enrolled in a technical diving course and I will be making my certification dives on these trips under the supervision of my instructor.

<u>   </u> 6. **I am physically fit for deep technical scub diving** and I will
initial not hold any of the above named persons or entities responsible should I be injured as a result of heart problems, lung problems, or other illnesses or medical problems which might occur while diving, or aboard the dive boat.

<u>   </u> 7. I understand that being under the influence of prescription
initial drugs, illegal drugs, many over the counter drugs, or alcohol is a contraindication of diving and could cause my inuury or death, therefore **I agree to refrain from drug or alcohol use prior to the dive trip** or I will refrain from making my dive.

<u>   </u> 8. I will not hold Deep Explorers, Inc., IANTD, TDI/SDI, or
initial their officers, agents, servants, and/or their employees

responsible for providing me with any of my diving equipment or breathing gases, **including any gases I might need in an emergency,** and I understand that I am solely responsible responsible for inspecting all of my equipment, and analyzing my dive gases, prior to diving.

_____ 9. I will be present at and attentive to the safety briefing given
initial
by Deep Explorers, Inc., their officers, agents, servants, and/or employees, and if there is anything that I do not understand or am not in agreement with, I will notify Deep Explorers, Inc., and the boat Captain immediately.

_____ 10. Should I notice any unusual condition that might adversely
initial
affect my safety, or the safety of the vessel or the other passengers, I am obliged to notify Deep Explorers, Inc., **and** the boat Captain immediately.

_____ 11. I understand that I have a duty to plan and carry out my own
initial
dive and to be responsible for my own safety and should I elect to dive with a buddy, it is to be an arrangement solely between that buddy and myself. Deep Explorers, Inc., IANTD, TDI/SDI, and their officers, agents, servants, and/or employees are not responsible for providing me with a diving partner or in any way coordinating my dive with another diver.

_____ 12. I fully understand and am fully aware that the dive boat is
initial
extremely limited in its rescue and emergency medical response capabilities and that the dive site is in a remote location. As a result, in the event of illness or injury, rescue and/or appropriate medical assistance may be significantly delayed and **I could sustain further serious injury, possibly resulting in death,** from this delay.

_____ 13. I fully understand that **it is my responsibility to make my**
initial
family aware, as I am, that scuba diving, especially when conducted deeper than 130 feet, is an ultra-hazardolus activity and to accurately portray to them the risk of my injury or death.

<u>   </u> 14. I authorize Deep Explorers, Inc. to use, in whole or in part,
initial my name, likeness, image, voice, biography, interview, and
performance in connection with SEEKER, in all manner and
media, as Deep Explorers, Inc. shall determine in its sole
discretion.

<u>   </u> 15. **I have been given the opportunity to review this document**
initial **with both my family and legal counsel.**

<u>   </u> 16. It is my intention that **this document be admissible in any**
initial **and all legal proceedings, or lawsuits,** that might arise from
my scuba diving activities.

<u>   </u> 17. **I have read and understand the foregoing in its entirety.** I
initial agree to the terms and conditions of each of the initialed,
numbered sections above on behalf of myself, my heirs, and
my personal representatives.

Signature _____ Date_____

Print Name _____

Address_____Notary Stamp & Seal

_____

_____

Witnessed by _____

Notary Public

2000

APPENDIX C

ANDREA DORIA FATALITIES

Compiled by Gary Gentile during the Summer of 1995
Verified by John McAniff
of the National Underwater Accident Center

	Year	Date	Boat	Fatality
1.	1981	July 1	*Sea Hunter*	John Barnett (DB = Stan Smith) (recovered by Gary Gentile and Stan Smith)
2.	1984	July 15	*Wahoo*	Frank Kennedy (DB = Mike Moore) (floated to the surface unconscious, died on board)
3.	1985	July 31	*Wahoo*	John Ormsby (DB = Billy Deans, Lou Delotto) (recovered by Gary Gentile and Rick Jaszyn)
4	1988	July 13	*Seeker*	Joe Drozd (DB = Kevin England, P. J. Haney)(recovered by John Moyer and Clint Zineker)
5.	1992	July 1	*Seeker*	Matthew Lawrence (DB = Nick Caruso)(recovered first by Bart Malone, then by John Chatterton and John Hildeman)

6. 1992 July 15 *Seeker* Mike Scofield (DB = Wings Stocks) (recovered by John Chatterton and Danny Crowell)

7. 1993 July 12 *Sea Hunter* Robert Santuli (DB = Pete Haralabatos)(recovered by Steve Gatto and Tom Packer)

Addenda

8. 1998 June 24 *Seeker* Craig Sicola (DB = none) (floated to the surface with no vital signs)

9. 1998 July 8 *Seeker* Richard Roost (DB = none) (found and brought out of the wreck by Gary Gentile and John Moyer, then sent to the surface by Danny Crowell and Greg Mossfeldt)

10. 1998 August 4 *Seeker* Vince Napoliello (DB = Denis Murphy)(separated from buddy, floated to surface next to *Sea Inn*)

11. 1999 July 21 *Seeker* Christopher Murley (DB = Joe Jackson)(reached anchor line but did not descend, had heart attack on the surface)

12. 1999 July 28 *Seeker* Charlie McGurr (DB = Pete Wohlleben, Darryl Johnson) (dropped off anchor line between 160 and 170 feet, without reaching the wreck) (recovered by Danny Crowell and J. T. Barker)

ACKNOWLEDGMENTS

John Barnett, Frank Kennedy, John Ormsby, Matthew Lawrence, Craig Sicola, Richard Roost, Vince Napoliello, Chris Murley, Charlie McGurr, Tony Smith, and Tony Maffatone. They are the names of the men whose deaths have come to haunt me. By looking into their lives as trailblazing divers and studying their untimely deaths and chronicling them in this book, I hope to give them a bit of recognition, and if nothing else a modest memorial to their lives. Hopefully, something will be learned from their tragic deaths to prevent future ones. My deepest sympathy goes out to their family and friends.

Obviously there are many among the living whose generous contributions, recollections, advice, and direction were invaluable in my undertaking. Captains Steve Bielenda and Dan Crowell are foremost among them. I am grateful for their patience and time in recounting the history of diving the *Doria*, the technical aspects of diving operations, getting me out and back safely to the dive site, and reliving the painful memories of the accidents on the *Doria* that have left indelible imprints on their psyches.

Billy Deans, a good friend of mine, was particularly gracious in opening up his home and his heart to me. I appreciated Gary

Gentile's always controversial and intelligent input. I am indebted to them.

There are many others who contributed by delving into their memory banks. In no particular order, they are: John Chatterton, Jennifer Samulski, Gary Gilligan, Sally Wahrmann, Captain Hank Garvin, Captain Janet Bieser, Rick Jaszyn, Joel Silverstein, Kathy Weydig, Captain Howard Klein, Captain John Lachenmeyer, Captain Sal Arena, Captain Robert Meurn, USMM, Mike de Camp, Evelyn Bartram Dudas, Pete Manchee, Richie Kohler, Rick Kleinschuster, Dr. Bob Jackson, Brett Gilliam, Vincenzo Della Torre, Bob Decker, Dr. Bill Hamilton, David Murphy, and Rich Hickey.

Special thanks to Lt. Tim Dickerson, USCG, and Bob Higgins for taking time from a busy schedule in explaining the official inquiries and positions taken by the Coast Guard.

The photographs between these covers were shot by a variety of sources besides myself. I would like to thank the following for their generous contributions: Mike de Camp, Steve Bielenda, Dan Crowell, Jennifer Samulski, Steve Gatto, Jon Hulburt, Billy Campbell, Billy Deans, Joel Silverstein, and the Mariners Museum in Newport News, Virginia.

The competent reporting by Joe Haberstroh of *Newsday* made my research infinitely easier.

I relied on Joel Silverstein's technical expertise in the proofing of the book's manuscript. He also supplied editorial advice culled from his own publishing experience and as a result made *Deep Descent* a better book.

Deep Descent would have never been undertaken had it not been for my agent, Jane Dystel. Thank you, Jane, for seeing book potential in a magazine article. Her guidance through the shoals of book publishing was, in a word, invaluable.

Mitchell Ivers, my editor, did a masterful job with his red pen. It is a rare occurrence when a writer is in total agreement on recommended changes in his prose, and I was. I look forward to working with him in the future.

This book is dedicated to my father, Joseph P. McMurray, and my wife, Victoria McMurray. My appreciation of their support and belief in the project and my ability to deliver can never be underestimated. Kelly and Kaitlyn, my beautiful daughters, thank you, too. My love and gratitude go out to them.

Kevin F. McMurray